Excommunicated from the Union

THE NORTH'S CIVIL WAR
Andrew L. Slap, series editor

Excommunicated from the Union

*How the Civil War
Created a Separate
Catholic America*

William B. Kurtz

FORDHAM UNIVERSITY PRESS
NEW YORK   2016

Portions of Chapters 1, 2, 5, 6, and 7 were published originally as "Let us Hear No More 'Nativism': The Catholic Press in the Mexican and Civil Wars," in the journal *Civil War History* 60(1), March 2014. Copyright © 2014 by The Kent State University Press. Reprinted with permission.

The author and publisher gratefully acknowledge permission to reprint, in revised form, previously published material from the *U.S. Catholic Historian*: "'The Perfect Model of a Christian Hero': The Faith, Anti-Slaveryism, and Post-War Legacy of William S. Rosecrans," 31, no. 1 (Winter 2013): 73–96, which is partially reprinted in Chapter 8.

to my wife, Erin

Contents

Introduction   1

1   The Mexican War
and Nativism | 9

2   Catholics Rally to the Flag | 29

3   Catholic Soldiers in the Union
Army | 52

4   Priests and Nuns in the Army | 68

5   Slavery Divides the Church | 89

6   Catholics' Opposition
to the War | 108

7   Post-war Anti-Catholicism | 129

8   Catholics Remember
the Civil War | 144

Conclusion | 161

Acknowledgments   165
Appendices   167
Notes   171
Bibliography   211
Index   227

EXCOMMUNICATED
FROM THE UNION

Introduction

The Confederate attack on Fort Sumter, South Carolina, on April 12, 1861, unleashed a patriotic fury across the northern United States. American-born men, immigrants, and later African Americans rallied to support the Stars and Stripes and save the Union. Men of all faiths answered the call enthusiastically, among both the Protestant majority and the growing but significant minority of Roman Catholics. Orestes A. Brownson, the leading Catholic intellectual of his day, was an outspoken critic of southern secession. "The American citizen who seeks to overthrow the American government is not only a traitor, but . . . a dis-humanized monster not fit to live or to inhabit any part of this globe: he has no suitable place this side of hell." Brownson believed that his fellow Catholic northerners were overrepresented in the army and that their service would promote their integration into American society. Their loyalty, he argued, was a natural corollary of their religion, which obliged Catholics to do their "duty" in defense of the nation.[1]

Other pro-war Catholic leaders across the North similarly spoke out to both support the war and celebrate Catholic men who volunteered for military service on behalf of the Union cause. Patrick Donahoe, the Irish American proprietor and editor of the most important and widely circulated Irish Catholic newspaper in the United States, the Boston *Pilot*, argued the bloodshed of Catholic soldiers during the war was irrefutable proof of their patriotism and valor. "Let us hear no more '*nativism*,'" he declared, "for it is now dead, disgraced, and offensive, while Irish Catholic patriotism and bravery are true to the nation and indispensable to it in every point of consideration." By nativism, Donahoe meant the widespread prejudice against immigrants in American society, culture, and politics. Catholic Americans like Donahoe believed that nativism was not only anti-immigrant but also inherently anti-Catholic.[2] Catholic elites were intent on proving their community's patriotism because, at that time, many American Protestant leaders openly feared that Catholicism was incompatible with the nation's republican government.[3] In response to such apparent hostility and in order to preserve their ethnic traditions and faith, Catholics had often segregated themselves from the rest of American society. Perhaps the war, however, would be a chance for them to assimilate on their own terms while maintaining their religious and ethnic identities.[4]

Anti-Catholicism had had a long presence in American history, religion, and thought, dating back to the earliest foundations of the original colonies by Great Britain. The colonies were overwhelmingly Protestant and seen as a means to counter Catholic French and Spanish economic and religious influence in the Western Hemisphere. In the eighteenth century, American Catholics faced wide-ranging discrimination in nearly all of the colonies in British North America. Even in Maryland, a colony originally founded to ensure religious freedom for Catholics, Anglicanism became the official religion by 1702 and Catholics were kept from voting and holding office and were forced to attend Anglican services.[5]

The Revolutionary War, however, convinced many state governments and many Americans that Catholics could be trusted and should enjoy more of the freedoms open to Protestants. Charles Carroll of Carrollton, Maryland, served in the Continental Congress and became the only Catholic signer of the Declaration of Independence. Prominent among Catholic patriots were Washington's cavalry chief, General Stephan Moylan, and Captain John Barry, who gained fame for his exploits in the fledgling American navy. In 1790 President George Washington addressed a letter "To Roman Catholics in America" praising their "patriotic spirit" during the war and affirming his belief that "all those" Catholics who were "worthy members of the Community [were] equally entitled to the protection of civil Government." The contributions of Catholic Americans to independence during the Revolutionary War thus helped foster a remarkable period of tolerance during the early years of the new American republic.[6]

During the antebellum period, however, many native-born Americans, especially those who had taken part in the recent evangelical religious revival known as the Second Great Awakening, became increasingly alarmed by the rapid growth of the Catholic Church in the United States. Many Americans believed that the assimilation of Catholic foreigners would be difficult, and they feared that unchecked immigration threatened to replace familiar customs and religious practice with foreign and Catholic ones. Many anti-Catholic Americans also distrusted the Catholic Church because it was both hierarchical and led by a foreign ruler, the bishop of Rome, known as the pope. Some Protestants denounced the pope as the "anti-Christ" and the Catholic faith as "popery," a common derogatory term at the time for Roman Catholicism. They frequently denounced the Catholic Church in general as the "whore of Babylon." For many

Protestant Americans, freedom of conscience was essential for the proper worship of God, and Catholic insistence on obedience and dogma was seen as inherently antidemocratic and un-American. For them, it seemed impossible to reconcile American liberty with Roman despotism.[7]

Anti-immigrant and anti-Catholic Americans formed the Native American[8] Party in the 1840s to preserve the republic from being corrupted by foreigners and popery. Later this party was succeeded by the even larger and better organized "Know-Nothing" Party, which also sought to pass anti-Catholic or anti-immigrant legislation at the local, state, and even national levels. Despite Catholic immigrants' antebellum protestations that the conservative nature of their religion, their respect for law and order, and their rejection of radical abolitionism made them just as loyal and democratic as their non-Catholic neighbors, some Americans insisted on depicting them and their faith as a threat to American republicanism.[9]

The Catholic population probably numbered about 3.1 million in 1860, representing about 10 percent of the nation's total population. Most of them, perhaps around 90 percent, lived in the states that remained within the Union in 1861. The church's incredible growth, particularly in the North, was made possible only by the increasingly large number of immigrants, overwhelmingly Irish and then German, who immigrated to antebellum America. Some of these immigrants were well-off or settled successfully in rural areas because they were skilled in a trade or profession, were well educated, or had brought property with them to the United States. Yet most, especially the Irish who were the predominant ethnic group in the church, were unskilled, ill educated by American standards, and poor. They congregated in urban areas where they put a strain on local institutions and what passed for social services in the nineteenth century. They refused to give up their ethnic customs upon arrival and often tended to cluster into separate ethnic communities. This reinforced the entrenched belief that Catholicism was a religion only fit for foreigners, something that made even native-born Catholics very uneasy. Catholic immigrants and their clergy insisted that their religious rights be respected in the public sphere, most noticeably in public education, where their criticism of explicitly Protestant teachings made them anathema to many educational reformers. In short, Catholics were already creating a separate subculture in the United States in the decades before the Civil War.[10]

When the Civil War began, Catholic Americans had a remarkable chance to prove their loyalty to the nation and perhaps foster a new period of tolerance for their religion and community in the post-war nation. Approximately two hundred thousand Catholics served in the Union Army, at least fifty-three priests worked as army chaplains in regiments or hospitals, and hundreds of nuns worked in wartime hospitals. Though bishops and lay leaders did not coordinate their efforts on a national scale, pro-war Catholics hoped that their community's wartime patriotism would end anti-Catholicism and nativism in American politics and society. After the war, they wrote histories and built monuments meant to preserve the memory of Catholic Americans' bravery and bloodshed on behalf of saving the Union. The most important of these efforts was the erection of a monument to Father William Corby, a Holy Cross priest from South Bend, Indiana, who served with the Irish Brigade at the Battle of Gettysburg. Dedicated in 1910, this monument was meant to symbolize the church's patriotism once and for all on what the nation remembered as the most important battlefield in the struggle to defeat the Confederacy.[11]

During the conflict, however, Catholic Americans did not react to the conflict or the government's wartime policies with a single pro-war voice. For most Catholic northerners the Civil War and its aftermath were ultimately alienating experiences that further isolated them from the rest of American society. These Catholics supported the Union as it was, but disagreed with what they saw as their political and religious enemies' attempts to use the war as an excuse to remake society in a radical way. In resisting emancipation, denouncing the abridgment of civil liberties, and attacking the draft, anti-war Catholics joined other Democratic northerners in asserting that their defense of the Constitution made them, not the Republicans, the true patriots in the conflict. By the middle of the war, horrific casualties suffered in battles such as Antietam and Fredericksburg caused many of these Catholics to reconsider their support for the war. Most northern Catholics were Democrats, and a majority of their leaders came to sympathize with the Democrats' anti-war faction. In addition, Catholics from the slaveholding Border States—Kentucky, Missouri, and Maryland—were early opponents of Republican President Abraham Lincoln and the war from the very beginning. Catholics' unwavering support for the Democrats in the 1864 presidential election left them open to the invective of their enemies in the Protestant and Republican press. Their efforts on behalf of the Union seemingly paled in comparison to the enthusiastic support of many northern Protestants for the war, emancipation, and Abraham Lincoln's Republican government.[12]

These internal divisions among Catholics demonstrated the lack of unity within the Catholic Church over the Civil War and had a major impact on the future development of a separate American Catholic subculture in the United States. Opposition to the war hindered efforts by pro-war Catholic apologists to forge an unassailable narrative of patriotism and sacrifice to counter nativ-ism and anti-Catholic prejudice. Many Catholic leaders responded to criticism of their community during the war with an instinctive defensiveness born out of their encounter with antebellum nativism. Their anger over the public's appar-ent lack of appreciation for their wartime sacrifices and the resurgence of anti-Catholic nativism after 1865 accelerated the development of a separate Catholic subculture in the North. In the late nineteenth century, Catholic apologists still tried to use their wartime patriotism to counteract religious bigotry. However, their efforts were directed at a narrow audience and were only successful in reas-suring the Catholic community that it had done its part to save the Union. The heroic stories they wrote in books and the heroes they commemorated in bronze statues had little effect on American society in general. By contrast, southern Irish Catholics, whose war record was similarly mixed, partially redeemed them-selves after the war by opposing Reconstruction, aiding in efforts to erect monu-ments to the Confederate past, and embracing the Lost Cause version of the war and its meaning.[13]

Until recently, religion was relatively neglected by Civil War historians, who, when they have examined the subject, have focused on the Protestant major-ity in the North and South. Difficulty in finding letters and manuscripts from Catholics seems to be largely to blame for their exclusion from histories of the Civil War. As one recent scholar explained, a "dearth of primary sources" forced him to consign Catholics to the periphery of his study along with the much smaller Unitarian and Swedenborgian denominations.[14] While some notable studies have begun to include Catholics, there is still very little known about how the war affected Catholic northerners and their place in American society in the second half of the nineteenth century.[15] Benjamin Blied's *Catholics and the Civil War* is the only book-length treatment of the subject, but it does not deal with the post-war period.[16] Studies of northern Catholic immigrants such as the Irish also tend to focus on ethnicity and class issues more than religion. Prominent among these studies are Susannah Ural's *The Harp and the Eagle* and Christian Samito's *Becoming American under Fire*. Samito emphasizes the ways in which the conflict secured Irish Americans' citizenship rights and helped to assimi-late them into the American mainstream. By contrast, Ural argues that the war was primarily an alienating experience for Irish Catholic northerners. While the question of the war's assimilating effect on foreigners is certainly not an either/or proposition, it is clear that the trend in current scholarship is to argue that the war was not a melting-pot experience for the Irish, Germans, or other immigrant groups.[17]

To the extent that historians have addressed how the war affected Catholics, they are also divided over whether the Civil War should be seen as a turning point in American Catholic history. Did the Civil War help promote Catholics' acceptance into the broader American society and culture, or did it merely reinforce existing prejudice? While scholars have made some notable strides in understanding various aspects of the Irish Catholic experience of the war, little is known about other ethnic groups or the ways in which the war shaped perceptions of the Catholic Church in America. The Civil War's effect on Catholics of American, Irish, and German ethnicity in the United States (the North and the slaveholding Border States that remained within the Union) demands further investigation and a new analysis.[18]

In an effort to represent as broad a range of views as possible from across the North and Border States, I rely heavily on the opinions expressed in Catholic newspapers. Though a historian must always be careful not to consider such opinions as equal to that of the public in general, the wide range of views expressed by Catholic editors does accurately portray the spectrum of Catholic opinion on the conflict. Patriotic editors spoke to and were patronized by pro-war Catholics, while anti-war editors, who appealed to anti-draft and poorer Catholics, expressed sentiments that were certainly held by many of their readers. As Orestes Brownson, himself the most prominent Catholic editor of the time, noted in the run-up to the 1860 presidential election, "No periodical with us can live except on condition of pleasing the special public it addresses." American journalists were not just expected to "tell what is true, right and just, but to defend [their community's] opinions, prejudices, sympathies and antipathies." "Even the Catholic public," he declared, "would soon drop a journal that constantly contradicted its political convictions and sentiments." Brownson spoke from experience, having lost many of his readers for being too outspoken on immigrants and Catholic theology. The truth of his statement explains why prior to the war other Catholic leaders generally avoided controversial domestic political issues such as slavery.[19]

I also rely heavily on the views of elite Catholic laypeople and clergy. Exploring the Civil War–era lives of nonelite Catholics, both native- and foreign-born, is a difficult task made more so by the paucity of extant wartime letters and diaries they left behind. Many Catholics, like other Americans who were poor or illiterate, left behind few personal records that survive to the present.[20] Even from the archives of religious sisters, who all cherish the memory of their communities during the war, the amount of letters, account books, religious diaries, and other manuscripts that have been lost far outweigh the number that remain.

Major American Catholic repositories such as the archives of the University of Notre Dame contain sources that focus on elite and especially clerical voices to the exclusion of lay, poor, female, and non-Irish ones. Thus it is easy to understand why James McPherson's study of Civil War soldiers' motivation, *For Cause and Comrades*, quotes from only a handful of Catholics, all of them Irish. Because the Irish left behind relatively more Civil War sources than did German or native-born Catholics, the *Irish* experience of the war has been conflated into the experience of *all* Catholics during the war.[21]

Ultimately, the war alienated most northern Catholics and their leaders, causing them to seek refuge in a separate Catholic subculture after the war. My first chapter examines antebellum anti-Catholicism during the 1840s while arguing that the question of Catholic patriotism during the Mexican War and Know-Nothing crisis was a dress rehearsal for a similar debate during the Civil War. The second chapter explores Catholic responses to the election of 1860, the secession crisis, and the attack on Fort Sumter while arguing that initial Catholic unity in favor of the war helped lessen prejudice against them in 1861. The third argues that the service of so many prominent and rank-and-file Catholic Union soldiers was a source of pride for members of the community, who were shocked to find how little their sacrifices were appreciated. The fourth argues that the church's hierarchy failed to provide enough spiritual support for its men, particularly so because priests were essential to the religious lives of Catholic soldiers. It also asserts that more so than the bravery of Catholic soldiers or priests, sister nurses by far had the largest impact on dispelling prejudices against their faith through their devotion to the health and recovery of thousands of Union and Confederate soldiers in all theaters of the war.

The fifth and sixth chapters argue that battlefield casualties, conscription, and emancipation combined to turn many northern Catholics against the war effort. This story is much more complex than it is often depicted, as one of Irish Catholic racism toward African Americans.[22] By the end of the war, Catholics had become disenchanted with the Republicans and vice versa, leading to attacks on Catholic loyalty and talk of a religious civil war. Chapter 7 argues that continued Republican attacks on Catholics as a threat to national well-being underscored how little the war changed attitudes about the compatibility of their faith with being an American. Finally, Chapter 8 asserts that Catholic veterans and apologists attempted to create a positive memory of their church's role in the Union war effort, but that their efforts were primarily directed at their own community and had no great success in lessening anti-Catholicism in post-war American society or culture.

In the end, pro-war Catholic leaders and soldiers were unable to convince other Americans that their religion posed no threat to America's republican government and institutions. Major internal divisions among Catholics themselves ultimately undermined all efforts to promote tolerance of their religion through their participation in the war. No amount of belated post-war unity between Catholic veterans, leaders, and apologists proved able to defeat new forms of nativism in the late nineteenth or first half of the twentieth century. Thus the American Civil War played a pivotal role in accelerating the antebellum trend in American Catholicism toward isolation and separatism. Alienated by a hostile society that showed no appreciation for their wartime sacrifices, that continued to attack them and their faith as not fully American, Catholics sought refuge for themselves and their faith in a subculture of their own making.

1

The Mexican War and Nativism

The Mexican War (1846–48) set important precedents for the Catholic experience of the Civil War. Some Catholic leaders hoped that by fighting in the Mexican War, American Catholics would prove their loyalty and promote tolerance for themselves as they had done during the American Revolution. Many of the arguments developed during the Mexican War to counteract nativism and anti-Catholicism were later refined and put into service again in the Civil War. Catholics' efforts to portray themselves as loyal, however, were complicated by the alleged corruption and immorality of the Mexican Catholic clergy, Protestant anger over the appointment of Catholic chaplains to the army, and most importantly the presence of Irish Catholic deserters in the Mexican Army. By 1848 the Catholic community was distracted by famines and revolutions in Europe and grew weary of anti-Catholic coverage of the conflict. In the end, most hoped that the war would end quickly in order to save the Mexican church from further destruction at the hands of the invading U.S. Army.

Because few of the poor Catholic volunteers who belonged to the U.S. Army before the war left behind personal records, and because most bishops ignored the war as a peripheral matter not related to the running of their dioceses, Catholic newspapermen and the stories and editorials they wrote about the war form the best body of evidence for opinions within the Catholic community about the conflict with Mexico. In 1822 the first Catholic diocesan paper in the United States was published, and by 1845 there were fifteen Catholic periodicals. This number continued to grow steadily, with forty-one serials published in 1850. While exact circulation figures for the years of the Mexican War are hard to find, it seems that many newspapers had a circulation of only a few thousand local subscribers, with only a few papers—like *The Pilot* and *Brownson's Quarterly Review*, both published in Boston—enjoying a truly national audience. Laymen published and edited most of these papers. However, some of these newspapers were the "official organs" of their dioceses, and their local bishops had varying degrees of censorship over them. Many Catholic newspapers experienced frequent changes in ownership during the mid-nineteenth century. Prior to and during the Mexican War, the *New York Freeman's Journal* saw several different editors before James A. McMaster took over in 1848 and held his editorship well beyond the Civil War.[1]

Almost every editor, of whom Irish Catholics composed the majority, expressed orthodox religious views, and, in actual practice, both priests and laymen often had a wide degree of editorial freedom to publish on religious, ethnic, and political issues. While editors who did discuss the Mexican War generally supported it patriotically, others ignored the conflict, commented on it only rarely, or merely reprinted military reports from secular journals. Still, in both advocating the war as a chance to prove Catholic loyalty and in criticizing it for its excesses, the Catholic press foreshadowed how it would later cover the American Civil War.[2]

The failure to defeat anti-Catholic nativism during the Mexican War left room for the resurgence of an even greater political threat, the Know-Nothing or American Party. The party grew in popularity across the North and South primarily due to unprecedented levels of immigration from Ireland and Germany. Know-Nothings feared the corrupting influence of uneducated immigrants on politics and the growing power of a religion that they saw as fundamentally antidemocratic and un-American. Although other issues such as slavery and reforming state constitutions motivated the party, Catholics saw it as being fundamentally animated by religious prejudice. Taken together, the experience of the Mexican War and 1850s nativism encouraged Catholics to seek protection for their community and religious beliefs by increasingly walling themselves off from the seemingly hostile forces surrounding them in secular and Protestant American society.

The Mexican War began in May 1846 after Mexican soldiers attacked American troops stationed just north of the Rio Grande River. The effect the Mexican War had on the American Catholic Church is a subject that has received only intermittent attention from historians. Historian Robert Johansen famously called the Mexican War "an exercise in self-identity" in the young life of the United States, in that Americans were able to define themselves against an alien culture. However, this depiction of the war does not adequately describe the American Catholic experience of the war. After all, Catholics in the United States shared a common faith with Mexicans, who lived in an overwhelmingly Catholic nation. Manifest Destiny, the then common belief that the United States should stretch from the Atlantic to the Pacific, was influenced by anti-Catholicism and the desire to make the West safe for Protestantism. American Catholics could patriotically have supported westward expansion sought by the nation's Democratic administration, but they could not have fully supported the religious goals of many of those calling for territorial enlargement. Though military historians have analyzed the experience of the U.S. Army and its officers in both the Civil and Mexican Wars, by trying to show how lessons learned in Mexico influenced the generalship of Civil War leaders such as Ulysses S. Grant or Robert E. Lee, they have generally not linked the two conflicts in terms or ethnic or religious history.[3]

Many American Catholics took an active role in supporting the U.S. war effort against Mexico. From 1840 to 1850, the nation's Catholic population increased from approximately 663,000 to an estimated 1.6 million. Some estimates reported that a significant portion of the pre-war U.S. Army was composed of foreign-born Catholics. One historian records that 2,135 Irishmen were in the army in 1845, 2,644 more became regulars during the conflict, and slightly more than 1,000 served in short-term enlistments. Though it is not clear how many of these Irishmen were Catholic, there were probably at least few thousand Catholics of Irish, German, or American ancestry in the army.[4]

From the beginning of the conflict, some Protestant and secular editors questioned American Catholics' loyalty to the United States. One paper reported that few Catholics had volunteered to fight for the United States because priests were telling their parishioners that "they must not fight against their church." Protestant ministers and editors also blasted Polk's appointment of "unnaturalized foreigners" as Catholic chaplains to the U.S. Army: two Jesuit priests from Georgetown, Fathers Anthony Rey and John McElroy. One minister argued that the Catholic chaplains and soldiers were a liability to American success in the war, stating, "They cannot fight against their religion." A Presbyterian publication saw the Catholic chaplain appointments as proof of "a jesuitical influence about the President and his Cabinet." Some, like the *Christian Advocate and Journal*, hoped that the war would provide an opportunity to redeem Mexicans from the "degrading superstition" of Catholicism. The *Cleveland Plain Dealer*, a Democratic paper, predicted that greed as well as patriotism would motivate volunteering: "There is wealth and treasures enough hoarded in vaults and used in the service of their Churches to defray the expences [sic] of subjugating that whole nation." Even the *Washington Daily Union*, a secular paper with close ties to Democratic President James K. Polk, dared to suggest that the wealth of the Mexican Catholic Church should perhaps be "sequestered" by U.S. forces because the Mexican government allegedly used it to fund the war effort.[5]

Many evangelicals in both the North and South saw the war as an opportunity to strike a blow at Catholicism by converting Mexico. At the front, some Protestant American soldiers shared or developed the anti-Catholicism expressed back home in Protestant newspapers. Protestant soldiers were also more likely to blame Mexico's problems on its clergy than were Catholic soldiers. American volunteers singled out Catholicism to justify their belief that Mexico "was a barbaric and backward nation." Major Henry Lane of Indiana called Mexican Catholicism a "monster which is miscalled religion" and predicted that "ignorant and bigotted" Catholics of Mexico would inevitably fall before the "all conquering genius of genuine Americanism." Some were also enticed into service by the idea of being enriched by plunder from Mexican churches. A popular song set to the tune of "Yankee Doodle" promised volunteers their pick of "gold and silver images, plentiful and handy. Churches grand, with altars rich." One Protestant soldier, Frank Edwards, dismissed the lavish feast day ceremonies of Mexican Catholicism as "ridiculous mummeries." Like many American soldiers, Edwards despised the wealth of the church vis-à-vis Mexican poverty and denounced the immorality of the Mexican priests that he had allegedly witnessed firsthand. To such men, Catholicism seemed to be about the performance of empty ritual and did little to uplift the morality of Mexican peasants.[6]

Many, perhaps having personally encountered Catholicism for the first time in Mexico, might have assumed that it was exactly the same in the United States, especially when they saw their American Catholic comrades diligently attending Mass in Mexico. Disputes between anti-Catholic and Catholic soldiers in the U.S. Army occasionally turned violent. For example, in August 1846, a fight broke out between the two groups on board the *Corvette*, a troop transport headed to the front. Protestant army chaplains often arrived in Mexico armed with tracts and Bibles to spread the true faith of Protestantism to ignorant Mexicans. One Kentucky chaplain went further, explicitly linking the war against Mexico to the war against Catholicism in his state.[7]

Protestants in the U.S. Army, however, held a variety of perspectives on Catholicism; many were negative, but there were some positive views. Raphael Semmes noted that Protestant soldiers often prayed alongside Catholic ones in Mexican churches, and that even General Winfield Scott sought to inculcate good feelings from the populace to the U.S. Army by kneeling at Mass. Even as Protestant soldiers criticized Mexican Catholicism, they often wrote home about how impressed they were with the grandeur of Mexico's Catholic ceremonies, religious music, and churches and cathedrals. Some commented favorably on the equality of Mexican churches, in which worshippers of every class prayed next to one another with no pews set aside for the wealthy. The devout Protestant Kentuckian Robert Anderson, later to defend Fort Sumter, admitted to enjoying the singing

Archbishop John Hughes of New York, widely acknowledged to be the preeminent leader of the American Catholic Church during the mid-nineteenth century (Library of Congress).

and preaching at Mexican churches even though he could not understand Spanish or Latin. Not all disliked the American Catholic priests in the army, either. Army Major Henry Lane, who had deep-seated prejudices against Catholics, grew to respect Father McElroy as a preacher, later writing, "If all Catholic priests were like him there would not be half so much prejudice again[st] Catholicism."[8]

Fortunately for Catholic Americans, President Polk acted to eradicate any notion that the administration viewed the war as one against Mexico's religion. At the beginning of the conflict, he sought the help of the Irish-born bishop of New York, John Hughes, in attaining priests to accompany the armies of Generals Taylor and Scott. There was even talk of Hughes going to Mexico as a representative of the United States government, though nothing came of it. U.S. Catholic newspapers such as the *Freeman's Journal*, *Catholic Miscellany*, and *Catholic Telegraph* all approved of the priests' appointments, with the latter applauding reports that Polk had ordered Taylor to punish anyone "guilty of plundering the property of churches or individuals in the Territory of Mexico." These assurances of safety for Catholic property in Mexico eased fears that nativists might extend such violence to the American church's property after the conflict.[9]

Though the United States government never officially sequestered church property, American Catholics still worried about the potential for such anti-Catholic abuses during the war. For example, the *Freeman's Journal*, published in New York City, supported the war but feared it would become an excuse to exploit Mexican Catholicism and spread anti-Catholicism in the United States. The paper advocated a limited war, not for the purpose of checking the extension of slavery (as the Whig Party's "No Territory" position did), but rather to spare Mexico and its religion from irrecoverable harm. While defending the president's actions in sending troops to the disputed area, it argued that the war should be prosecuted with "generous treatment" of the Mexicans to ensure that American goals were achieved without causing lasting "hatred." In particular, the *Freeman's Journal* was shocked to hear that a onetime opponent of the Native American Party had actually advocated the "leveling of [Mexico's Catholic] temples to dust." Having seen nativist violence do just that during the Philadelphia riots only two years earlier in 1844, its editor clearly feared that the Native Americans would try to benefit from any religious animosity stirred up during the war. The New Orleans paper *Le Propagateur Catholique* condemned "les feuilles bigotes du Nord" for denouncing the appointment of Catholic priests to the army, an act of "justice et d'impartialité" to Catholics in the American army.[10]

Catholic editors and journalists, most of whom supported the war effort, consistently criticized anti-Catholicism during the war while defending the patriotism of their faith community. Boston's *The Pilot* denounced suggestions that Irish Catholics had deserted in large numbers to Mexico. Its Irish American editor, Patrick Donahoe, mocked nativists, asking if they would now join the fight as the men of the Irish Catholic Montgomery Guard of Boston were expected to do. Donahoe sarcastically asked why, "in time of peace we Irish are not fit to enjoy life, liberty, and the pursuit of happiness, but when the country needs our aid, we are capital, glorious fellows! *Vive la republique!*" The *Catholic Telegraph* called for Catholics to rally to the national cause, regardless of right or wrong, until the war had been won. It urged them to put aside any feelings of hesitation over going to war with a Catholic nation, arguing that U.S. interests were at stake and should be upheld as a general principle even if it meant fighting the "Roman States" of the pope himself: "We believe most truly, that if any field of battle be lost in the present war, it will not be through the cowardice or faithlessness of the Catholic citizen." A Catholic editor from New York pointed to the kindly reception that American Catholic chaplains received from their fellow Mexican clergymen in an attempt to undermine the idea that the Mexican Catholic Church, and by association the American Catholic Church and its clergy, were hostile to the United States. Charleston's official Catholic paper, the *U.S. Catholic Miscellany*, denounced attempts by Whigs to poison Catholics against the war and predicted that Catholics would unite with Protestant Americans to defeat Mexico.[11]

The one major exception to this chorus of pro-war voices was an influential but unusual Catholic voice, Orestes Brownson. Like other Catholic editors, Brownson agreed that citizens had a responsibility to support the government now that it had gone to war, and he hoped that "our government . . . will remember the distracted state and weakness of Mexico, and show its moderation." At first, he largely shared the basic concerns of fellow Catholic editors for the safety and welfare of Catholic Mexico. A year later, however, he adopted a strong anti-war position, denouncing the lust for Mexican lands an "insane rage" that would only cause greater conflict between the North and the South over slavery. "Mexico must not be dismembered," he wrote, because land acquired from it would certainly lead to greater divisions in American society, possibly leading to an American "civil war." Brownson was one of the few Catholic public figures to denounce openly the morality of the conflict itself in terms of the larger national debate over expansion and slavery.[12]

Brownson's vigorous criticism of the war was unmatched in the Catholic journalistic community. Still, some Catholics in the U.S. Army appeared to share his lack of enthusiasm for the conflict. Lieutenant William S. Rosecrans, a recent native-born convert to Catholicism, never saw action during the Mexican War because he apparently made no effort get himself reassigned to the front from his noncombat engineering posting in Rhode Island. Rosecrans's close friend from West Point and later his chief of staff in the Civil War, Julius Garesché, similarly showed a lack of enthusiasm for the war, which his son later said his father had found to be of "doubtful justice." Though Garesché served in the war, he never saw combat, silently decried the war, and was angered by American volunteers who abused Mexican citizens and their churches. Likewise, another Catholic army friend of Rosecrans, Eliakim P. Scammon, admitted that he did not want to go to war. "Perhaps I am unpatriotic," wrote Scammon, "but it is not a welcome Sound to me—to fight against my brethren in Xt. [Christ]." Another Catholic, Thomas J. Curd, apparently lost his desire to remain in the service and instead left the army to become a priest. Apparently some Catholics, as their critics claimed, did not have their hearts in the conflict.[13]

Yet these men were not representative of all Catholics in the army, many of whom distinguished themselves during the war. The Irish General, James Shields, the most prominent Catholic serving in the U.S. Army, served with distinction at the battles of Cerro Gordo, Churubusco, and Chapultepec. Colonel William Selby Harney, a convert to Catholicism, had the duty of overseeing the execution of members of the San Patricio Battalion, a group of American soldiers allegedly composed entirely of Irish Catholics who had deserted to fight for Mexico. He forced them to watch the Mexican colors being hauled down and replaced with the Star-Spangled Banner before their execution. Meanwhile, the Maryland Catholic Raphael Semmes, later to gain fame as the bane of the northern merchant fleet during the Civil War, wrote two books about his wartime experiences, titled *The Campaign of General Scott* and *Service Afloat and Ashore*. Both went through several printings. Another future Confederate officer, Pierre Gustave Toutant Beauregard, a French Catholic Creole from Louisiana, also showed much promise during his service south of the border.[14]

These Catholic officers and their evident patriotism during the war stood as a direct refutation of the anti-Catholicism of 1840s nativists. Sigma, the alias of the *Freeman's Journal*'s correspondent in Washington, argued that the courageous service of these Catholics "gives the lie direct to those fanatics" who argued that they could not fight against a fellow Catholic nation. Sigma believed that no Catholic could rightly refuse his country's call to help defend the republic from attack, whether the war was "just or unjust." The editors noted with pride that the Catholic religious press supported the United States in its war against Mexico, while the Protestant press "have generally leaned to the other side, and condemned the 'Mexican war.'" The *Freeman's Journal* reminded the editors of *The Presbyterian* that Catholics were fighting valiantly in the U.S. Army in Mexico just as they had in Washington's army. "We yield to none in discharging all the duties of good citizens," declared the *Freeman's* editor.[15]

While most of the American Catholic press wrote in English, there were also a small but growing number of Catholic newspapers printed in German. Although German immigration did not accelerate until after the Mexican War, when it surpassed that from Ireland, the Midwest and the major northeastern cities already had significant numbers of German Catholics—estimated as representing one-third of all German immigrants to the United States at that time. The oldest U.S. German Catholic paper was *Der Wahrheits Freund* (*Friend of Truth*), published in Cincinnati since 1837, and the second oldest, begun in 1846, was Baltimore's *Katholische Kirchen-Zeitung* (*Catholic Church Newspaper*). Both German-language papers catered to a wide, nearly national audience, and though neither commented extensively on the war, the *Wahrheits Freund* openly disputed charges that Catholicism and American democracy were incompatible. It prominently published a letter that cited testimony from Alexis de Tocqueville and George Washington as proof that Catholicism was no threat to America. In July 1847, the paper reported a memorial speech given in honor of a German Catholic, Lieutenant Matthew Hett, who had died in battle near Monterrey, Mexico, the previous September. The speech praised Hett's battlefield death as proof that a German Catholic could be a "true citizen" of the republic.[16]

In order to emphasize the real patriotism of Catholics, other editors similarly highlighted their battlefield sacrifices and compared them favorably to seemingly less patriotic Americans. *The Pilot* attacked opponents of the war, including antislavery critics of the conflict, as worshiping "no gods but money and pleasure," and of having in wartime chosen to "shirk from [the nation's] defense, and sympathize with its enemies." Its editor further argued that the accusation of divided loyalty leveled repeatedly against Catholics was nothing but "libel" and that "nearly all these anti-Popery folks are shirking from the support of the war" while the paper's subscribers patriotically went off to fight. A letter published by the Pittsburgh *Catholic* pointed to the sacrifice of a Catholic officer with pride and praised the willingness of Father McElroy and Father Rey to serve as chaplains. *The Pilot* published a letter to the editor that hailed the "gallant exploits" of the Irish in the war's early battles, and later reprinted an article listing Irish and German battlefield casualties, which "left on record an eloquent argument against the charges of Nativism." Similarly, the *Freeman's Journal* reprinted a story which stated that the majority of American casualties at Monterrey had been loyal Irish

Catholic Americans, thus illustrating the absurdity of Native Americanism's insistence that Catholics were disloyal. Another correspondent defended the loyalty of Irish Repealers (Irishmen and Irish Americans who sought the peaceful dissolution of Ireland's political union with Great Britain), asserting that the real traitors were the followers of the "fanatic" abolitionist, William Lloyd Garrison, who they alleged sought the dissolution of the American Union itself. Thus some Catholic Americans defended themselves against accusations of disloyalty to the United States by pointing out the real threat to American society: radical abolitionism.[17]

The desertion of immigrant and Catholic soldiers diminished whatever reputation Catholics gained for patriotism during the war. They left throughout the war for a variety of reasons including religious prejudice in the American army. In particular, the Irish Catholic deserters serving in the Mexican Army's San Patricio Battalion threatened to undermine American Catholic leaders' attempts to portray their community as unequivocally loyal. Numbering more than two hundred by July 1847, the San Patricios were composed largely of American deserters of foreign birth but also included native-born Americans as well as Mexican citizens. Led by the Irish-born and Catholic deserter John Riley, it was "named for the Irish patron saint and fought under an emerald flag emblazoned with the Irish harp and shamrock." Though a tiny group of men when compared to the total number of Irish Catholic soldiers who remained loyal to the United States during the war, Protestant soldiers and American nativists saw them as undeniable proof of American Catholic treachery. Many Catholic journals dealt with these deserters by simply ignoring them.[18]

The Pilot, however, actively took up the subject, arguing that the number of Irishmen in the unit had been exaggerated. Furthermore, it claimed, the unit's leader, John Riley, was actually English, not Irish. Borrowing enlistment data from a New York paper, *The Pilot* tried to show that most of the deserters were actually nativists, not Irishmen. A Catholic soldier in the American army in Mexico, who claimed to have been present at the execution of sixteen former soldiers of the San Patricio Battalion, insisted that only five of the condemned men were actually Catholic. Historian Robert Miller similarly has concluded that the Irish ancestry and Catholicism of the San Patricios has been exaggerated by both their American critics and their Mexican supporters. Miller found that only two-fifths of the San Patricio Battalion were from Ireland and that the Catholic connection was emphasized more by the Mexicans than by the San Patricios themselves. While no data on the religious affiliation of each of its members exists, the fact that so few were from Ireland makes it likely that many, if not most, of the members of the battalion were not Catholic. Nevertheless, some American nativists would use the San Patricios after the war to question Catholic patriotism.[19]

As peace negotiations dragged on after the capture of Mexico City in 1847, many Americans, including Catholics, became weary of the conflict and hoped for its quick termination. A Catholic writer for the *New York Sun*, Jane Storm, begged Bishop Anthony Blanc to intercede with the clergy of Mexico to end the "grief and anxiety" of the war. *The Pilot*, while blaming Mexico for the start of hostilities, feared that the war was simply becoming a tool of "Protestant propagandism at the point of the bayonet." At the end of 1848, Philadelphia's *Catholic Herald* agreed, chiding Protestants for thinking that the war would accomplish the "introduction of that Gospel to that benighted people" of Mexico. Echoing this fear, a Catholic army officer named E. P. Scammon guessed that his Catholic army friends Thomas Curd and R. W. M. Johnston had resigned because they had become so "disgusted with this warfare & pillage to such an extent th[a]t they can no longer bear arms with a clear conscience."[20]

Although Father McElroy later remembered his service fondly as helping to care for Catholic soldiers while also dispelling anti-Catholic "calumnies," he admitted that he was not always as positive about his experience at that time. In the spring of 1847, he readily obeyed his superior's call well before the war's end that he return to the United States even though it meant leaving no one behind to care for the souls of Catholic soldiers still in service. The death of his fellow chaplain, Father Rey, who had been waylaid and killed by Mexican bandits on his way to Matamoros, probably hastened his return. "It is one of the most melancholy events, connected with the war," wrote Father McElroy as he informed New Orleans's French-born archbishop, Anthony Blanc, of his plans to return. "Zealous, pious, laborious, Father Rey, had promised a life of usefulness—now he is no more! cut off in the prime of life, the 39th year of his age R.I.P."[21] Increasingly many other Catholics lost their fervor for a war that they believed should have ended long ago and was simply becoming an excuse for attacking the church and its property in Mexico.

In fact most Catholic editors, such as those in charge of the *Miscellany*, *Le Propagateur*, *Der Wahrheits Freund*, and the *Catholic Herald*, had little to say about the conflict. In general, they merely reprinted war news from other papers. For a war against a Catholic country, full of religious intensity and passion in both Mexico and the United States, many Catholic editors demonstrated an amazing level of indifference to the conflict. More pressing events in their former European homelands quickly drew the Catholic community's attention away from the war. Compared to coverage of the Irish potato famine or the 1848

revolutions in Europe, the final peace negotiations with Mexico paled in importance. One newspaper, content to clip from other Catholic papers' news on the
war, even admitted that since it had not deemed it worth its time to examine the
merits of the conflict, "we forbear to express an opinion upon the war."[22]

In the end, Catholics left behind a mixed record of support for the war. On the
one hand, reports of priests urging their parishioners to stay home, of chaplains
aggressively converting American Protestants, and of the Irish American deserters in the San Patricio Battalion cast a pall over the entire Catholic community.
On the other hand, there were numerous reports of the patriotism and sacrifice of American Catholic soldiers and officers on Mexican battlefields. Bishop
Hughes's willingness to support the government diplomatically if necessary and
to help find Catholic chaplains for the army showed that at least one church leader
had actively supported the American cause. Even for those American Catholic
soldiers who fought bravely in Mexico, however, the pillaging of churches and
continued religious discrimination in the U.S. Army itself may have hindered
the Americanization of Catholics soldiers. While a few editors, leaders, and laypeople saw the war as an opportunity to prove Catholic patriotism, the actual
experience of the conflict demonstrated the limits of relying on military service
to defeat anti-Catholic nativism. The resurgence of political nativism in the mid-
1850s clearly demonstrated that the war had little positive impact on tolerance for
Catholicism in American society.[23]

With the end of the Mexican conflict, European events accelerated the growth
of American anti-Catholicism. Pope Pius IX, initially seen as a reformer, fled
Rome in 1848 after a popular revolution overthrew his government in the Papal
States. Many Americans saw this revolution as the work of the Roman people
and praised it as a triumph of democracy. They later denounced the pope's return to power thanks to the intervention of the French Army in 1849. When
Pius returned, he was determined to oppose both revolution and anti-Catholic
reform in Europe. Following the other failed European revolutions of 1848, democratic exiles—including the anticlerical German radicals known as the Forty-
Eighters—immigrated to the United States where they continued to attack the
Catholic Church. Alessandro Gavazzi, a former Italian priest turned Roman
revolutionary, toured American cities giving anti-Catholic lectures to receptive
Protestant audiences. The anti-Catholic message of these radical exiles strengthened many Americans' dislike for the tyranny of the pope and his potential influence in American affairs.[24]

With the triumph of reactionary aristocratic forces over democratic revolutionaries in Europe, American Protestants increasingly attacked Catholicism as
antithetical to the United States and its republican values. As the famed Protestant leader Alexander Campbell put it in 1837, Catholics were "abject slaves
to their priests, bishops, and popes." Catholicism, he declared, was "essentially
anti-American, being opposed to the genius of all free institutions, and positively
subversive of them, opposing the general reading of the scriptures, and the dif-
fusion of useful knowledge among the whole community, so essential to liberty
and the permanence of good government." Rev. William S. Balch took umbrage
at Bishop John Hughes's claim that Catholicism had furthered the progress of
liberty and republicanism in the United States. In his opinion, this argument was
merely one of the "old tricks of Jesuitism," for Hughes would gladly overthrow
democracy if he had the power to do so. Theodore Parker, a prominent Protestant minister, castigated Catholicism for denying Catholics the free use of their
own conscience, stating that it was "therefore the foe of all progress; it is deadly to
Democracy." If Catholics could not interpret the Bible for themselves, and if they
were spiritually subservient to the pope, who could say that Catholics could not
be manipulated into overturning America's democratic institutions? For many
Protestants, Luther and the Reformation were synonymous with prosperity, true
religion, and progress; the pope and Catholicism with poverty, ignorance, and
crime. Interpreting the Bible using one's own private judgment was just as American as voting in an election. After all, Americans were the chosen people of a
Protestant nation entrusted with the divine mission of redeeming the world from
Old World corruption. Roman Catholicism, the most obvious example of this
corruption, clearly had no role to play in America's status as a divinely appointed
redeemer nation.[25]

Hard economic times, nativism, and anti-Catholicism all contributed directly
to the establishment of the American Republican Party in 1843 in New York. The
party spread throughout the country, particularly in the North, by 1844. Also referred to as the Native American Party, it supported amendments to naturalization laws (making immigrants wait twenty-one years before becoming citizens)
and the use of the Protestant King James Bible in public schools. Despite some
initial success, the party could not survive a strong public backlash against the
role its members played in burning Catholic churches and fomenting violence in
Philadelphia in mid-1844. Only one Native American was elected to Congress in
1846, and by the following year the party was no more. Compared to the Know-
Nothing movement of the following decade, the American Republican Party was

a mere "footnote" in American history. Still, the very existence of an openly nativist party in American politics was a troubling sign for Catholics.[26]

The remarkable growth of the Catholic Church contributed to widespread
fears that it was a pressing threat to the United States. By 1850 Catholicism had
become one of the largest denominations in America. It achieved this remarkable distinction because of an unprecedented level of immigration during the
late 1840s and early 1850s, primarily from the European countries of Ireland and
Germany, and because the largest mainline Protestant denominations had split
over the issue of slavery. However, the Catholic Church's growth set the stage
for the nativism and anti-Catholicism of the mid-1850s. Continued fears of immigration, and the apparent arrogance of some Catholic bishops in the common school debates, fueled the growth of anti-Catholicism, particularly among
working-class Americans who already felt threatened by the rise of the market
economy, its periodic financial downturns, and inflation that hurt their ability to
purchase goods and services. The additional prospect of lowered wages due to
competition with large waves of European immigrants led many to lash out at
Catholic foreigners as a threat to their personal livelihoods as well as the nation's
well-being.[27]

Everywhere nativists looked they seemed to find more and more evidence
of how Catholics were threatening American democracy. An ill-timed visit of a
Vatican diplomat, Italian Archbishop Gaetano Bedini, to the United States from
the end of June 1853 to February 1854 raised the familiar if far-fetched specter
of a papal takeover. Nativists and anti-Catholics greeted Bedini with violence
and insults. At the end of his tour of the United States, the archbishop had to be
smuggled out of New York in order to leave the country safely. The last straw for
many nativists was Whig candidate Winfield Scott's courtship of the Catholic
vote in the 1852 presidential election. With both the Democrats and Whigs trying
to curry favor with Catholics, many anti-Catholics became frustrated with both
parties. They sought to create their own political party, which became the Know-
Nothing Party in the mid-1850s.[28]

The Know-Nothing Order, whose members later referred to it as the American Party, was a secretive organization that opposed the growth of Catholic immigration and the Catholic Church's power in the United States. By 1854 Know-
Nothingism spread across the country and became an important force in U.S.
politics. The growth of the Know-Nothings in Massachusetts was particularly
impressive. Galvanized by Catholic opposition to state constitutional reform, the
prominent role played by Irish Catholics in returning runaway slave Anthony
Burns to slavery, and the fear of the growing power of the naturalized Irish Cath-

olic vote, antislavery and pro-reform politicians joined forces with the Know-Nothings to win impressive election victories in 1854. The Massachusetts party won that state's governorship, all the seats in the state Senate, and all but two seats in the state House of Representatives. Even though many in this nativist coalition were reform-minded or antislavery, the new Know-Nothing legislature revealed its anti-Catholicism by sponsoring harassing visits to Catholic colleges and convents. Utilizing many of the standard anti-Catholic prejudices of the day, Know-Nothings described the Catholic Church as a threat to American republicanism and blamed Catholicism for corrupting American politics. They attacked both the Democrats *and* the Whigs for pandering to immigrants and the Catholic Church, and expanded quickly into the North, South, and Border States. While it may be tempting to see the party's success as short-lived and a mere side story to the rise of the Republican Party, one scholar has pointed out there "seemed to be a likelihood" in 1854 that nativism might replace slavery as the "focal issue in American political life."[29]

In the House of Representatives, anti-Catholic congressmen, such as William R. Smith of Alabama and Nathaniel P. Banks of Massachusetts, warned that the pope would try to enlarge his temporal power by invading the United States with the aid of traitorous Jesuits. While at the national level nativist politicians could not muster enough votes to enact their agenda, Know-Nothings found greater success at the state and local level. For instance, the Know-Nothing governor of Connecticut disbanded Irish militia units, while Massachusetts's Know-Nothing legislature passed laws requiring passages from the King James Bible to be read in schools. Massachusetts Know-Nothings also barred state funds from being used for parochial schools. These and other measures passed around the country aimed at limiting immigrant and Catholic power while also trying to stimulate Americanization. While Know-Nothings cared deeply about other issues as well, such as slavery and political reform, many Catholic leaders understandably focused on the anti-Catholic and anti-immigrant policies of the party, both those that were enacted and those that were proposed but failed to be passed into law.[30]

At first, Catholics themselves were unsure of the danger or the extent of the Know-Nothing threat. During the very height of Know-Nothingism in late 1854, Stephan Bell, a Catholic farmer from Germany living near Madison, Wisconsin, wrote a glowing letter to his family about the advantages of immigration to the United States. "The people are all brothers here," he noted, remarking that both the "English" and "Germans" were friendlier in America than in Germany. The president of Mount St. Mary's College in Emmitsburg, Maryland, Father John

McCaffrey, was confident that as long as Catholics were "prepared to maintain their just rights" they would defeat the nativists. McCaffrey even claimed that the Know-Nothings were already retreating in the face of Catholic unity. Baltimore's Archbishop Francis P. Kenrick, who had been the bishop of Philadelphia during the riots of 1844, however, was less sanguine. "Times still look bad, though perhaps not quite so gloomy as recently. We should all be ready for martyrdom, and preparing our flocks for the trial," Kenrick wrote to Cincinnati's Archbishop John Purcell in August 1854. Clearly fearful of a repeat of the violence he had personally witnessed a decade earlier, Kenrick warned his friend, "You are in a station of eminent danger, but none of us is safe." Many Catholic leaders believed caution was the best policy given past violence against their church in previous decades.[31]

Despite such caution, Know-Nothings resorted to violent measures to get rid of Catholics or actively sowed division within the church whenever possible. The American-born bishop of Louisville, Martin J. Spalding, stood by helplessly while a nativist mob unleashed a "reign of terror surpassed only by the Philadelphia riots" and attacked an Irish neighborhood in his city, burning property and killing innocent families. The following year he complained that Know-Nothings had rigged elections and that his parishioners were "leaving [Kentucky] by the score." A Know-Nothing mob in Ellsworth, Maine, seized and tarred and feathered the future founder of Boston College, Father John Bapst, S.J. This caused at least one other priest in nearby Bath to flee the state as well or suffer a similar gruesome fate. In Cleveland, the French-speaking bishop Amadeus Rappe complained that Know-Nothings were actively encouraging German Catholics in their attempts to wrest control of a local parish from its priest. In Cleveland, then, just as at New Orleans where nativists actively recruited disaffected Catholic creoles into their ranks, Know-Nothings seemed determined to deprive the church of its essential unity.[32]

Catholics relied heavily on the support of their own ethnic and religious communities to help them weather this latest nativist storm. Many agreed that the "primary agency for the Catholic defense was the newspaper." The Catholic community had a growing number of Catholic newspapers and journals edited by distinguished laymen, priests, and bishops to defend their interests and their faith. They clearly saw the Know-Nothings as motivated by both anti-immigrant and anti-Catholic prejudice, and they believed that Protestant immigrants were welcome in the organization. Editor and newspaper proprietor Patrick Donahoe took the Know-Nothings seriously enough to recommend that all of his readers become naturalized before naturalization laws could be changed. Donahoe quoted anti-Catholic nativist diatribes from non-Catholic Irish American radicals and Know-Nothing papers alike to show that Catholicism's growth in the United States had provoked the movement's growth. A number of Know-Nothing lodges and associations allowed foreign Protestants to join or cooperated politically with them against their common papist foe.[33]

Other Catholic newspapermen emphasized that religious prejudice, not antiforeign sentiment, was the primary motivating factor behind the Know-Nothing Party's growth. James McMaster, an American-born descendant of Scots–Irish Presbyterian immigrants who had converted to Catholicism in 1845, strongly attacked Know-Nothingism with a convert's zeal for denouncing the enemies of his faith. He used his paper, the *Freeman's Journal*, to appeal to well-meaning Protestant Americans to take notice of the "forbearance and quiet moderation of the entire Catholic community during the whole movement of this fanatical crusade." He bitterly opposed the Know-Nothings and their "anti-Popery crusade," which McMaster claimed was linked to "anti-Slavery propagandism" by the two movements' common origin in England. His readers needed no help in further understanding that any organization that was British in origin was inherently unfriendly to Irishmen and Catholics alike. McMaster counseled against the idea of forming an anti-Know-Nothing Party, instead calling on moderate non-Catholics to join their Catholic neighbors in refusing to support the Know-Nothings. Baltimore's *Catholic Mirror* characterized the secrecy of the movement as antithetical to American republican values and harshly criticized Protestants for supporting it. Though the paper did not go so far as to blame "all Protestants" for the Know-Nothings, it did firmly state, "We believe the Protestant religious press favors generally the growth of the huge fungus called 'Know Nothingism.'" No matter, opined the editor, "The Church never thrives more than under persecution and proscription." Thus the Catholic press reaction to the Know-Nothings was a mixture of aggressive criticism and confidence that the threat would eventually disappear, leaving the church stronger than before.[34]

Because they believed Know-Nothingism was just as anti-Catholic as it was nativist, most Catholic leaders, both clerical and lay, did not hesitate to attack American-born Catholics who expressed any sympathy for the anti-immigrant biases of the Know-Nothings. In July 1854, Orestes Brownson wrote a notorious editorial that portrayed the nativists as primarily motivated by antiforeign sentiment. He argued that the un-American behavior of some nominally Catholic Irishmen had directly contributed to the growth of nativism and anti-Catholicism in the 1850s. He strongly urged foreign Catholics, specifically the Irish, to assimilate in order to promote greater tolerance of Catholicism by eradicating the notion that Catholics belonged to a foreign religion unsuited for the United States.

He admonished them to "understand . . . that they must ultimately lose their own nationality and become assimilated in general character to the Anglo-American race." A small number of foreign and native-born Catholic voices, including that of the Boston *Pilot*, supported Brownson's arguments, at least initially. However, despite his best intentions, it soon became clear that most Catholics hated his ideas only slightly less than those of the Know-Nothings themselves.[35]

Brownson's "Native Americanism" article alarmed many foreign-born Catholics by its strong criticism of their ethnicity. The *Catholic Mirror* accused Brownson of holding views that were "wrong and injurious to Catholic interests." The *Catholic* expressed disapproval of Brownson's views, with its editor writing that Brownson could benefit from a "great amount of Christian humility." Perhaps the most critical of Brownson was the "second-most important Catholic editor" in the country, James McMaster. McMaster attacked Brownson for asserting "Anglo-Saxon" superiority over the Irish, and he criticized Brownson's distinction between native and naturalized Americans. McMaster found the article to be "objectionable," "very poor," and full of "fallacies." One Louisville correspondent warned Brownson that "Native Americanism" had angered Catholics of native and foreign birth, "particularly" the Irish. Bishop Spalding of Louisville was incensed that Know-Nothings utilized Brownson's article to attack Catholics, and he called for the removal of the American bishops' letter of endorsement of Brownson's journal that was printed on the back of every edition of Brownson's *Review*. By attacking Brownson's ideas so sharply, Catholic leaders forcibly and unequivocally restated their belief that Know-Nothings were primarily motivated by religious prejudice.[36]

The debate over Brownson revealed divisions within the Catholic community not just about how to deal with nativism, but also over the extent to which Catholics should participate in or remain separate from the larger American society. Many of the more political Catholics, most particularly the Irish, reacted to anti-immigrant or anti-Catholic sentiment by wedding themselves more closely to the immigrant-friendly Democratic Party. Being a Democrat in the mid-1850s meant belonging to the last truly national political party. It allowed Catholic immigrants, in one historian's phrase, to experience "a sense of Americanness by being part of a nationwide organization." Catholic leaders did not want their flock to completely separate themselves from American life, politics, and culture. For example, Bishop Hughes, who was often active in all three, opposed Catholic colonization schemes in the West not only because he believed there were inadequate steps being taken to provide for their faith but also because he feared they would hinder immigrants' assimilation. Catholic leaders including Hughes celebrated their faith's and its members' contributions to American society and government, while repeatedly praising the American value of religious freedom. Hughes wanted a balance between assimilation and cultural retention that would allow the faithful to be good Americans while remaining good Catholics.[37]

Still, nearly all Catholic leaders including Hughes and much of the devout laity believed that some degree of separation was necessary given the traditional hostility of WASP culture. The vast majority of Catholics saw no need to give up many of their ethnic customs or assimilate on Protestant Americans' terms to be considered truly American. Thus leaders such as Hughes rejected other groups' attempts to "Americanize" Catholicism and built up large and powerful Catholic institutions to challenge those run by non-Catholic Americans. Many Irish and German bishops and priests in turn encouraged the founding of Catholic schools, aid societies, and parish organizations as alternatives to American ones under the control of Protestants. German Catholics in particular fiercely clung to their language and customs as a means of preserving the faith of their children in a religiously and linguistically alien environment. This question during the 1850s of just how American Catholics could be without ceasing to be Catholic would again play itself out even more dramatically during the Civil War.[38]

Despite its impressive rise to power, starting in 1855 political nativism suffered serious reverses that eventually led to the collapse of the Know-Nothing Party. The Know-Nothings, just as some Catholic periodicals had predicted, were discredited for their violent ways and ultimately failed to pass their legislative agendas at the national level and in most states. At their national conference in Philadelphia in June 1855, the Know-Nothings split into sectional factions because they could not withstand the divisive force of the preeminent issues of the day: slavery and its westward expansion. Though the American Party ran former president Millard Fillmore in 1856 and gained an impressive, and alarming as far as Catholics were concerned, 25 percent of the popular vote, he finished third in the election. Catholics knew that the American Party's electoral defeat did not spell the end of anti-Catholicism in the United States. Many looked with distrust on the Republican Party, which they accused of all too willingly welcoming former Know-Nothings and well-known anti-Catholic abolitionists into its fold. For example, the successful candidacy of Republican Salmon P. Chase relied heavily on Know-Nothing votes to win the Ohio gubernatorial election in 1855.[39]

From a historian's point of view, it is tempting to dismiss the anti-Catholic Know-Nothings as a short-lived phenomenon that inevitably gave way to the antislavery Republican Party. Catholics living at that time, however, could not know that the Know-Nothings would not be replaced by a new anti-Catholic, anti-immigrant party. Similar religious and social constituencies in the North supported both nativism and antislaveryism, and these groups would prove to be prominent in the Republican Party. As one prominent historian of the Republican Party asserted, Republicans were primarily antislavery, but they also consciously fostered the identification of Catholics with the Democratic Party while refraining from pursuing Catholic votes. Such tactics allowed Republicans to court Know-Nothings who continued to hold nativist views even after their party had died. "Both the Republican party's rhetoric and membership gave it an anti-Catholic image" of which Catholic Americans like the American-born bishop of Buffalo, John Timon, were well aware. Timon reported that while the Know-Nothings had almost died out in his diocese by the end of 1855, he feared the moderately anti-Catholic Republican Party even more. This fear of nativism was often in the background of their reactions to the political events surrounding the 1860 election, the secession movement later that winter, and the Republican-led Civil War itself. The fact that nativist politicians such as Daniel Ullman, Schuyler Colfax, and Nathaniel Banks held prominent positions in the Republican Party certainly did not help Lincoln garner many Catholic votes. If the constitutional rights of slaveholders could be ignored by abolitionist Republicans, so the argument went, then the nativists in the party would be able to attack the Catholic Church as well.[40]

2   Catholics Rally to the Flag

In response to political nativism, and despite the official neutrality of the clergy and many religious newspapers, Catholic laymen strengthened their ties to the Democratic Party prior to the election of 1860. Other factors certainly influenced this decision, including local, ethnic, and economic ones. But Catholics' faith and religious worldview, which emphasized stability over reform, also made them predisposed to favor a conservative and national party. When secession came, church leaders and laymen argued that they had avoided the slavery issue altogether and could not be blamed for the sectional crisis. Most Catholic leaders opposed forcible reunion with the Confederacy.

The Confederate attack on Fort Sumter on April 12, 1861, however, ended hopes for a peaceful settlement of secession and unleashed an unprecedented, united patriotic fervor across the North. Lincoln called for troops to put down the rebellion a few days later and soon four more slave states left the Union. Ironically, for all of the Catholic claims of having done nothing to cause disunion, it was a French Creole Catholic, General P. G. T. Beauregard, who commanded the Confederate attack on the fort. Border State Catholics, caught in the middle, were forced to make the difficult choice between their kinship with the slaveholding South and the Union, now composed overwhelmingly of free states. By and large, they chose to remain neutral.

Northern Catholic leaders and editors, like most of their neighbors, supported the war throughout 1861.[1] Both native-born Americans like Orestes Brownson and foreign-born leaders such as the Irishman James A. Mulligan rushed to uphold the Union against southern treachery. Their patriotism did not go unnoticed, as the Republican and Protestant press praised their willingness to bear arms in defense of the Stars and Stripes. If the war had ended in 1861, as many thought it would, Catholic loyalty and patriotism would have been beyond question. But defeat at the First Battle of Bull Run in the summer ensured that the war would not end quickly, and disputes over the measures necessary to ensure the Union's eventual triumph caused some Democrats and Catholics to begin questioning Lincoln's wartime policies. Although generally limited to exceptionally strident voices such as James McMaster's, these early signs of dissent hinted that many Catholics had a limit to what they would tolerate and sacrifice to keep the Union intact.

Even as the country became increasingly divided over slavery, the Catholic population of the United States continued to grow in size and influence. According to one estimate, by 1860 there were approximately 3.1 million Catholics in the United States, with most living in the states that would remain within the Union. Although immigration was slowing down from its peak in the mid-1850s, the Irish dominated the church's hierarchy and laity. Though there were signs of increasing social mobility, the Irish still "were concentrated at the bottom of the occupational hierarchy." After the Irish in importance came native-born and German Catholics, with French- and Spanish-speaking members making up a tiny proportion of the larger community. The Catholic press continued to expand as well, increasing from forty-one to sixty-two periodicals from 1850 to 1860.[2]

Throughout the 1850s and into 1860, many Catholic journalists and bishops continued to confine themselves to religious subjects and to avoid domestic politics as much as possible. Such a course of action, they hoped, would not only prevent their own church from splitting (as the Baptists and Methodists had done over slavery in the 1840s), but it would also allow them to keep a low profile and avoid a recurrence of anti-Catholic nativism. In 1858 Catholic bishops attending the Ninth Provincial Council of Baltimore implored their priests to refrain "prudently" from commenting on political issues. Whereas Baptist and Methodist ministers had joined the Know-Nothings in large numbers, and northern clergymen such as Henry Ward Beecher frequently weighed in on slavery, Catholic priests were notable for abstaining from partisan politics. Brownson, despite having supported Democratic candidates in his *Review* in the past, agreed with his fellow editors that religious papers should not side with one party over the other. Since none of the political parties was Catholic, he continued, the church should not form an alliance with any of them. "The Church," wrote the editor of a Philadelphia Catholic paper, was the "promoter" of all private and public virtues, including patriotism. Catholics, "above all other people," intoned the editor, "should prefer patriotism to party" and should support the maintenance of the Union. As the editor warned his readers, Catholics would be the "first victims" of the "rage and violence" of the disunionists.[3]

Despite this official political neutrality from church leaders, the great majority of Catholics remained loyal to the Democratic Party. McMaster's *Freeman's Journal* and Donahoe's *Pilot* were openly allied with Illinois Senator Stephen A.

Douglas's presidential campaign, supporting Douglas Democrats and the Catholic Church with an equal fervor. For most Catholics, abolition and nativism often seemed to be advocated by the same people who supported the new Republican Party. They refused to join a party prominently supported by evangelical Protestant reformers, whom they believed were a threat to both the Catholic Church and the maintenance of the American Union. The Democratic Party's defense of immigrants' rights, its status as a national party, and its opposition to abolitionism helped to retain the allegiance of most Catholic voters. Most northern Catholics favored Douglas, while those in the slave states were divided between other candidates, such as John Breckinridge, the southern Democrats' first choice, and John Bell, the conservative candidate of the Constitutional Union Party. Very few Catholics supported the Republicans. The most notable Catholic to vote for Lincoln was the ever-independent-minded and increasingly liberal Brownson, who before had always voted for the Democrats. Johann Dieden, a German Catholic immigrant who sympathized with other Germans just as much as he did with other Catholics, also broke the mold by supporting Lincoln as "the man of freedom, the enemy of slavery, the man of equal rights." Both men, however, were the exception to the tacit rule that Catholics should be Democratic voters.[4]

Few Catholic commentators bothered to comment on Lincoln's victory in November 1860, but they freely expressed their opinions about the ensuing secession crisis that began with South Carolina leaving the Union the following month. The *New York Tablet* denounced secession as "diabolical" and predicted that thousands of citizens would rally to the flag to defend the nation should the need arise. Likewise, a German Catholic editor from New York published a strong editorial in favor of the Union, warning its readers that "the first disunionist was the violent Cain," and that "no good citizen can go against the Union." Another editor likened the actions of South Carolinian disunionists to those of anti-Catholic English liberals and Hungarian rebels, who in their selfishness sought to overthrow stability and promote chaos and anarchy in Europe. The secession crisis was more proof, he continued, that Catholic editors should stay out of political affairs and confine themselves to defending the faith.[5]

For Catholic leaders the solution to sectionalism was clear: the Catholic Church. McMaster, for one, argued that the nation's salvation lay in accepting the truth of the Catholic Church, which had not "split upon the negro," and its universal principles that would bind the country together again. Taking a stand in defense of the Union, he assured his readers that the church had never been treated better than it had in the United States. Likewise, Louisville's Catholic newspaper, the *Guardian*, commended "to the sober attention of Americans" the church's refusal to agitate the slavery question that was threatening to sunder the Union. This Border State paper, while less willing to criticize secessionists, nevertheless stood by the Union and agreed with the editors of the *Catholic Telegraph* that Protestantism's emphasis on "private interpretation" produced irreconcilable differences over slavery and thus brought ruin to the country. Brownson blamed a lack of "spiritual discipline and culture" that directly resulted from Americans' rejection of the Catholic Church in favor of an "easy sort of religion," for having rent asunder the Union. Thus this apolitical anti-Protestant commentary on the causes of the war was found in both free and slave states.[6]

Whereas Brownson placed blame on both sections of the nation, many conservative Catholics actually agreed with their southern counterparts that the Republicans and abolitionists deserved most of the blame for secession. Even before South Carolina voted to leave the Union, Donahoe criticized abolitionist and Protestant preachers alike, declaring that "Northern aggression on the principle interest of the Southern States has been the cause of the treasonable sentiments on the right to secede, which is now so dangerously inflaming those important members of the Republic." "Slavery is an evil," asserted Donahoe, "but the distraction of the nation, consequent on its agitation, is a greater evil; and, neither in itself, nor in the manner in which it exists here, is there any repugnance to the Divine law." Baltimore's Catholic paper likewise lashed out at Republicans, declaring Lincoln's opposition to slavery harmful to the maintenance of the Union while asserting that it had already inspired slave unrest even prior to his election. Slavery was *"an evil,"* but it was "inseparable from humanity"; only by the states minding their own business could the Union be saved. Its editor, a former slaveholder named Courtney Jenkins, publicly supported peaceful secession if the North did not give into southern demands.[7]

As the secession crisis wore on, Catholic commentators consistently weighed in on domestic political developments with a single message: *Dona nobis pacem*. Grant us peace. President James Buchanan's declared fast day of January 4, 1861, was widely supported by Catholic leaders. Donahoe warmly praised the bishops for supporting the fast day, never doubting that the prayers of the "three millions" of American Catholics would be heard by God, who would restore peace in the country just as He had done many times in European history. McMaster happily reported that the Church of St. Lawrence in New York City was full of Catholics at specially appointed Masses for the country and that a number of bishops had likewise encouraged observance of the fast day. He warned his readers that their work was not done, however, and enjoined Catholics, as "especial servants of God," to continue to pray for God's intercession. It was "foolish" to think that the Catholic religion would not suffer for the downfall of the Union and urged his readers to "redouble" their prayers. In Louisville, Bishop Spalding preached a neutral sermon expressing hope that the "conservative action of all lovers of their country, North and South," would soon end the political and financial chaos afflicting the United States.[8]

Thus northern and Border State Catholic leaders worked to promote fasting, penance, and an increased reliance on God during the secession crisis. Virtually no Catholic leader wanted to restore the Union by force. As the *Catholic Telegraph* put it, "We condemn secession as a cruel wrong done to the cause of human rights . . . but coercion, by renouncing the principle of self-government, would shatter [our free government] to fragments, and scatter its poor ruins to the winds." On April 11 Spalding wrote his superior in Ohio, "God avert Civil War, & restrain such fanatical firebrands as your own Chase & Dennison, to say nothing of the preachers!" Despite his prayers and those of millions of other Catholics, the war began the very next day with the Confederate attack on Fort Sumter in Charleston Harbor.[9]

Catholic reactions to the outbreak of war were shaped by geography, politics and their religious and ethnic backgrounds. Catholics in the Border States in particular deplored the outbreak of violence and continued to oppose coercion to save the Union. In Kentucky, the *Louisville Guardian* followed the lead of Bishop Spalding, who preached a sermon the Sunday after Fort Sumter calling for peace. The paper saw the war as a calamity of brother against brother and offered up a prayer to God, who "alone can help us in this direst of all calamities." When Spalding traveled across the Ohio River in late April to attend the Third Provincial Council of Cincinnati, he was shocked at how the city had been transformed into a "fortified camp." Spalding wrote the council's pro-peace pastoral letter and fervently hoped it would help ease tensions stoked by warmongering fanatics.[10]

Spalding's consistent opposition to the war as the bishop of Louisville (and later as archbishop of Baltimore) was based primarily on two factors. First, Spalding came from an old slaveholding Maryland family and, as bishop of Louisville, owned twenty or more slaves. As one biographer put it, "Slavery for Kentucky Catholics was a fact of life," an institution that the church did not condemn as immoral. Thus Spalding culturally sympathized with slaveholding Confederates and had no love for abolitionism. Second and perhaps most important, for Spalding the church and its mission of salvation were always paramount over wartime politics. Though he privately favored the Confederate cause, he remained officially neutral long after his state of Kentucky did. He saw no inherent conflict in letting the rabidly secessionist French-born bishop of St. Augustine, Florida, Augustine Verot, preach in his cathedral in October while also providing priests and nuns to attend to the spiritual needs of Union soldiers. Though such a policy may have dismayed partisans on both sides, to Spalding it was both principled and the only one faithful to his religious duties that he could have taken.[11]

Many Catholics in the Border States probably shared the neutrality of the *Louisville Guardian* and Spalding, though some openly supported secession. One Catholic wrote to the *Louisville Guardian* to argue like Spalding that Kentuckians should continue to work for peace and resist calls for secession, at least until every effort had been made to end the conflict peacefully. In Baltimore, the *Catholic Mirror* meanwhile credited the Catholic Church for having nothing to do with spreading the "discord" that had ruined the nation. However, it also was much more openly critical of the North and its role in the conflict. Southerners, it editorialized, would be fighting "for altars and homes" while northerners were preparing "for conquest." "War will bring no good to any parties, but misery and destruction to all," it declared. "The North and the South cannot live in peace together, then why not part in peace?" In Wheeling, West Virginia, Bishop Richard V. Whelan, a native-born Marylander who privately sympathized with the Confederacy, repeatedly denounced both the war and the North in letters to Archbishops Hughes and Francis Kenrick. Whelan pleaded with Hughes not to encourage Catholic northerners to fight on behalf of the Republicans, a party "that contains [Catholics'] most deadly enemies, abolitionists, infidels & red republicans." Whelan's lack of discretion in expressing his pro-Confederate views later forced Archbishop Kenrick to intervene personally on his behalf with President Lincoln to keep the Wheeling bishop from being arrested.[12]

The cultural affinity of Catholic Marylanders for their fellow southerners led many of them to sympathize with the Confederacy. Baltimore priests refused to pray a traditional prayer for the Union, and when Archbishop Kenrick insisted on reading it himself, many of his congregation stood up and left or "expressed their dissent . . . by a great rustling of papers and silks." Violence that erupted on April 19, 1861, between northern troops marching through Baltimore on their way to Washington and a pro-secession mob probably only hardened the pro-southern views of Maryland's Catholics. It also forced the cancellation of a regularly planned provincial council in the city. Soon after the riots, the *Catholic Mirror's* editor noted that the state "is now thoroughly southern in her tendencies and sympathies." Kenrick took a more conciliatory approach and called for peace prayers to be added to every Mass. Privately, however, he declared that Marylanders were being "treated as a conquered people," and he increasingly resented the

Lincoln administration's heavy-handed policies. While he professed his love for the Union and did not care for the *Catholic Mirror*'s increasingly pro-southern viewpoint, stating that he wished that "secession had never been thought of," he also adamantly refused to interfere with his paper's editorial policies.[13]

Many Border State Catholics immediately blamed Lincoln and the abolitionists for the outbreak of war. If they did not become Confederates themselves, then some did their best to obstruct the new administration's wartime policies. Such was the case with Chief Justice Roger Taney. Taney, the most politically powerful Catholic in the nation, took sides against the administration after it suspended habeas corpus and resorted to martial law to keep Maryland's legislature from voting the state out of the Union. Intervening in the arrest of a Confederate sympathizer named John Merriman in the early days of the war, Taney used the power of the Supreme Court in a manner called "officious and improper" by the Republican *New York Times*. Taney's insistence on trying this case himself was probably the result of his desire for a direct confrontation with Abraham Lincoln over the constitutionality of his actions during wartime. His sympathy for the South and his subsequent efforts to undermine Union war policy, whether it was the blockade or emancipation, ensured that Taney was one of the most prominent of all anti-war and obstructionist Catholic voices in the United States. Lincoln ignored the *Merriman* ruling and routinely used the War Powers Clause of the Constitution vigorously to prosecute the war despite Taney's objections.[14]

In sharp contrast to their coreligionists along the border, the vast majority of northern Catholics made an abrupt about-face and joined in the patriotic outburst sweeping through the North after the attack on Fort Sumter. Immigrant Catholics soon showed that their support for the war was equal to that of any native-born American. Prior to Sumter, Irish American leaders had criticized the idea of Irish participation in an American war as detrimental to the cause of Ireland. Among these was Thomas F. Meagher, who was involved in the Irish revolutionary group known as the Fenians, who worked for the independence of Ireland from Great Britain. Meagher and other Fenians, however, pragmatically changed their minds and supported the war effort both to stave off potential criticisms from native-born Americans and to acquire military experience.[15]

German Catholics similarly reacted with a patriotic fervor to Fort Sumter. Maximillian Oertel of New York's *Katholische Kirchen-Zeitung* declared, "No good citizen can go against the Union." Faced with the threat of secession after Lincoln's election, Oertel implored religious protection over the "magnificent Union." "May God preserve us from this calamity and let the Union rather survive yet a long time." Likewise, *Der Wahrheits Freund* reminded its readers of their "Pflicht" (duty) to their country, regardless of whether they agreed with Lincoln's politics: "It is therefore the duty of every good citizen, in the carrying out of the measures [to suppress the rebellion], which the highest authorities find suitable to take, to contribute and to facilitate them, as the best he can." While the exact numbers of German Catholic soldiers who served is unknowable, it is likely that many served in German-speaking regiments during the conflict.[16]

Some northern Catholic voices that had previously denounced the idea of coercion soon became some of the strongest proponents of the war. Perhaps the most dramatic shift after hostilities commenced was made by what ultimately became one of the administration's strongest allies, Archbishop Purcell's *Catholic Telegraph*. After the news of Fort Sumter reached Ohio, the paper, now edited by Purcell's brother, the Irish American Rev. Edward Purcell, and General William S. Rosecrans's brother, the native-born Bishop Sylvester Rosecrans, called for Ohio Catholics to fulfill their "solemn duty, as good and loyal citizens to walk shoulder to shoulder with all our fellow-citizens in support of the laws and the national honor." Cincinnati's Catholics turned out in large numbers to support the Union at an April 19 meeting at the city's Catholic Institute. Speakers pledged their fidelity for the Union, called for able-bodied men to volunteer, and passed resolutions condemning secession and in favor of the Union. This very vocal support for the Union by the laity seemed to contrast with the recent provincial council's enjoinders "to pray fervently for peace and prosperity to our beloved country." Bishop Spalding wrote to his friend Purcell to convey his "pain" over reading about the Union meeting and seeing the *Catholic Telegraph* "favoring civil war against Southern brethren at the biding of black republicans." Nevertheless, Purcell's paper argued that naturalized citizens owed their allegiance to their newly adopted country and soon became a strong supporter of the federal government against southern disunion that threatened the nation with anarchy. Purcell also actively supported the cause of Catholics in the army, including General Rosecrans's friend, E. P. Scammon, who had been dismissed from the antebellum army due to a drinking problem.[17]

While many northern Catholics condemned the South and even enlisted in the Union Army, many also understood the war from their point of view as Democrats. From the beginning, McMaster blamed the Republican Party for the opening of the conflict and judged the administration's recourse to arms as a sign of its "complete incompetence." Promising to oppose the designs of the "abolitionized Black Republican Party," McMaster hoped that soon opponents of the war would so frustrate the designs of warmongers "till that happy day comes when the American people—having buried alike the abortions of Lincoln-ism and Jeff Davis-ism, will reinaugurate once more an *American* policy, adequate to the wishes of the country, and worthy of our history and our governmental experience." As for the war, "We hiss and flout all who promote it."[18]

McMaster's extreme opposition to the war had a few parallels in the Catholic press at the beginning of the war. Perhaps the closest were the German Oertel and the Irish American John Mullay, both fellow Catholic editors from New York. It took Oertel little more than a month to renounce his formerly pro-Union rhetoric, oppose calls for additional troops, and forcefully come out in favor of peace. "We vote for peace, the Church votes for peace, calm citizens vote for peace, common sense votes for peace," wrote Oertel. "It is therefore even for every true citizen, who means well for the fatherland, a joyful omen, amid the noise of war however even still to hear the voices of peace." Striking a much less enthusiastic tone than Archbishop John Hughes, the Irish layman Mullay, who ran his diocese's official paper, the *Metropolitan Record*, called for Catholics to act on their convictions as citizens as they best saw fit. He moreover was in full agreement with McMaster, anti-abolitionist Democrats, and Hughes that the war must be prosecuted on a limited basis solely to preserve the Union and not for conquest or to further the ends of abolitionists.[19]

By contrast, Donahoe, like many Irish Catholic Americans, became a War Democrat. This meant that he supported the war as a means to preserve the Union, but not necessarily all of Lincoln's military and political policies. In the wake of Sumter, *The Pilot*, which had unfurled the American flag above its office in Boston, declared it was everyone's duty to stand by the administration regardless of who was in power. Unlike McMaster, Donahoe cared more about defending the honor of Irish Catholic Americans against the slanders of secular newspapers like the *New York Tribune* and the *Boston Transcript* than he did about assigning blame for the conflict. The editors of these papers had accused Archbishop Hughes of encouraging Catholics to betray their oaths of allegiance to the United States in order to avoid military service in the event of war. To the contrary, *The Pilot* noted, Hughes had encouraged support of the government, and Irish Catholics had turned out to volunteer on behalf of the Union despite such gross insults and the disbanding of Irish militia units "under the know-nothing-republican rule of 1855." No "greater lie" or more "wicked imputation" had ever been spread against Irish Catholic citizens, declared Donahoe, who knew such criticisms were aimed not simply at Irishmen's foreign birth and ethnic customs, but at their religion as well: "The Catholic Church has always countenanced loyal submission to legitimate rule; and in this, as in every other principle, no people listen so readily to that infallible guide, as the Irish." For Donahoe, both Irish ethnicity and Catholic religion, so tied up in one another as to be virtually inseparable, were reasons to trust the Irish, not to suspect them of being secret traitors to the national cause.[20]

The pro-war *Pilot* was much more typical of the initial reaction of northern Catholic Democrats to the conflict. For example, the *New York Tablet*—a weekly edited by the Irish Catholic brothers, Dennis and James Sadlier—blamed the war on the secessionists' rebellion while declaring that the duty of the government as well as "every true man" was to put it down. Taking an uncompromising position on secession, the *New York Tablet* gloried equally in the coming together of Republicans and Democrats against secession, the patriotism of the 69th New York Infantry Regiment, and Archbishop Hughes for flying the flag above both St. Patrick's Cathedral and his own residence. The Sadliers touted the benefits of the war for the nation, namely, its ability to unite Americans for the first time across ethnic, religious, political, and social divides to achieve one common goal: to preserve the Union and defeat sectionalism once and for all. "We shall also, with God's help, come out of the fiery ordeal, a *nation*." The *Catholic Herald* of Philadelphia, like *The Pilot*, pointed to the patriotic response of Catholics as proof that charges of their disloyalty were completely "unfounded." Not only had flags been seen flying from the spires of many churches across Pennsylvania, boasted the editor, but one pastor had preached a sermon urging his male flock under the age of forty-five to enlist. Another gave a "very patriotic speech" at a flag-raising ceremony at his church, "enlivened by the singing of several national airs by the pupils of the parochial schools."[21]

Southern Catholic criticism of pro-war Catholic northerners only strengthened the latter's support for the northern cause. Writing to Archbishop Hughes shortly after the First Battle of Bull Run, Charleston's Irish-born bishop, Patrick Lynch, advised northern Catholics, "The Separation of the southern States is un fait accompli. The federal government has no power to reverse it." Blaming "black republicans" for the conflict, Lynch told Hughes to keep Irish Catholics out of the conflict and boasted that the South could never be militarily subjugated. Hughes, however, was a firm advocate of the Union from the beginning. In his publicized response to Lynch's letter, Hughes, in a conciliatory yet firm way, denied that the southern states had acted justly in seceding. He further dismissed Lynch's idea that the conflict was now one of northern "conquest" and opined that "foreigners now naturalized, whether Catholics or not, ought to bear their relative burthen in defense of the . . . country." Hughes's outright rejection of secession, which was published in Catholic periodicals around the country, added considerably to his reputation as a northern patriot.[22]

Hughes put his patriotic words into action by agreeing to serve as the unofficial agent of the Lincoln administration in Europe in the winter of 1861–62. Although this appointment did not sit well with some Catholics at home or abroad, Hughes believed his mission would promote peace as well as the best interests of both North and South. As he later told Cardinal Alessandro Barnabo, the head of the church's Rome-based missionary organization, the Sacred Congregation for the Propagation of the Faith (Propaganda Fide), to not accept would have called into question Catholic loyalty. Besides, the government intended the appointment both as a "great compliment" to Catholic Americans and a firm repudiation of the Know-Nothings that would be emulated by future administrations.[23]

Like their coreligionists from New York and Boston, Pittsburgh Catholics were also known for their patriotism. Pittsburgh's Catholic newspaper labeled the South the "aggressors" and defended Lincoln's policy as merely retaking federal property and defending the national capital. Calling the "Catholic sentiment" "unmistakably true" in the present crisis, the editor explained that for Catholics the choice to the support the Union "cannot be for a moment doubtful." When forced to choose between "the duty we owe to the United States" and "sympathy for a Confederacy which as its Vice President declares, has African Slavery for its corner stone," Catholics would naturally choose the former. Soon church officials hoisted American flags over the city's cathedral, many churches, and even the city's Catholic seminary. The Spanish-born bishop of Pittsburgh, Michael Domenec, preached a patriotic sermon urging naturalized citizens to "rally around the Union" and ordered that the local Committee of Safety's address be read from the diocese's pulpits. Later, while serving in an unofficial diplomatic capacity, Domenec would help represent the government's interests in Spain.[24]

Northern Catholic patriotism, however, was not always spontaneous or deeply felt. Sometimes, it was prompted by pro-war Americans who pressured them to support the Union cause more openly. Pittsburgh Catholics' patriotism must be qualified by the fact that it was also partially coerced. Writing to Archbishop Kenrick, Domenec begged him not to allow his "patriotic" homily printed in his own diocese's paper to be published in the *Catholic Mirror*. Not only did it misrepresent his words, Domenec claimed, but he had preached the homily mostly to placate arsonists who had threatened to destroy the city's Catholic churches. This, rather than spontaneous patriotism, was the real reason why the flags were raised in Pittsburgh, Domenec claimed. He assured Kenrick, "I hate to meddle myself about politics, but for the safety of our churches it was necessary to do some thing at the same time."[25]

A pro-war mob also visited the office of Philadelphia's Catholic newspaper and forced it to fly an American flag as well. The editor, an Irish American veteran of the War of 1812 who had previously compared the southern cause to that of the American colonies, was not cowed for long and began criticizing the war just as Pittsburgh's Catholic leadership threw its support wholeheartedly behind the Lincoln administration. Significantly, Bishop Domenec remarked that the Pittsburgh church, thanks to its patriotism, was now safe for the time being. After the Pittsburgh Catholic leadership had made clear its support for the Union cause, even the "most bigoted protestants" and the "greatest enemies of our church" had toned down their anti-Catholic rhetoric. They had even begged "our pardon," wrote Domenec, for having ever "said or done anything against the Catholic church." Regardless of the true origin of the patriotism of Pittsburgh Catholics, their devotion to the Union cause, so Domenec argued, had helped to dispel religious prejudice, and *The Catholic* continued to support the Union cause throughout the war.[26]

Orestes Brownson was by far the greatest Catholic supporter of the Union cause. Writing a few months after war began, Brownson praised the northern people and government for their patriotic and energetic response to Sumter. "The star-spangled banner was thrown to the breeze from every public edifice, from every church steeple, and almost from every house; and the mighty heart of the Free States rung out the battle-cry, 'The Union must and shall be preserved,'" he declared. Slavery was not the cause of the war, he argued further, for the South had seceded because it felt its power over the federal government slipping away. For Brownson, like many Republican commentators, the war was not so much about African slavery as it was about the slavery of the North to the South. In this respect, his understanding of the causes of the war very much fit the "Slave Power Conspiracy" paradigm identified by historians as one of the principal beliefs of the Republican Party. Now that the South had thrown down the gauntlet, the North could do nothing but stand up to them "without abdicating their manhood, and standing branded in history as the most miserable cravens and dastards that the world has ever known."[27]

Later in October, Brownson first articulated his vision of a better future for Catholics in the post-war world resulting from their support for the Union cause. He claimed that Catholics, bound by their "Catholic duty" to faithfully support the Union, had turned out in disproportionate numbers to volunteer in the federal armies. He predicted that after the war Catholics would finally be accepted as equals in American society. He argued that "both Catholics and non-Catholics will mutually feel that they are citizens of a common country, and form but one

Orestes Brownson, famous editor and theologian, was by far the most enthusiastic Catholic leader on behalf of the Union and emancipation (University of Notre Dame Archives).

political people" after the war. Despite its controversial nature, for he had also endorsed emancipation as a war measure, Brownson's piece was hailed by a number of pro-war Catholics, including his personal physician, Dr. Henry Hewit, who later became a surgeon on General Ulysses S. Grant's personal staff. One group of Union men thought his article "the clearest in thought and expression that has appeared on the momentous question treated," and they took the liberty of reprinting it and sending to other like-minded men in Missouri. Brownson's uncompromising pro-war attitude was similar to the vast majority of patriotic Protestant editors. In his *Quarterly Review*, Brownson strongly and consistently supported the Union cause throughout the war.[28]

If Brownson had a clerical doppelganger among the northern bishops in 1861, it was certainly Josue Young, the American-born convert who was the bishop of Erie, Pennsylvania, and had been mentored by Archbishop Purcell. He was unique in the American hierarchy in that he had been known to favor abolition as early as the beginning of the 1850s, a fact that contributed to him being recommended by his peers for a northern diocese rather than one closer to the South. Shortly after the attack on Fort Sumter, Young preached a fiery patriotic sermon in his cathedral that the *Erie Weekly Gazette* credited with encouraging local Irish enlistments in the army. He even refused to approve of a priest's proposed appointment as bishop because of the man's well-known sympathy for the "Southern Revolution." Young explained that he could not regard the Confederates' rebellion as "anything else than a most criminal & treasonable outrage." A correspondent of General William T. Sherman's wife, Ellen, Young praised her brother Charles Ewing for serving in the Union Army in a struggle over "the life & existence of the country." According to Ellen's paraphrase, "[Bishop Young] compares the rebels to an ingrate who strikes at the heart of his mother." A true patriot throughout the conflict, Young's small diocese and his desire to avoid conflict with other bishops, however, ensured that he played a relatively minor role during the war.[29]

Such expressions of northern Catholic patriotism did not go unnoticed. The war initially helped Catholics, Protestants, and nativists put aside old prejudices to work together toward the common goal of restoring the Union. One Buffalo paper cheerfully praised the Catholic Church for raising the Union flag above its churches and for being free from all sympathy with the rebellion whether in the North or South. Union soldiers on board a steamer making its way past Cape Girardeau, Missouri, were pleasantly surprised to find themselves saluted by the inhabitants of the local Catholic convent who gave "three cheers for the Union." The *New York Times* approvingly printed Archbishop Purcell's pro-war speech at the Catholic Institute at Cincinnati, in which he called the Union cause "just and holy." Harvard even awarded the Irish-born bishop of Boston, John B. Fitzpatrick, an honorary doctor of divinity degree. "This would not have been done," noted one prominent Harvard administrator, "were it not for the loyalty shown by him and by the Irish who have offered themselves freely for the army."[30]

Most of all, Irish Catholic Americans' initial enthusiasm for joining the Union Army earned them the gratitude of their fellow patriotic Americans. Grateful businessmen in New York City contributed $1,500 to a fund for the poor families of the soldiers of the 69th New York Infantry so that the husbands, fathers, and sons could go off to war knowing that their families would be taken care of for the three-month terms of their enlistment. All of these seemed welcome signs of what might be a new wave of religious toleration to match that which had followed the American Revolution. Later, the writers of the early-twentieth-century *Catholic Encyclopedia* praised Archbishop Purcell for flying the Union flag about his cathedral despite the "sympathy" of "many Catholics" for the anti-war faction in the North. "The event showed the wisdom of his course," they wrote, "[for] the last vestige of insane Knownothingism and its hatred of the Church disappeared."[31]

State and federal leaders showed their appreciation for Catholic service, and perhaps their simultaneous desire for more Catholic votes, not only by giving them prominent positions in the military but also by intervening in the army and navy to make sure that Catholics could practice their faith without undue harassment. This marked an important change from the antebellum years when Catholic soldiers and sailors had frequently complained of religious discrimination. Governor John A. Andrew of Massachusetts was especially vigilant in making sure that Catholics were given every opportunity to practice their faith without hindrance from strict army regulations. While Lincoln personally requested and appointed Catholic chaplains for the army and hospitals to show his government's religious impartiality, Congress went a step further by revoking naval regulations that had forced Catholics to attend Protestant services. This important change allowed Catholics to hold their own services and to be buried at sea with traditional Catholic rites. Although Lincoln did not appoint any official Catholic chaplains to the navy, these important steps corrected long-standing complaints from before the war.[32]

Ultimately, it was the Catholic Americans' service in the Union Army that seemingly put to rest questions about Catholic loyalty to the Union. Raising flags, printing patriotic editorials, and denouncing secession from the pulpit could only go so far in defeating the Confederacy and reconstructing the Union. If Catholics were to prove they were true Americans, they would have to back up their words by putting on the Union blue. German- and English-speaking Catholic editors across the North published editorials encouraging their male readers to enlist and thereby do their duty to the nation. Such reminders were hardly necessary, for already thousands of men, particularly the Irish, rushed alongside their fellow native-born citizens to enlist in order to save the Union. Catholic men from Boston formed the 9th Massachusetts, others from Cincinnati and Chicago the 10th Ohio and 23rd Illinois, respectively, and, most important, the Irish Catholic members of the 69th New York State militia formed the famous 69th New York Infantry Regiment. So many men rushed to join the latter regiment that reportedly over five thousand were left behind when its Irish American colonel, Michael Corcoran, led the 69th off to the front in Virginia. Regardless of the motives for this initial outpouring of patriotism by Catholic men and their families, it led Brownson to make the exaggerated claim that "Catholics have, considering their numbers, more than their proportion in the regular army and volunteer forces of the Union."[33]

As more and more young Catholic men left school to join the nation's armies, many Catholic colleges emptied out at an alarming rate. Many secular as well as religious colleges consequently had to deal with low enrollments that caused them to endure considerable financial difficulties. Catholic colleges in the North and Border States were thus no exception, and especially those in the latter area suffered when the war put them close to the battlefront. Low enrollment forced St. Joseph's College in Somerset, Ohio, to close in July, and Bardstown College in Kentucky was forced to close for similar reasons as well. Georgetown College, situated on the outskirts of the nation's capital, saw its enrollment drop to fifty students by May, with many of the southerners having returned home. Those who were left still overwhelmingly supported the South and helped the school gain a reputation as pro-Confederate by burning Abraham Lincoln in effigy.[34]

Mount Saint Mary's College in Emmitsburg, Maryland, also gained a pro-Confederate reputation due to the southern boys who boarded there. Its president, Father John McCaffrey, insisted that he was "no secessionist" but that he could not support the war or Lincoln's "unconstitutional courses" that had reduced Marylanders to "slaves." Similarly, at Jesuit-run Saint Louis University in St. Louis, Missouri, several priests on the faculty gained reputations as secessionists. Many Irish Catholics, including an Irish-born priest, John Bannon, who later became a chaplain for the Confederacy, were among those pro-Confederate forces captured at Fort Jackson by Union commander Nathaniel Lyon. The affair probably did not help the school's already poor reputation for loyalty.[35]

If the passion the Georgetown students showed for the Confederate cause had its pro-Union match, it was certainly found among the pupils of Notre Dame, a small college run by the Congregation of the Holy Cross in South Bend, Indiana. Founded in 1842, Notre Dame had partisans of both sides enrolled, although the majority of the students at the beginning of the conflict were northerners. One student, the commander of the college's cadet company named William F. Lynch, addressed his peers with such a fiercely patriotic address that many of them, of age or not, wanted to volunteer immediately. The school's president, Father Edward Sorin, urged restraint, however, reminding the boys that many were too young to enlist without their parents' permission. Though a number of students including Lynch left, Notre Dame's enrollment, like that of secular state colleges in the Midwest such as the University of Michigan, eventually recovered and reached record numbers. Swelled from pupils sent from the Border States to be as far from the war as possible, pro-Union and pro-Confederate students eyed one another warily as Holy Cross priests and brothers managed to keep political passions under control.[36]

Confidence that the war would be won quickly was shattered by the Union Army's defeat at the First Battle of Bull Run on July 21. Confederate forces under General Joseph E. Johnston and General P. G. T. Beauregard dealt the army led by Major General Irwin McDowell an unexpected and heavy setback, leading to a disgraceful Union rout. McMaster, who had already called for an "honorable and just peace" in May, continued to promote a cessation of hostilities as the only way to restore the Union in the wake of the disaster in northern Virginia. More fighting would only further the dissolution of the Union, he claimed, an opinion shared by the equally pro-compromise, anti-war Catholic editor in Baltimore. McMaster became such an outspoken opponent of Lincoln and the war that Secretary of State William Henry Seward shut McMaster's paper down and he was thrown in jail in the fall of 1861. Released after six weeks, McMaster was not allowed to publish his paper again until April 1862. The experience did little to alter his opinion of the war or Lincoln's government, and he continued to criticize both for the rest of the conflict. Though extreme in comparison with most other Catholic papers in the war's first year, if the number of complimentary letters in his columns was any indication many of his Democratic and Catholic readers wholeheartedly approved of his uncompromising advocacy for peace. His fellow editors Mullay and Jenkins likewise stepped up their criticism of Lincoln's government after the battle.[37]

Pro-war Catholics, like many patriotic northerners, criticized the way the battle had been handled. However, this did not mean that they no longer supported the war effort. In the wake of the battle, Father Purcell publicly criticized the anti-war *Catholic Mirror* for showing too much "anxiety . . . for the success of the rebellion against legitimate authority." Archbishop Hughes, though disturbed by reports of the defeat, wrote an encouraging letter to his friend, Secretary of State Seward, urging the government to use the reversal as a reason to raise even more troops to win the war. As he assured the secretary, "[The defeat] may be providential, and I think that it is, and its benefits should be to make the federal government more alert in meeting the difficulties without regard to cost of men or money." Maria T. Ewing, the Catholic wife of the powerful Ohioan War Democrat Thomas Ewing, told her son Charles of the family's relief that the battle had not been as bad as reported and expressed their family's "deep determination to assist by every means in their power to hasten the day of reckoning in store for rebels and traitors."[38]

Many pro-war Catholics reaffirmed their commitment to the Union cause even in defeat. In particular, northern Catholics took great pride in the heroism the soldiers of their faith had displayed. For Donahoe the bravery of the 69th New York in the battle was yet another proof of "Irish valor" against their enemies at home and abroad. Patrick Guiney, an Irish Catholic officer in the 9th Massachusetts, boasted to his wife that the 69th "is praised by everybody here. They fought bravely—they charged against the enemy's lines repeatedly and at every point swept the rebels before them." Likewise the ultra-loyal *New York Tablet* strongly echoed Guiney's and other Catholics' praise of the 69th and its leader, Corcoran. The 69th soon became the cause célèbre of the English-language Catholic press. Rosecrans and Purcell of the *Catholic Telegraph* remarked on the irony of so many newspapers praising the Irish of the regiment when they had in years past repeatedly printed the "most atrocious calumnies on the Irish . . . on account of their religion." Though ever alert to such prejudice, in one instance calling for foreigners not to enlist until an alleged order dismissing foreign naval yard workers was rescinded, they remained strong proponents of the Union cause. Mullay's *Metropolitan Record* also attacked the hypocrisy of the Republican *New York Tribune* for its praise of the Irish after accumulating a long record of anti-Catholicism and as an "intolerant sheet toward everything that bears the Irish name." As before the war, ethnic and Catholic commentators were on the lookout for perceived or real insults.[39]

The war brought tremendous challenges to Catholic communities across the United States, leading many men to rush to volunteer to show their patriotism, while others viewed the conflict as an unwelcome intrusion on their lives and families. As editors and bishops sought to define the church's attitude toward the war, the laity struggled to cope with the changes in their lives the war wrought. German Catholics, whose language further isolated them from mainstream America, were particularly conflicted about the war, which many of them saw as the result of radical Forty-Eighters meddling in internal American social affairs. On the one hand, for the Dünnebacke family in Michigan, the war brought unwelcome inflation. On the other, the Pack family, living outside Pittsburgh, welcomed the higher wages the war brought the miners in his community, which offset some of this inflation. Others seemed to hardly notice the war. One German Catholic farmer in Iowa claimed that the conflict had little effect on his daily life, which went on much as before. "Where I am it's just like at home when there was a war in Baden or Holstein," he informed his mother and sister in Germany. "You never noticed it at all, and it's like that here too." Some recent Catholic immigrants used their status as unnaturalized immigrants to avoid both volunteering for the army as well as the draft when it began in 1863.[40]

Economic motivations as well as ethnic loyalties played a large role in how Irish Catholics responded to the conflict. Nationalist Irish Americans agreed with the Fenian leaders such as Meagher that the war was an opportunity to prove their valor and gain military experience for the coming struggle with England. As historian Susannah Ural has argued persuasively, they had "dual loyalties" to both countries that influenced how the Irish understood and participated in, or avoided entirely, the Union war effort. But many Irish civilians, who had additional loyalties to family and faith, recognized that whether they fought for Ireland or the Union they had much to lose from the conflict. After the initial rush to enlist in the 69th New York, a collection had to be taken up because the "majority of the soldiers leave large families in very poor circumstances." Thus, as a matter of survival, many poor families of Irish Catholic soldiers must have hoped for a quick and relatively bloodless conflict. While some avoided the war for economic reasons, other Irishmen may have joined because it was the only work they could find. Bounties paid for volunteers later on in the war certainly made serving in the army financially appealing. There were thus practical limits to their devotion to the Union that went beyond feelings of patriotism or party loyalty. Even their bishops wrote frequently to Europe complaining about how the war had hurt their dioceses financially, contributed to their inability to pay their debts, and overwhelmed them with requests for relief from poor, needy Catholic families.[41]

The opinions and motivations of nonelite Catholic laywomen at the start of the war have been even harder for scholars to determine than those of their men.

Like other working-class immigrants, they left behind few personal letters or diaries. From those that still exist it is clear that they, like their husbands, sons, and relatives, refused in many cases to subjugate the interests of their families to that of the nation. The wife of a noncommissioned Catholic officer in the 28th Massachusetts complained about him using patriotic stationery and clearly did not share her husband's enthusiasm for the war. While one Irish Catholic woman wrote to Father William Corby thanking him for attending to her husband during his death, another inquired after money that her husband had supposedly left with the priest. None of these women showed much interest in the Union cause; all were much more preoccupied by the daily concerns of feeding themselves and their children. Such an apparent lack of pro-Union sentiment from working-class women led many observers in the North to criticize women's patriotism in contrast to that of southern women.[42]

Although working-class civilians warily weighed the costs of the war, many elite Catholic northerners supported the war effort and successfully encouraged others in their faith community to do likewise. For example, Charles Daly, a prominent judge and Irish Catholic leader in New York City, became a strong supporter of the war and the government. At a gala held at Willet's Point on behalf of the 15th New York Engineer Regiment in June, Daly joined fellow Catholic Orestes Brownson in speaking out against secession and commending the nation's citizen–soldiers for their defense of the Union. Daly's support for the national cause was widely recognized among the city's entire population and won him the special acclaim of pro-war Irish Catholics. Later, in his honor, they named a company the Judge Daly Guards in one of the regiments of the newly formed Corcoran Legion in 1862.[43]

Similarly, working-class women's apparent indifference about the war was not shared by all Catholic women, as some, especially from the middle class, became fierce patriots. Mary Noyes, a Catholic laywoman from New York City, sent Rosecrans, "our Christian Patriot," a St. Joseph medal to wear while another Catholic laywoman from Yonkers composed a poem in the martyred Colonel Garesché's honor. "Dear Gen'l Rosecrans, it grows very dark all around, but tho' the darkness I feel there is coming, not only the temporal, but the spiritual salvation of our beloved People. Blessed are you who can so gloriously aid in both," Noyes wrote. At Saint Mary's College in South Bend, Indiana, northern girls, including General William T. Sherman's daughter Minnie, insisted on wearing patriotic symbols even though the school forbade the practice. Goaded by Sherman's wife, Ellen, they refused to back down and soon came to fisticuffs with their southern classmates.[44]

Ellen Ewing Sherman was a fierce advocate of her husband and the Union cause (University of Notre Dame Archives).

Ellen Sherman was just as patriotic as her brothers and her husband, all of whom were northern generals. Accusing Democrats of "skin deep" patriotism, Ellen angrily told her brother Charles that Benedict Arnold was a "saint" compared to the Confederates. Defeat at Bull Run only increased her patriotic fervor, instilling in her a new visceral "loathing and hatred of the men that are desolating our country without cause." "For the first time in my life," Ellen continued, "I wish that I had a man's strength that I might use it against the traitors." Ellen's hatred of southern rebels stemmed in part from her atypical, for a Catholic woman, hatred of slavery. "A catholic should be governed somewhat by the fact that the Church has always treated Slavery as an evil which should be abolished by wise & moderate means," she wrote. She found it hard to understand how anyone "could sacrifice country & honor for the privilege of whipping negro wenches." Despite her antebellum "dislike [for] the Abolitionists," she told her husband that "their folly sinks into insignificance when compared with the treason of the South."[45]

Elite and middle-class Catholic women helped support the war effort just like other women of their class by organizing tables and displays at local sanitary affairs. In the last months of the war, Ellen Sherman, Mrs. Stephen A. Douglas, Mrs. James A. Mulligan, and other Catholic women organized a "Catholic Department" at the Chicago Fair on May 30, 1865, not just to help the soldiers but also to prove to the nation that Catholic women had and were doing their part for the national cause. By staffing their effort entirely with laywomen, they implicitly likened their efforts on behalf of "Christian charity" and the nation to the Catholic men and officers in the army and the nuns in hospitals. Their appeal, for "everything rare, useful or ornamental . . . all the stores of the farm and garden," undoubtedly was directed at other laywomen across the Midwest. Participating in such relief activities, which saw them working side by side with their Protestant sisters, presented Catholic women with direct opportunities of aiding the war effort and becoming part of "a nationwide community of female supporters."[46] When taking into consideration their less patriotic and poorer sisters, however, it is clear that Catholic laywomen, just like their men, were divided over the war. Some seized on the conflict as a way to show their patriotism while others eagerly awaited the war's end.

Many pro-war northern Catholic leaders saw the conflict as an opportunity to prove their patriotism to their nation. In so doing, they would put to rest once and forever the lies of Know-Nothing politicians and anti-Catholic Protestant editors. A layman writing to the archbishop of Baltimore in December clearly had this concern in mind when he thanked the bishop for ordering that the "good old patriotic prayer before Mass . . . be used in all the churches <u>without</u> <u>alteration</u>." And although he believed that "all good" Catholics were loyal to the "Constitutional authorities," he still was "disappointed and grieved to see so many <u>Catholics</u> & even <u>priests</u> failing in their duty at this crisis." He feared that their failing, rather than the loyalty of most Catholics, "will be remembered against us at a future day."[47] Catholic apologists such as Brownson and Donahoe could only hope that the American people would prove him wrong, by remembering the true and loyal Catholics, both citizens and soldiers, over those few Catholics who were either apathetic about the war or outright opposed it.

Though the vast majority of Catholics supported the war initially, the luke-warm responses of many Border State and even some northern Catholics proved harbingers of coming division within the church over the war and its goals. The growing apathy of some Catholics, especially among the clergy and foreign-born, for the Union and its cause angered some Republicans and reinforced deep-seated anti-Catholic and anti-immigrant prejudices among some northerners. Even some pro-war Catholics such as Ellen Sherman admitted that "most of the Catholic clergy of Cin[cinnati]" were "Secessionist[s]." Despite her devotion and respect for the clergy as a whole, she told her husband, "I hope vengeance will fall on them yet for being false to their country." Starting in 1863, Catholic apathy over the Union war effort would be remembered "at a future day" by their en-emies, and all the hard work and sacrifice of Catholic soldiers, priests, and nuns would do little to counteract the larger community's apparent lack of patriotism during the Union's most desperate hours.[48]

3   Catholic Soldiers in the Union Army

Many Catholic men from the Midwest to the Northeast turned out enthusiastically in support of the Union in 1861 and 1862. Scholars have generally portrayed Catholic northerners as overwhelmingly antiwar, thereby obscuring their early patriotic fervor and willingness to serve in the Federal Army in order to save the Union. Ethnic, religious, and political allegiances proved no check on their early volunteering. In rushing to support the flag, they responded like most northerners did, as patriotic Americans willing to give their lives for the nation. Soldiers carried their Catholic faith and identity with them into the army, and many devout men tried to practice their religion as faithfully as possible under difficult circumstances.[1] Defeating prejudice, however, was a minor concern for most Catholic volunteers, who more often cited ethnicity, politics, a desire to save the Union, or economic need to explain why they enlisted. Still, their willingness to die in the service proved their commitment to the United States and its democratic institutions. While the patriotism of Catholics was not the first thing on most northerners' minds in 1861, some did take notice and applauded them for their willingness to serve.

Unfortunately, when scholars have looked at Catholics soldiers' experiences, they have almost exclusively examined the Irish Brigade,[2] while other predominantly Irish Catholic regiments, such as the 10th Ohio, the 35th Indiana, 23rd Illinois, and even the 9th Massachusetts, have been comparatively neglected. Even worse, the focus on Irish Catholics means that German- and American-born Catholics in the army have faded completely into the background. In order to reveal the full story of the Catholic soldier in the Civil War, all three ethnic groups of Catholic soldiers must be examined in a comparative context.

In examining the neglected story of Catholic officers and soldiers at war, five key aspects of their experience in the army stand out. First, they turned out in larger numbers at the beginning of the war and tried to serve in homogeneous units when possible to be with other men who shared a common ethnicity or religion. Second, the Catholic community back home paid close attention to their military heroes, particularly high-ranking officers and the Irish Brigade, and took great pride in them as examples of their faith's compatibility with patriotism. Third, while even the most famous Catholic units were in reality often ethnically and religiously diverse, for many soldiers it was important to be able to practice their religion. They were often frustrated in this goal by a shortage of priests in the army or, on occasion, harassment from non-Catholic superior officers. Fourth, Catholic soldiers on the whole were much more likely to embrace radical measures such as emancipation as a means to end the war than were their Democratic friends and family at home. Finally, at the end of the war, after having made considerable sacrifices on behalf of the Union, they and the larger Catholic community would be shocked to find just how little their service was appreciated.

When the nation called on its military-age men to enlist in order to save the Union, Catholics at first willingly volunteered in large numbers. It is estimated that more than two hundred thousand Catholics served in the Union Armies during the Civil War. Union muster rolls did not record religion, thus making it impossible to track easily all their casualties, rates of desertion, rates of reenlistment, or average length of service. While German and American-born Catholics also had their heroes, cowards, martyrs, and deserters, it was the Irish, who composed the majority of the Catholic Church in America and were thus the most visible representatives of the Catholic military-age population. Although not all Irish Americans soldiers were Catholic, the fact that approximately 144,000 Irishmen served in the Union Army suggests that they made up the greatest percentage of Catholic troops fighting for the Union. The Irish Brigade's members, who were predominantly Catholic, acquitted themselves heroically on the battlefield despite suffering heavy losses at places like Antietam, Fredericksburg, and Gettysburg. Comprising the 63rd, 69th, and 88th New York, as well as the 28th Massachusetts and 116th Pennsylvania, all of the brigade's regiments fought hard and consequently suffered heavy casualties. While in most Union regiments two men died of disease for every man who died in combat, this casualty ratio was reversed in the Irish Brigade. The Irish Brigade was by far the most important Irish Catholic unit during the war and received the largest share of press in both Catholic and non-Catholic newspapers.[3]

While there were a number of distinctively Irish Catholic units in the army that had been assigned Catholic priests as chaplains, there were no regiment-sized units, perhaps not even company-sized, that were majority German Catholic. While a number of German Protestants and Forty-Eighters such as General Carl Schurz achieved prominent commands during the war, there were no Catholic German Americans who achieved a similar rank in the Union Army. When Germans congregated in one unit, such as in the 11th Corps of the Army of the Potomac, they seemed to be mixed between Protestants, religious freethinkers, and Catholics. In general, German Republicans, who were in many cases Forty-Eighters or Protestants, were more likely to enlist than were German Catholics, who were mostly Democrats. Though most Catholic Germans were Democrats and thus less likely to serve, some historians have recently argued that "it [is] doubtful that a segment as large as the Catholics, at least one-third of the total, was made up of consistent slackers." Likewise, native-born American Catholics seem not to have congregated together in any appreciable size in the army or navy.[4]

Like other groups of northerners, Irish Catholic leaders and politicians took leading roles in forming regiments. Irish American men such as Thomas F. Meagher, James A. Mulligan, and Michael Corcoran actively recruited Irishmen from New York to the Midwest by appealing to their patriotism for both the United States and Ireland. They promoted their regiments as particularly Irish, referring to the Irish Brigades of past European wars and such past battlefield glories as the Battle of Fontenoy in 1745. Many men, especially those of the Fenian Brotherhood, understood that their service would not only save the Union but that their experience could be used after the war to help liberate their native land. Such recruitment efforts also sought to reassure devout Irish Catholics that they would be able to practice their faith in the army. Thus one recruitment poster for the 9th Massachusetts reassured volunteers that they would have access to "a chaplain of the old faith to minister to [their] spiritual wants and dispense the priceless blessings of religion." Thanks to the efforts of their leaders at the local level, Irish regiments were formed in many northern states in 1861. Recruitment efforts continued throughout the war, appealing both to Catholic patriotism and increasingly to their pocketbooks by promising them bounties in exchange for their service.[5]

There were many similarities between the service of Catholics and that of other men from the North and Border States. Catholic soldiers and officers of all ranks braved the same dangers in battle and endured the same boredom. They, like others in the Union Army, enlisted for a variety of reasons, such as patriotism, adventure, masculinity, and money. Despite efforts to raise ethnically homogenous units, most Catholics probably served in religiously and ethnically mixed regiments formed in their home states. The shared experience of serving in the army, some historians have argued, may have helped to Americanize ethnic soldiers. While this is probably true in a number of cases, many Catholics preferred to enlist in regiments with other men of their own faith and ethnicity and with priests who provided them the sacraments essential to Catholicism. A few even saw their service as promoting tolerance for their faith, their ethnic group, or both, in the post-war world. This motivation played a large role in the foundation of the Irish Brigade and other similar if less famous Irish Catholic units. For most soldiers, however, this goal only became important to them as veterans after the war.[6]

By serving in these Irish Catholic units, men could also insulate themselves somewhat from anti-Catholicism in the army. Colonel James Mulligan, already considered a hero for his service at the Battle of Lexington, Missouri, in the fall of 1861, received a letter marked "Private and Confidential" from a captain of the 14th "Irish Regiment" asking for permission for the entire company to transfer to the "Irish Brigade" (23rd Illinois) that Mulligan was then recruiting. The man complained that his regiment was "incompetently officered, and to go to battle under them is certain disgrace and death." Noting that his unit also was "partially American and bigotedly Protestant," the captain begged Mulligan to help him get his company transferred to the 23rd, "where we can be with and amongst our own race and people."[7]

Protestant officers' bigotry seemed to be a common complaint among Catholics who wanted to practice their faith. According to Irish-born chaplain Father Paul Gillen, Colonel William R. Lee of the 20th Massachusetts prevented Irishmen in his unit from leaving on Sundays to attend Mass for fear that they would find whiskey along the way and get drunk before returning to the regiment. Dennis Duggan, a private in the 78th Pennsylvania, grew more and more indignant at the slander directed at the unit's chaplain, Father Richard Christy, who had the unusual distinction of serving in a largely non-Catholic regiment. According to Duggan, "It kills them [Protestants] to think that a Catholick' Priest should be the Chaplain." Enraged to hear "an expression which is too ignorant for any man to use in this enlightened 19th Century" uttered on a Sunday, he expressed further dismay to hear of an alleged comment by a fellow soldier that Christy "would make fifty dollars that day." Anecdotes of such antiforeign and anti-Catholic sentiment from before and during the war's first year thus reinforced many Catholics' desire to serve in separate segregated units.[8]

While German Catholics could serve among their fellow Germans in German-speaking units, they did not (as the Irish did) have any real options of enlisting in units with Catholic priests who spoke their language. The fact that German Catholics were not concentrated in regiments made it difficult to find places for German-speaking priests in the Union Army. Father Gustavus Miettinger, who

served as a chaplain in the 2nd New York Infantry, resigned his commission after less than a year because the United States War Department could not find
him a position in a predominantly Catholic German-speaking regiment. Many
German Catholic soldiers could only receive the sacraments when near a local German parish. Conscientious nuns in hospitals and devoted priests like the
Union chaplain Father Francis McAtee appealed to their superiors to get German-speaking priests for German soldiers but succeeded in securing them only
on a temporary basis. The dearth of such priests, in turn, made it very hard for
German Catholic soldiers to practice their religion while serving in the army. As
one German Catholic man, Corporal Adam Muenzenberger, told his wife, "Here
one sees no church or religion—nothing but woods and soldiers." With no opportunity to practice his faith in his native tongue, he resorted to asking his wife
to read her tea leaves to him. Most German-speaking chaplains in the army were
Lutheran; only a handful of German Catholic priests served during the war. Additionally, many may have been wary of serving in German units led by radical
Forty-Eighters like Schurz, for these were the same men who had attacked the
church back in Germany. A devout German Catholic, aside from political and
social reasons, would have to think twice about enlisting in the army without the
sacraments necessary to his salvation being readily at hand.[9]

Regardless of whether they supported the war, many Catholic editors and clerics, especially Irish ones, championed the cause of ethnic Catholic soldiers in
the army. Some commented ironically on the fact that suddenly their services
as soldiers were in such high demand whereas they had been so despised by
native-born Americans less than ten years before. "Every effort was there made
to throw odium and distrust on Irishmen" during the 1850s when Irish militia units were disbanded as untrustworthy. Now "the times have changed" and
Governor John Andrew of Massachusetts boasted to President Lincoln of his
"two thousand unflinching Irish soldiers." The overwhelming sense of pride that
the Catholic community showered on its soldiers more than overshadowed this
sense of bitterness. Perhaps Catholics had been scorned in the past, but now was
the perfect time to show anti-Catholic and nativist Americans just how wrong
they had been. Patrick Donahoe's *Pilot* boasted that it was the Irish Catholic bishops who had first spoken out for the Union and that Catholics across the country
had remained true to the nation in its time of peril. Like other Catholic weeklies,
it particularly promoted the cause of the 69th New York Infantry Regiment and
later the Irish Brigade during the war.[10]

Orestes Brownson, dismayed by the pro-southern position of some priests and Catholic editors, applauded what he saw as the patriotic response of the Catholic laity to the war despite their overwhelming adherence to the Democratic Party. In particular, the editor was cheered by the response of Catholic men to Lincoln's call for volunteers. "Catholics have, considering their numbers, more than their proportion in the regular army and volunteer forces of the Union," he boasted. "And Catholic soldiers, whether we speak of officers or men, are surpassed by no others now in the field." Brownson took heart that the service of these brave Catholic men, two of which were his own sons, would eclipse the disloyalty of Confederate Catholics and destroy forever questions of Catholic fealty to the nation. After the war, they would join with their fellow non-Catholic citizens to "form but one political people."[11]

Contemporary newspapers, as well as historians since the war, focused their attention on prominent Catholic officers who gained a name for themselves during the war. For example, *The Pilot* ran a column called "Records of Irish American Patriotism," from 1862 through the end of the war that tracked the progress of Irish Catholic units and officers including General Phil Sheridan, Colonel Patrick Guiney, and Corcoran. Major General William Rosecrans was known even by non-Catholic Americans to be a devout soldier, and his victory at Stones River in early 1863 made him a popular northern hero. *Harper's Weekly* praised him as a strategist who was "second to none," while the *New York Times* declared, "Gen. Rosecrans, if success be the standard, stands at the very head of the Union Generals." The *Catholic Herald* portrayed his success and piety as a model for young Catholics, while also declaring that "the nation owes to the great element of his character this latest and greatest victory of the war." Father Peter Paul Cooney, the Irish American chaplain of the 35th Indiana Regiment, declared him "the perfect model of a Christian hero" who made "Catholicity respected and the name *Catholic* honorable" in the army.[12]

Catholic soldiers who died on the battlefield became martyrs, celebrated for demonstrating their religious and ethnic communities' patriotism by shedding their blood on behalf of the nation. Colonel Julius Garesché, Rosecrans's chief of staff, became particularly well-known for the pious way he knelt to pray shortly before he died on the first day of the Battle of Stones River. General Amiel W. Whipple, a convert to the Catholic faith from before the war, was a less well-known but equally pious man who received last rites before dying from battlefield wounds at Chancellorsville. Finally, Colonel James Mulligan, a particularly popular Irish Catholic officer, was lauded across the North for his defense of

General William S. Rosecrans, the highest-ranking devout Catholic in the Union Army (Library of Congress).

Lexington, Missouri. Even the Republican *Harper's Weekly*, not known to be friendly to Irishmen or Catholics, published a short biography that declared Mulligan to be "worthy of all praise," stating, "A purer, better man does not live in the State of Illinois." He became an even greater symbol of Irish and Catholic patriotism when he was mortally wounded in the Shenandoah Valley in 1864. His famous last words, "Lay me down and save the flag," were widely repeated and a source of great pride to Irish Catholics.[13]

Even more popular within the Irish Catholic community were the two commanders of the only Irish Catholic brigades in the Union Army, Thomas Meagher and Michael Corcoran. As commander of the 69th New York Regiment, Colonel Corcoran was famous even before the war for refusing to parade his troops in honor of the Prince of Wales. His patriotism and devotion to the Union cause in the wake of his capture at Bull Run enhanced his reputation, with *Harper's Weekly* dedicating its front page to the "gallant" Corcoran upon his release. His popularity among Irish- and native-born alike also helped propel him to the head of a new Irish Brigade, the "Corcoran Legion" in 1862. General Meagher also became popular for his rousing speeches on behalf of the Union and Ireland and proved instrumental in organizing the Irish Brigade after Corcoran's capture at Bull Run. "He is doing a yeomen's service in rousing the enthusiasm of his countrymen, and enlisting their service in this contest for the Constitution," remarked the Republican *New York Times*. The service of these men, identified as Catholic regardless of the level of their personal piety, became a source of pride for many Catholics during and after the war. At least initially, such heroes helped Irish Catholics to improve their image in American society and gain a degree of toleration and acceptance. Both the Republican *Harper's Weekly* and the *New York Herald* praised the patriotic example both men set for their larger community. The very fact that local and state governments now actively encouraged the formation of ethnic units in 1861–62, which Know-Nothing legislatures and governors had disbanded in the mid-1850s, spoke volumes about how the war had changed perceptions of ethnic Catholics in the North.[14]

As with officers of other ethnic and religious groups, Catholic officers were not all brave or even competent, and there was always the danger that such failures would leave behind a legacy of shame for the larger community. Major General Robert Patterson, an Irish American veteran of the Mexican War, failed to prevent General Johnston from moving his army to the Bull Run battlefield, which proved decisive in the Confederate victory. The *Chicago Tribune* laid the defeat solely on "Patterson's head" while *Harper's Weekly* remarked that "few will regret his retirement to private life." Another Mexican War veteran, General

James Shields, bickered over rank and the size of his command with the Lincoln administration before he took command in the Shenandoah Valley. Shields attributed his lack of recognition to the president's abolitionist supporters. He ultimately resigned from the army in 1863 in "disgrace" after losing the Battle of Port Republic the previous June. His supporters argued that prejudice against the Irish and Democrats had led to his undoing. Newspaper editorials commenting on Patterson's and Shields' resignations, however, did not bring up their ethnicity or their religion.[15]

Patterson and Shields were by no means the only Catholic officers with questionable records. Despite their wild popularity, both Meagher and Corcoran were suspected of the old Irish vice of intemperance. The former was said to have imbibed too much on several occasions, most notably at Antietam, and the latter during a deadly confrontation with a subordinate and later prior to a fatal fall from his horse. Worst of all, General Charles P. Stone, a conservative Democrat and an outspoken opponent of abolition, became a scapegoat for Radical Republicans after the embarrassing Union defeat at Ball's Bluff in the first fall of the war. Accused of treason, his name dragged through the mud and his career ruined, Stone received a minor posting in New Orleans from which he retired before the end of the war. Like his Irish coreligionists, Stone's faith apparently was never directly attacked and thus Catholic newspapers did not bother to mount any defense on his behalf. By contrast, as soon as his career ran into trouble, critics attacked Rosecrans's faith, which was well-known inside and outside the army. After his defeat at Chickamauga in September 1863, the *New York Times* alleged that he was "subject to fits of religious depression." Critics of his leadership in his subsequent posting to Missouri charged him with treating pro-Confederate Catholics lightly. In both cases, his friends sincerely believed that religious prejudice had played a major role in his relief from duty.[16]

Reconstructing and evaluating the wartime service of Catholics in units like the 69th New York or 10th Ohio that were largely Catholic is difficult; finding Catholic men in mixed units is nearly impossible because muster rolls did not record religious affiliation. The Irish Brigade, despite its plethora of priests and its reputation, was not made up entirely of Catholics or even Irishmen. For a short time the largely non-Irish 29th Massachusetts served with the unit, and the 116th Pennsylvania was a mixed unit of Americans, Irish, and other foreign-born soldiers. For example, Privates Daniel Chisholm and his brother, Alex, both of whom joined the 116th Pennsylvania as new recruits in the spring of 1864, were of Scottish descent and never commented on the Irish Catholic identity of their unit.

Their letters make no mention of religion at all. Instead, they were much more interested in politics, military affairs, and the day-to-day experience of camp life and battle. Certainly many Protestant, Jewish, and Catholic soldiers likewise focused on such temporal concerns to the exclusion of spiritual ones. Private William McCarter, an Irish Protestant immigrant from Derry, went out of his way in his published account of his service in the Irish Brigade to dispel what he called a false "impression [that] prevailed in many parts of the country" that all the brigade's men were Catholic. He claimed that some of the brigade's chaplains were actually Methodist and that "twenty [men] attended the Protestant services for every two who went to Mass." Thus McCarter and the Chisholm brothers demonstrate that even the Irish Brigade was not completely "Irish Catholic."[17]

Perhaps more typical of the religious affiliation of the majority of the men in the Irish Brigade was Private Peter Welsh, a Catholic member of the 28th Massachusetts. Later promoted to sergeant in September 1863, Welsh repeatedly demonstrated his deep faith and intense patriotism in the letters he wrote to his family throughout the war. Welsh, like many Irishman, hated the "fanitics of the north," whom he blamed for provoking the South into rebellion. Yet he told his wife that this was not "sufficient cause" to justify disunion; citing St. Paul and alluding to Archbishop Hughes's famous letter on the subject, Welsh firmly asserted that the rebels had no "just cause" in starting the war. He believed the struggle was one "in which the people of all nations have a vital interest." This was a war, the "first test," to determine whether a "modern free government" could survive a "matured rebellion." "All men who love free government and equal laws are watching this crisis," he wrote, hoping to see the Union prevail. "If it fails," he warned his wife, "then the hopes of millions fail and the desighns and wishes of the tyrants will succeed." What he lacked in spelling and grammar, Welsh made up for in the intense patriotism of his prose, espousing a belief in the Union that other Catholics such as Colonel Patrick Guiney of the 9th Massachusetts would have applauded. Praising the men of the Union Army for having "draw[n] their swords from motives of a noble patriotism to fight for our Republic," Guiney continued to justify his service to his wife in patriotic terms until a battlefield wound led to his discharge from military service in 1864.[18]

Welsh applauded the United States for the relative tolerance it showed Catholicism. Asserting that "the most important of all rights enjoyed by the citezen of a free nation is the liberty of concience," Welsh argued that there was nowhere else but Rome in which "the Church enjoys such fredom as in the United States." Sounding much like Orestes Brownson, Welsh argued that not even Catholic France or Austria were as hospitable to Catholicism as the United States. Sharing

Welsh's high estimation of the nation's protection of religious liberties, Sergeant Walter Elliott—a member of the 5th Ohio, a native-born Catholic American, and a future Paulist priest—declared his brother William's death during the war to be a "sacrifice" to the cause of "freedom and religious toleration." Both Welsh and Elliott believed that the country's free institutions and democracy were boons to the cause of their religion and not a threat (unlike many conservative Catholics in Europe at the time).[19] Saving the Union was a holy cause and one in which thankful Catholics enjoying freedom of worship should be willing to lay down their lives.

Welsh's letters reflect a strong faith in God and provide an enlisted man's perspective about the Catholic religious world in the Army of the Potomac. His own regiment had a chaplain, Father Laurence McMahon, who apparently was sick often and served for less than a year with the 28th. Although not a member of the 88th New York, Welsh knew its chaplain, Father William Corby, who helped him send money back to his wife. When she expressed concern that he was not taking care of his religious obligations, Welsh was quick to assure her that "we have a priest continually with us[.] father Corbit of the 88th is always with us where ever we go and always ready to do anything he can for any one of the brigade." Welsh greatly appreciated Corby's efforts on behalf of his and his comrades' spiritual welfare.[20] Amid the horrors of war, Welsh found comfort and peace in his faith.

German Catholics in the army, however, rarely enjoyed such access to the rituals and comforts of their faith or the comradeship of other Catholic men who spoke their language. While there were several German-speaking priests who served as chaplains, the only attempt to recruit a German Catholic regiment and equip it with a German-speaking priest was an utter failure. In response to General Braxton Bragg's forces advancing into the neighboring state of Kentucky in the fall of 1862, a call went out in Cincinnati for volunteers to help repel a potential invasion. One such unit was to be the 108th Ohio Infantry Regiment. Local Catholic papers such as *Der Wahrheits Freund* and the *Catholic Telegraph* advertised that it was to be German Catholic and would have a priest as well. The Hungarian-born Father Aloysius Hatala volunteered to serve as chaplain with Bishop Sylvester Rosecrans's approval. Despite the enticement of a priest who spoke their language, however, the city's German Catholic population responded with little enthusiasm for the project. Although the regiment was formed anyway, its eventual chaplain, Rev. Robert Koehler, was a minister from the German Reformed Church.[21] In the end, there were simply no German Catholic equivalents of the Irish Brigade, 10th Ohio, or 35th Indiana, and no German Catholic commanders of equal rank to Generals James Shields, Philip Sheridan, or Thomas Meagher.

At the start of the war, many Catholic soldiers, like the majority of white northerners, believed that blacks were inferior to whites and wanted little to do with abolition. A few months after Congress made it illegal to return runaway slaves to their masters, the men of the Irish Catholic 10th Ohio did just that. Daniel Finn, one of the unit's musicians, noted in his journal on May 28, 1862, "Sent our niggar home to his master with a letter stating we were no abolitionists." Irish Catholics frequently used degrading terms to describe blacks and treated them poorly. Even the abolitionist Orestes A. Brownson's own son, Edward, regularly referred to blacks as "darkies" and in other belittling ways. William White, an Irish Catholic private in the 69th Pennsylvania, was willing to believe even the flimsiest of rumors that painted African Americans in a negative light. During the siege of Yorktown, White reported that the rebels "have got two Regiments of niggers down here they took t[w]o wounded prisoners of the 3rd Vermont and riddle them with bullits all the men around here swear they will drive every nigger out of Philadelphia." Robert O'Reilly, a surgeon who joined the army in late 1863 and served primarily in hospitals in Chattanooga, also spoke disparagingly of blacks. Telling his mother of his hope of "buying a contraband for a body servant," he complained, "The worst of these niggers is that they are so very unreliable." Coupled with Irish Catholics' dislike for blacks was a hatred for the "black" Republican Party shared by many Catholic Democrats. Private White grew so incensed at the radicals after some Union troops were "cut to pieces" during the Peninsula Campaign that he promised "if them black republicans dont stop their heating they will see the bloody 69th coming up on them on a charged bayonets."[22]

As the conflict dragged on, a few Catholic soldiers came to support the Republican administration and some of its more controversial policies, such as emancipation as a means to win the war. General Meagher grew disgusted with his countrymen for their "gross stupidity" in blindly following the Democratic Party. "To have been a Democrat in the days of Andrew Jackson was to have been an American citizen in the boldest and proudest interpretation of the word," Meagher wrote to his friend Patrick Guiney. "Now-a-days," he continued, "it is to be the partisan of a selfish and conscienceless faction, which under the captivating pretexts of State-Rights, Habeas Corpus, and the popular claims and rights of the kind, would cripple the national power." Captain Edward P. Brownson, a wartime Republican like his father, even supported General John C. Frémont's candidacy, whose chances of election he felt were better than Lincoln's.[23]

Similarly a few German Catholic soldiers broke ranks with their conservative communities back home and supported the Republicans' emancipation policy. Private Carl Ruff, a German Catholic immigrant who because of his antislavery views was arrested and then forced to flee New Orleans shortly before the war broke out, enlisted in 1864 in the 41st Missouri Volunteers as a private "to take revenge on these wretched rebels and to do my part in the fight for freedom." Similarly, Anton Bullenhaar of Westphalia declared that "the object of the war is the abolition of slavery." "Hura for the Union en the Sisechen gohn tor Helle," he wrote, closing the same letter with "Lord keep and preserve the United States *of the* America in the indivisible bond of unity." Bullenhaar came to believe so strongly in the Union cause that he enlisted as a private in January 1862. He was killed on the second day of the Battle of Chickamauga.[24]

Though Sergeant Welsh referred to blacks as "nigars" and reported an "intensely strong" feeling against them in the army as the "principal cause of this war," he still supported Massachusetts Governor John Andrew's proposal to raise black troops. In late 1862, Welsh wrote that "if slavery is in the way of the proper administration of the laws and the integrity and perpetuety of this nation, then i say away with both slaves and slavery[.] sweep both from the land forever rather then the freedom and prosperity of a great nation such as this should be destroyed[.]" Welsh's support for black troops and his opposition to slavery is remarkable given his observation that antipathy toward blacks was "especially strong in the Irish regiments." His conversion to emancipation as a means to win the war made him like many other Union soldiers in the army who merely wanted to end slavery to save the Union, not because they liked African Americans. One Irish Catholic private named Joe Duff wrote his aunt that he, too, had "bitterly opposed" abolition at first, wanting only to defend "our Country and to restore the Union." People at home may feel like an abolition war was "imposed" on them, but as for those who were actually fighting "we seen that it was necessary to punish and weaken them, the South." Although some Catholic soldiers eventually supported emancipation as a war measure and later condemned antidraft riots that took place in New York in 1863, many continued to support the Democrats just as they had before the war.[25]

Faced with repeated setbacks in the war against the rebellion, many Catholic soldiers still remained confident in ultimate victory. If only every man would "doe their duty fully and bravely," argued Sergeant Welsh, "this war would [have] been ended before now." Disgusted at shirkers and cowards among his regiment, Welsh was optimistic that the war was "now being pushed forward" to ultimate victory for the Union. He gave thanks to God that he had been "lucky" enough to remain unscathed despite the carnage of the recent Battle of Fredericksburg while his friends were killed or wounded. In the wake of this disastrous fight, Guiney wrote to his wife that should the army fail the nation's tombstone would read "The Republic which had the world at its service, expired for the want of a General to lead its armies." Guiney predicted that Union defeat would also be a personal defeat: "If we fail I never can be half the man. The charm of life will be gone. Even now the 'Star Spangled Banner' sounds like a wail to me." Ultimately, his faith was what gave him hope for the future. "God is above us, though, and no Christian should despair."[26] Badly wounded on May 5 at the Wilderness, Guiney gave thanks that "God gave me an opportunity and of which I availed myself, to shed my blood for our beloved Republic." Guiney believed that General Ulysses S. Grant was the man to finish off the rebellion, and he could rest knowing that he had "many times assisted in the damage and discomfiture of the Enemy."[27]

The war's bloody carnage took a heavy toll on many Catholic families, who could ill afford to lose their primary breadwinner. Peter Boffinger, a German from Ulm, was typical of soldiers whose families depended on their monthly pay to help make ends meet. Writing to his sister, Boffinger regretted that "I am not in a position to lend you a helping hand, because our government, so it seems, is short of fund and keeps us waiting for our money." Although he worked his way through the ranks and even reenlisted in 1864, his wounds from the Battles of Fairs Oaks and Gettysburg eventually caused him to be mustered out for disability in February 1865. Although he received a monthly pension as a disabled veteran, he died a poor man.[28]

Tragedy fell even harder on Sergeant Walter Elliot's family, for two of his brothers died while serving in the Union Army. The first to fall was William Elliott, who had just written home to his family on the morning of the day after the Battle of Gettysburg to report that he had escaped the fight unscathed. He was wounded later that day, however, and died on the fifth. Despite the "sorrow and gloom" hanging over the family, William, at least, died "a practical Catholic," having received last rites and a Catholic burial. Walter comforted his family back home by assuring them that William had "died a glorious death." William's passing was a "great sacrifice offered to God to leave yet on earth the great blessings of freedom and religious toleration." William, he continued, could not have met "[a] better death, a more becoming end for a soldier and a Christian." The following spring, their brother Robert died from wounds suffered during the

Overland Campaign. Heeding his grieving mother's request, Walter left the army in June.[29]

Nor did the war spare the family of the Union's greatest Catholic patriot, Orestes A. Brownson. His son Henry was badly wounded at Chancellorsville, returning to the army only after a long convalescence at the family's home. A year later, Brownson's other son Edward, known as "Ned" to his family, was wounded through the shoulder at the beginning of the Overland Campaign but recovered quickly to rejoin the army. Ned's luck did not hold, however, and he died gallantly while rallying Union troops at the Battle of Ream's Station. Shortly thereafter, another one of Brownson's sons, William, died while on his way to enlist in the Union Army. Apparently both sons died without receiving the reassuring last rites from a priest, though many New York clergy offered Masses on Edward's behalf.[30]

Margaret Welsh's worst fears were realized when her husband, Peter, died in 1864. Despite the fact that "every man that was near me in the right of the company was either killed or wounded except one," Welsh could still reassure his wife in the wake of Fredericksburg that "God is good[.] he brought me safe out of this last battle and he can as easily bring me safe home to you if it is his holy will." In the end, it seemed that God's will dictated that Welsh would never return home. He was wounded at the Battle of Spotsylvania Courthouse on May 12. Suffering complications from his wound, he died just over two weeks later, his wife having barely managed to reach him before his death. After burying her husband Margaret, who never remarried, depended on a small widow's stipend from the U.S. government for the rest of her life.[31] Given the sacrifices they and their families often made on behalf of the Union, Catholic veterans and their apologists would soon be shocked to see how quickly their service was forgotten and how little it had done to stamp out old religious prejudices in the reunited nation.

At the beginning of the war, there was no shortage of Catholic men willing to serve in the Union Army. Men volunteered for purely patriotic as well as economic, ethnic, and individual reasons, but their willingness to serve on behalf of the nation did not go unnoticed. Catholic civilians took great pride in visible symbols of their patriotism, from the famed Irish Brigade to famous generals like Rosecrans, Meagher, and Corcoran. Although most did not serve in regiments or companies that were made up of a majority of men of their faith or ethnicity, those that did, particularly the Irish, enjoyed life in the army relatively free from prejudice and with a greater chance of being able to practice their faith while under arms. Some were transformed by their desire to win the war to forego their old civilian prejudices and political affiliations and support the Republicans and even emancipation. In the end, the war proved very costly to them and their families, for many Irish units suffered particularly heavy casualties. As the war entered its third year, many back home began to doubt that the struggle was worth it, and eventually they came to resent the war's effect on their families, to resent the Republicans who directed the Union war, and to resent the lack of appreciation among the larger community for Catholic sacrifices on behalf of the nation.

4 Priests and Nuns in the Army

U nderstanding the religious lives of Catholic soldiers and how the war did or did not change attitudes toward members of their faith requires not only looking at the volunteers themselves but at priest chaplains and sister nurses as well. While some men made do with reading the scriptures or prayer books on their own, proper Catholic worship required a priest to celebrate the sacraments. A letter from an Irishman in the 78th Pennsylvania makes this point quite strongly: "[Fr.] Christy is with us here. I have not went to my [religious] duty since I left. You cannot imagine how rejoiced I was when I seen him come on the boat at Louisville." Unfortunately for devout soldiers, there were never enough Catholic chaplains in the army. Just over fifty Catholic chaplains received some kind of official appointment to regiments or hospitals. They were vastly outnumbered by Protestant chaplains in the Union Army. Of the few chaplains who did serve, their average term of service lasted for only eighteen months, further limiting their ability to serve adequately Catholic soldiers, let alone attempt to dispel nativist prejudices. While many priests served with distinction, bishops did not always send their best priests to the front.[1]

Catholic sisters, whose unmarried, cloistered lifestyle had been sharply criticized in antebellum America, served in many theaters of the war and numbered well over six hundred. Over time, the government and soldiers alike came to value them highly for their expert care of the sick and wounded. Catholic nuns may have constituted as much as one-sixth of all female nurses on both sides, and around 20 percent of all the nuns in the United States served as wartime nurses. This meant that they served in proportionally higher numbers than any other single group of women, lay or religious, North or South. In the end, it was the selfless devotion of these women and their careful neutrality in terms of religious faith and politics that did more to rehabilitate the church in the eyes of Protestant Americans than did the actions of Catholic chaplains or soldiers.[2]

From the war's start, local, state, and federal authorities recognized the need for chaplains to serve men of various Christian denominations. At first, some served as unofficial volunteers, but, as time went on, Congress passed laws and the War Department issued regulations that gave official status to chaplains working in hospitals and in Union regiments. In this respect, Catholic chaplains shared some common experiences with ministers from other denominations. To become a chaplain, a minister needed the approval of the colonel of the regiment in which he hoped to serve. Appointments were then confirmed by the War Department, which gave each chaplain an official commission. Chaplains received the pay of a captain of cavalry. Additionally, they were expected to make regular reports on the "moral and religious status of the regiment" and to officiate at services for deceased soldiers in their unit. Apart from those official governmental requirements, they provided religious services for their men as required by the chaplain's denomination.[3]

Catholic soldiers needed the clergy if they wanted to practice their religion fully and devoutly in the army. Only a Catholic priest could provide a soldier with the sacraments such as Holy Communion, Penance, and Anointing of the Sick that nineteenth-century Catholics believed were necessary for their salvation. During the war, having a priest in one's regiment was a crucial factor in whether a Catholic could receive the sacraments. Fears about the availability of chaplains seem to have deterred some Catholics from enlisting. Hugh Harlin, an Irish Catholic from Indiana, cited his fear of dying on the battlefield with "no priest perhaps" to ensure him a proper burial or last rites as one of the reasons he avoided military service. Devout German Catholics, who were not likely to find a German-speaking priest in the army, probably feared that dying for the Union was taking a huge risk with their spiritual salvation. This fear made the need for adequate spiritual support for Catholic soldiers a pressing concern, not only for patriotic Catholics putting themselves in harm's way but also for the government that wanted their support. One local priest in Washington, D.C., Father James Fullerton, was so concerned about the need for chaplains that he personally met with General McClellan and wrote to both President Lincoln and Archbishop Hughes about the matter.[4]

Despite a widely recognized need for chaplains, church authorities ran into difficulty in finding priests for the army and navy for a number of reasons. In an article calling for more chaplains, the pro-war Father Edward Purcell gave three of the most often cited reasons for why no more priests could be found. There were not enough men who were "qualified," few could handle "this very arduous department of the ministry," and, as Purcell admitted of his own diocese, "We have not a sufficient number of priests to supply destitute congregations." This last reason was the one the Paulists—a splinter group from the Redemptorist

order founded in the late 1850s by Brownson's friend, Rev. Isaac Hecker—gave
when they routinely refused all requests for priests from Bishop Hughes and
the American-born bishop of Hartford, Francis P. McFarland. Later in 1863, in
answering General Rosecrans's request for more chaplains, Archbishop Purcell
lamented that if he could only "manufacture myself into a decade of priests I
would so devote myself to the glorious mission of both White and Colored Men
whose immortal Souls there is such an oppty of now converting to the only true
& saving faith in yr. Department." "But alas!" continued Purcell, "it is equally
impossible to find priests in the Diocese as to do this multiplication." Archbishop
Hughes wrote Archbishop Francis Kenrick in April 1861 that he would not per-
mit more than one man from his diocese to serve as a chaplain due to the overwhelming need for priests in his parishes. In fairness to Hughes, when he later
offered the services of nuns and Jesuit priests to Union General Winfield Scott,
the general thanked him but declared they already had enough Catholic religious
from Georgetown College to fulfill the army's needs.[5]

In short, bishops put the needs of their flock at home ahead of those in the
field and never developed a common plan to deal with the problem. Despite
such excuses, years after the war was over Archbishop John Ireland of St. Paul,
a former Civil War chaplain, sharply criticized the hierarchy as being responsible for the tragic shortage of priests in the army. It would have been much
better, in his opinion, to have assigned temporarily priests to two parishes each
to free up enough men to send one Catholic chaplain for every Union division
in the field, than to have let so many men die without receiving the sacraments.
Of the roughly 2,300 regimental chaplains in the Union Army, only about forty
of them—less than 2 percent—were Catholic.[6] In total, about fifty-three priests
served in hospitals or regiments, which was only one priest for every 3,773 Catholics in the army, or one for every 41,509 federal soldiers. These ratios must have
fluctuated during the war, and visits from local priests certainly helped alleviate
the problem. Still, these figures are a strong vindication of Ireland's criticism.[7]

Politicians and military leaders took greater initiative in finding Catholic
chaplains for the army than the hierarchy did itself. For example, it was at the
behest of Minnesota's governor that John Ireland became the state's official Catholic chaplain, and a similar arrangement was worked out for Father Cooney of
the College of Notre Dame through the influence of Indiana Governor Oliver P.
Morton. In October 1861, Lincoln personally requested priests for the hospitals
from Archbishop Hughes. Hughes forwarded the request to Archbishop Kenrick of Baltimore, who, despite his lack of enthusiasm for the war, did promptly

recommend two priests for the duty. Rosecrans was not the only Catholic officer in the Union Army to take an active interest in the spiritual welfare of his troops. Colonel Julius Garesché in Washington, as well as Brigadier Generals Amiel Whipple and John Newton of the Army of Potomac, corresponded with the president of Georgetown at various times asking for chaplains, Catholic reading material, or religious items such as scapulars and rosaries for their men.[8]

The religious orders based at universities, not the diocesan clergy, provided the most reliable source of chaplains for the army. Not beholden to parish duty or the commands of hesitant bishops as were secular priests, the regular orders proved crucial in supplying men to units such as the Irish Brigade. The Jesuits of Fordham sent two priests, Fathers Michael Nash and Peter Tissot, to serve along the East Coast. Even Georgetown College, despite its markedly southern sympathies, sent one Jesuit to serve in a Maryland hospital, while two former faculty members served as chaplains in the Union Army. The college's president, Rev. John Early, proved willing to send additional priests when needed, dispatching three at Colonel Julius Garesché's request to take care of the wounded after First Battle of Bull Run. The relatively young community of the Holy Cross, founded in France in reaction to the French Revolution, with its American headquarters at the College of Notre Dame in South Bend, Indiana, sent seven priests, two of whom died from disease during the war. Writing to Archbishop John Purcell in early 1862, Rev. Edward Sorin said the four Holy Cross priests in the army "were all commissioned by the Department at the request of Colonels who knew them before & sent for them." Thus, even at patriotic Notre Dame, it was army officers who first thought of the spiritual needs of their men and initiated the chain of events that led Sorin to send so many of his priests away to the army.[9]

Whatever his motivations, Sorin's priests filled a vital need in the Union Army. At a time when many bishops were reluctant to spare even a single priest for the Catholic soldiers of their diocese, Notre Dame sent seven priests during the course of the war. As the school's chronicles attest, there was much hope at Notre Dame that the work of Catholic chaplains would help dispel the prejudices of many of the Protestant soldiers they met in the army. "Never had circumstances been more favorable to the progress of the Catholic religion," noted a Holy Cross cleric. Rather than taking sides on the causes of the war or who was in the right or wrong, the chronicles instead depicted the Union armies and hospitals as a vast mission field for the salvation of souls. The entry for 1862 boasted that the order's priests bravely "followed their regiments or their brigades amidst the bullets and all the dangers of the war." Notre Dame's chaplains—and the Holy Cross

Two of Notre Dame's priests, Rev. William Corby and James Dillon, sit with other Irish Brigade chaplains (Library of Congress).

Sisters, too—had gained for it a "more enviable position in the outside world," and the cause of Catholicism in the United States would profit from their remarkable services during the war.[10]

Not every priest sent to the front, however, was necessarily the exemplar of Christian piety, fortitude, and kindness. A bad chaplain might not only fail his spiritual charges in the army but also reconfirm old prejudices. Concerned about the influence of two defrocked priests serving in the Union Army, the Purcell brothers put out a warning in their paper in early 1862 that the men were operating without authorization. Another troublesome priest named Father Hugh Quigley, who had been involved in a legal controversy before the war with the Belgian-born bishop of Detroit, Peter Paul Lefevere, reportedly sold not only schnapps to federal soldiers at five dollars a bottle but also the clothes and boots of dead Union soldiers for a profit. "God help us!" exclaimed a scandalized Bishop Spalding when he learned of Quigley's misdeeds. On several occasions, Father Sorin received credible reports of chaplain Father Peter Paul Gillen's alleged drinking problem. A fellow priest in the army, Father James Dillon, feared that "should he [Gillen] repeat this thing a few more times then it would be decidedly injurious not only to the Congregation but to religion." In the spring of 1864, Gillen's drinking got so out of hand that Father Sorin seriously considered removing him from duty. Fortunately, with Father William Corby's help, Gillen mended his ways and received an honorable discharge at the end of the war.[11]

Sometimes bishops used the army to rid themselves of troublesome priests. Father William O'Higgins had nearly been expelled from the diocese of Cincinnati before the war because he had allegedly neglected his priestly duties. O'Higgins was spared dismissal when Purcell gladly accepted his request to become an army chaplain in the 10th Ohio. Likewise, Father Thomas Brady had been a thorn in the side of Bishop Lefevere, first by fighting a legal battle with the diocese for control of the Catholic church in Grand Rapids, Michigan, and then for bullying an order of Irish nuns he had brought to the United States to teach school. Lefevere must have been relieved by the priest's decision to become a chaplain for the mostly Irish Catholic 15th Michigan Infantry Regiment. The Irish American bishop John McCloskey similarly allowed one of his priests to serve in the 2nd New York "Troy Regiment," but, not wanting him to return, quickly agreed to allow him to leave for another diocese. Regardless of whether these men proved to be good chaplains, the bishops' desire to hold onto their good priests while sending such men to the army was a disservice to Catholic soldiers and probably to the church's reputation as well.[12]

On occasion chaplains could cause scandals not so much by inattention to duty or through vice but by being too *enthusiastic* in their new roles. Father Thomas F. Mooney, the first chaplain of the 69th New York, was known to be overly partisan in favor of his men and the federal cause. Although precedents had already been set in the Confederacy by Catholic authorities who had blessed battle flags of local Catholic units, Mooney crossed a line when he decided to bless the cannon of Fort Corcoran in June 1861. Likening the act to the baptism of a child, Mooney compared the squeals of a protesting baby to the cannon's anxiety to speak "in a thundering voice, to the joy of his friends and terror of his enemies." Mooney's flippant speech enraged Catholic authorities in Maryland, and the *Catholic Mirror* criticized his excessively "exuberant patriotism" that made him seem a poor example of a "disciple of the Prince of Peace." Kenrick wrote immediately to Hughes to have him recalled. In response, Hughes lectured Kenrick that Mooney had merely done what southern bishops had when they blessed flags or sang Te Deums after the Confederate victory at Fort Sumter. Still, Hughes removed Mooney from the army to satisfy the wishes of his more neutral colleague.[13]

Most chaplains performed their tasks well and often under trying circumstances. Poor working conditions and a lack of funds were constant problems for Catholic chaplains. Despite troubles getting a commission and thus receiving no pay for months, Father Francis McAtee somehow managed to acquire large numbers of religious books and items for his men. Being a successful chaplain also required a good deal of patience and improvisation. The rainy season in Florida often prevented the celebration of Mass at Fort Pickens, during which Father Nash had to make do with a small tent. Later his men constructed him a larger "church" out of barrels, boxes, and "pine boughs," a makeshift structure that was similar to those employed by others in the Army of the Potomac. In one instance, the men of the Irish Brigade could not find a single box or board, so they constructed "the rudest of altars" from some pine trees and provided it with shelter by attaching pine branches to a nearby tree. Father Corby later recalled the Mass he celebrated there as one "to rival that of the most destitute Indian missionary that ever put foot on the soil of the Huron Nation." Unattached to any particular regiment and seeking to attend to as many Catholics as possible, Father Gillen traveled throughout the Army of the Potomac saying Mass in the ramshackle buggy given to him by General McClellan. It was not a perfect solution, but Gillen made the best of it.[14]

Priests greatly benefited from serving under Catholic officers, who knew the duties of a priest and the importance of making the sacraments available to their men. Father Jeremiah Trecy, a missionary priest in Alabama who became persona non grata in his own parish after ministering to wounded Union soldiers, became General Rosecrans's constant companion. Trecy helped Father Cooney say Mass for the general on the morning of the first day of the Battle of Stones River and devoted himself to ministering to Catholics throughout the Army of the Cumberland. Major General John Newton of the Army of the Potomac often asked Father Francis McAtee of the 31st New York Infantry for help in getting religious books and items for Catholic soldiers. McAtee appreciated the attention and kindness he received from his patron, for whom he said daily private Mass. As a result, many priests became fiercely loyal to their Catholic leaders, especially to General Rosecrans. In November 1863, after Rosecrans was removed, O'Higgins reported that the general still "has a great number of enemies here from the highest to the lowest" and defended his former commanding general. After Rosecrans's removal, Father Cooney continued to work closely with Major General David Stanley, who frequently attended Mass and threw his support behind Cooney's temperance activities.[15]

Catholic officers had high expectations for their chaplains. When rumors reached Colonel Wilson that Father Nash thought of leaving for awhile to recuperate in New York, the colonel admonished him to stay at his post and not to "disgrace" the church by leaving. Even after Nash assured his commander he would not leave, Wilson implored him to stay and set a good example for the men, even if it meant dying there: "Father, to leave your bones here would be the greatest honor you could confer on our holy religion or on your order."[16] Catholic officers and chaplains often had a mutually beneficial relationship. The latter helped boost discipline and morale in their units, while the support of the former often reinforced a chaplain's influence and authority with the men.

After saying Mass, by far the most important occupation of the Catholic chaplain in camp was hearing confessions. This sacrament was most important, and thus in the greatest demand, right before a battle. Father Gillen devoted himself to hearing the confessions of the men of the 22nd New York the night before the Battle of Bull Run. The demand was so great that he had to give conditional absolution to many men from other units who were still waiting to see him when the order to advance was given. Prior to an expected clash with General Braxton Bragg's men in Kentucky, penitent soldiers kept Cooney up all night hearing confessions from a makeshift confessional made by stacking three muskets together and covering them on two sides with blankets. Though his men pitied him for having to sit thus for eight straight hours, Cooney claimed to his brother that he was joyful when he "considered how much God was doing with the hands of his unworthy son." Father Joseph Carrier's temporary appointment to General Grant's army proved invaluable to Catholic soldiers besieging Vicksburg who otherwise would have had no priest to take their confessions. One hospital-bound Irishman, who had despaired when there was no priest to care for him as he lay wounded on the battlefield, profusely praised Carrier for making him "now at peace with my Maker and with myself." This account is one of many examples from the war illustrating the importance of confession to the devout Catholic soldier.[17]

When there was not enough time for a priest to hear confessions, such as in Father Gillen's case before Bull Run, priests could also give absolution quickly to steel their men with the courage that, should they die in battle, their sins would be forgiven. Although Father Corby's general absolution at Gettysburg is the most famous, Father Gillen was probably the first to give absolution to Civil War soldiers, and this practice could be found throughout the Union armies. At the Battle of Williamsburg in 1862, Father O'Hagan had the Catholic soldiers of his regiment kneel and receive absolution before entering battle. Father Trecy likewise gave absolution to a group of Catholic soldiers while under fire before the first day of Stones River. Father Cooney was even more proactive. Every morning for five days at Stones River, Cooney stood in front of the 35th Indiana and had them all kneel and repeat a prayer and act of contrition with him. He then gave them absolution while they knelt. According to Cooney, General Rosecrans was so impressed that he ordered every chaplain, including the Protestants, to give a blessing to their men before battle.[18]

For reasons having to do with the preeminent position of Gettysburg in the memory of the Civil War, these battlefield absolutions, which all took place prior to the war's third summer, have largely been forgotten. Corby's absolution on July 2, 1863, however, has been constantly celebrated ever since and even memorialized in a bronze statue erected on the very rock that he stood upon when he pronounced the blessing. Just as the Irish Brigade was about to go into battle, Father Corby, realizing that his men had not had the proper chance to prepare themselves for the battle, proposed that the brigade halt so that he could give them general absolution. Standing on a rock and raising his right arm, he proceeded to recite the prayer for absolution in Latin. He said the prayer while "under fire" according to some accounts. Catholic and non-Catholic men alike reportedly all went down on their knees to receive the blessing. Even Major General Winfield Scott Hancock, Corby's corps commander, allegedly took off his hat and bowed his head during the prayer, which Corby later claimed was intended for all soldiers of all faiths in both armies. For devout Catholics in the Army of the Potomac, the inclusiveness of the absolution was fortunate because Corby was the only Catholic chaplain in the army at that point, meaning that most would not have been able to go to confession before the war's bloodiest battle. General St. Clair A. Mulholland of the 116th Pennsylvania later told Corby that his act had inspired one of his less-devout men to fervent prayer just before his death only twenty minutes later.[19]

Catholic priests risked their lives to tend to their wounded men in battle to help save both their lives and souls. This necessarily put them in harm's way, although only one priest died during the war while tending to his men. Father Nash found himself twice in the thick of battle in October and November 1861. On the first occasion he was almost captured and in the second he came under direct fire from Confederate artillery. Father Thomas Scully of the 9th Massachusetts was not so lucky and was captured on two separate occasions during the Seven Days Campaign outside of Richmond. Father Corby and Father Dillon, riding back and forth near the front lines, came under fire at the Battle of Fair Oaks. While stopping to hear a wounded man's confession behind a small home Corby likened the bullets hitting it to hail. Recalling the battle many years later, he took great pride in the fact that "as fast as our men dropped, they were seen first by the priest."[20]

Sticking with his men through the horror and slaughter of Stones River, Cooney was later commended for showing himself "cool and indifferent to danger." Cooney's reputation for staying "at the front" with his men, braving shot and shell to tend to them, won him the praise of two officers in the wake of the Battle of Nashville. Similarly, Father Trecy claimed to have taken a sharpshooter's bullet through his coat at the Battle of Chickamauga. Some priests paid the ultimate price for their service as chaplains. Notre Dame's Father Julien-Prosper Bourget had been in the country for less than two years from his native France when he succumbed to disease while serving at a military hospital in Mound City, Illinois. Two of the Holy Cross Order's sisters also died there in April and July of 1862. Father Joseph Leveque only served a short time as a Union chaplain before he also died in Jersey City in February 1862, apparently of exhaustion and disease. Father James Dillon, plagued by a lung disease he contracted while in camp, finally left the army in August 1864 and died only four years later from his chronic condition.[21]

Just as important as their work during a battle or in the camps was the work chaplains performed in hospitals. In all, at least thirteen Catholic chaplains served with the approval of President Lincoln in Union hospitals. Even though they generally served for only a few months, these men diligently took care of the spiritual health of both the patients and quite often the sister nurses as well. Even neutral bishops supported sending priests to hospitals, which they could do while presumably still running their parishes. Baltimore's Kenrick, at Lincoln's request, sent two local priests to take care of the wounded in Washington in October 1861. Father Edward McGlynn served at a hospital run by the Sisters of Charity in Manhattan's Central Park. Although most of the men were non-Catholic, McGlynn commended the nursing nuns for showing their patients "real Catholicism" and reported that many non-Catholics took part in evening Catholic services on Sunday, including the benediction of the Blessed Sacrament. Army chaplains likewise often divided their time between the camp and the hospital to tend to the wounded and sick Catholic men of their regiment. Father John Ireland constantly rode from hospital to hospital seeking out wounded Catholic men. Cooney's hospital experiences confirmed his deeply seated prejudice against Protestant ministers. Cooney claimed that the typical Catholic clergymen attended those most in danger of dying first, "irrespective of denomination or creed," and that he had personally baptized many dangerously ill men who had been passed over by Protestant clergymen.[22]

Despite the fact that both Protestants and Catholics were fighting the same war to the save the Union, religious bigotry continued in the army during the conflict. In one instance, Catholic men seeking to leave their regiment on Sunday to attend Mass with Father Gillen were stopped by a colonel, who claimed he was merely preventing them from getting drunk. Regardless of whether the colonel was telling the truth, Gillen still perceived it years later as motivated by religious prejudice. Upon arriving at the 6th New York's headquarters to become its chaplain, Father Michael Nash had little trouble gaining the support of its Catholic colonel, William Wilson. The other officers were all Protestants. Although he won them over, they admitted to him that they had never spoken to a Catholic priest before and had been leery of having him there until meeting him. After the regiment arrived at Pensacola, Nash remarked that, while most of the reinforcements were Irish Catholics, the men had nothing to read except Protestant tracts that made "low attacks on our faith." This was a common problem for Catholic soldiers as the church simply did not have the resources to match the Protestant journals and tract societies of the North. The problem persisted throughout the war, with one chaplain promising to say a Mass for any Catholic who donated Catholic reading material to the 69th New York. Whenever the devout among the men were fortunate enough to receive a shipment of rosaries, religious medals, and prayer books, they were very thankful.[23]

Catholic chaplains generally could hope to overcome bigotry only by turning the other cheek and to dispel prejudice by working hard on behalf of their men. Father Cooney reported that Protestants were attending his sermons in the open field "by thousands" and that "prejudice to the Church is almost gone." No doubt exposure to Catholicism through such public events convinced many such non-Catholic soldiers that the "Whore of Babylon" was not quite as fierce or evil as they had been led to believe. Sometimes, however, Catholic soldiers took matters into their own hands. The men of the 6th New York decided to punish a superior officer for insulting the Catholic faith during Mass. Forming a vigilante group, the men marched the offender off at the point of their swords and threw him into the ocean, promising to drown him if ever he acted up again. The newly penitent man soon had a changed disposition toward Fr. Nash and Catholicism.[24]

As this story implies, Catholics in the army sometimes went beyond defending their faith to criticizing Protestantism. Catholic chaplains likewise were certainly not immune to anti-Protestantism. Allegedly at General Rosecrans's request, Cooney and the four other priests in the Army of the Cumberland got together in the summer of 1863 to counteract the evangelization efforts of the United States Christian Commission among the army's troops. Cooney gleefully reported that these USCC representatives had little effect on the men after their initial appearance in camp. The commission's failure, Cooney stated, offered the "clearest proof of the impotency of Protestantism which has no power over the heart." Both Corby and Cooney expressed open disgust with liberal Protestant chaplains who told soldiers sentenced to death that they did not need baptism to be saved. Cooney claimed to have baptized such a man on the scaffold, while Corby barely managed to convince a chaplain nicknamed "Boots" to allow Corby to baptize his ward shortly before he was shot by a firing squad. Additionally, Cooney believed that Catholic priests willingly risked their lives at the front because they could offer the "treasures" of Catholicism—the sacraments—to their men. A Protestant minister, however, was "absent from the danger threatening his so called sheep as he has nothing for the conferring of which to risk his life." Such instances of unholy pride as Cooney's probably did little to endear Catholic chaplains to non-Catholic soldiers and chaplains.[25]

Nevertheless, Protestant and Catholic interaction in the battlefield often weakened religious prejudices on both sides. Despite the initial bigotry he encountered, Father Nash's career is a testament to this fact. Protestant soldiers often turned out in large numbers to Nash's Masses at Fort Pickens and were generally respectful during the ceremony. Impressed by the "zeal" of Nash's Catholic soldiers, the Protestant officers of a nearby regiment voluntarily vacated the wooden building they had been using for quarters and gave it over to the priest to celebrate Mass. Also known for his bravery, fellow Jesuit Father O'Hagan made a good impression on a Congregationalist chaplain, Reverend Joseph H. Twichell, who was also assigned to the Army of the Potomac. The men, sharing the same difficulties and dangers, soon became good friends, putting their religious differences aside to work for the spiritual welfare of their men. One night, after working to care for the wounded after Fredericksburg, the two men, exhausted, collapsed together, huddling for warmth and sharing blankets to ward off the harsh December cold. O'Hagan found the situation rather comical for a "Jesuit priest and a New England Puritan minister—of the worst sort—spooned close together under the same blanket. I wonder what the angels think." Pausing only a moment, the priest declared, "I think they like it."[26]

Catholic chaplains appreciated the praise they received from their former critics and often tried to do all that they could for Protestants in their units. In the West, Father Cooney's bravery even won him the recognition of a Know-Nothing officer, General Walter Chiles Whittaker. This officer praised him as a model chaplain who was "meek, pi[o]us, and brave as a lion" for braving the dangers of the battlefield to afford "the ministrations of his holy religion to the wounded and dying and giving words of encouragement to his fellow soldiers." This was high praise and exactly what Catholic apologists such as Brownson and

Donahoe hoped the war would achieve. In his memoirs, Father Corby claimed that the war had produced "excellent results" in "removing a great amount of prejudice." At some level, Corby believed that the "common danger" soldiers had faced in the war helped them to give up their religious prejudices against one another to the benefit of Catholics and Protestants alike.[27]

Father John Ireland's wartime and post-wartime career was a testament of the possibility of reconciliation across the religious divide. In 1862 Ireland joined as chaplain the 5th Minnesota, of whom only about one-third were Catholic. In addition to providing the sacraments to his Catholic soldiers, Ireland spoke highly of the Protestant soldiers he encountered, blaming most of Americans' anti-Catholicism on the poor behavior of Catholics. In a particularly telling case, Ireland came across a dying non-Catholic officer. Learning that he had been baptized, and seeing there "was not time to talk of Church," Ireland simply gave the man a nondenominational talk about "the Savior & of sorrow for Sin." Though Ireland did not convert the man, he recalled, "I have not doubted the Salvation of that Soul." At a time when Catholic doctrine still held that there was no salvation outside the church, this was a very liberal point of view. Long after the war he relished meeting his former comrades, both Protestant and Catholic, at reunions for veterans across Minnesota. "My years of chaplaincy were the happiest and most fruitful of my life," he remembered.[28]

Ultimately there were not enough priests, exemplary or not, in the Union Army to make any significant headway against anti-Catholicism in the North. The hundreds of nuns who served as nurses during the war, however, created a much greater positive impression of the Catholic Church among many of the soldiers and officers they encountered. Surprisingly, on the one hand major narratives of the war or gender studies of the conflict all acknowledge the then-new and remarkable presence of thousands of Protestant women volunteers in Union hospitals while overlooking or barely mentioning the contribution of sister nurses.[29] On the other hand, books and articles about Civil War nuns have dominated studies of wartime American Catholicism since the publication of the George Barton's *Angels of the Battlefield* in 1897. Although many Catholic laywomen certainly played important roles, and some, like Mary D. Lee of Maryland, nursed in hospitals alongside Protestant women, it was the nuns who made the greatest impression at that time and since.[30]

Nuns who served in hospitals as nurses do not easily fit into standard narratives of the war that traditionally see it as a watershed for northern women. Scholars have largely tended to celebrate the war as a chance to challenge existing

Daughters of Charity outside Satterlee Hospital in Philadelphia (courtesy of Daughters of Charity Province of St. Louise Archives, Emmitsburg, Md.).

gender norms. They have emphasized new or expanded roles for women in the public sphere, whether they were serving as hospital nurses far from their families, taking on leadership roles in local sanitary fairs, or speaking in public on behalf of the war or the Republican Party. While serving as a nurse was a new experience for many nuns who lived cloistered lives or were dedicated to teaching, many like the Daughters of Charity came from orders well trained and experienced in caring for the sick. The war brought them into greater contact with other Americans outside the Catholic community, and the nuns believed their work did much to eliminate antebellum prejudice toward them and their faith. Ultimately they saw themselves as continuing a pious tradition of Catholic sisters caring for the wounded and sick. Their goal was to save the body and souls of their patients, not to challenge Victorian gender norms or to assert new rights for themselves as women.[31]

Like chaplains, sister nurses served for various lengths of time in every theater of the war at the request of politicians, officers, and their religious superiors. At least 617 sisters served on both sides of the war, the vast majority of them in

Union hospitals. Almost all the sisters who served did so in hospitals staffed exclusively by other nuns from their own religious order or community. Communities of every size, region, and mission participated. One of the smallest, the Sisters of St. Joseph in Wheeling, West Virginia, numbered only a handful. They served in a Union hospital in Wheeling with the blessing of their bishop, who despite his extreme pro-Confederate views frequently said Mass at the hospital. The largest of these communities was the Daughters of Charity, who had considerable experience in nursing from before the war. Hundreds of nuns from this order served in hospitals in both the United States and Confederacy during the war. Next were the Sisters of the Holy Cross in South Bend, Indiana, who were a teaching order with no previous experience in nursing. By the end of the war this order had sent sixty-three women from Mound City, Illinois, to Washington, D.C., to serve as nurses. In all, perhaps as many as one-fifth of all Catholic sisters living in the United States in 1860 performed hospital service at some point during the war, a larger number proportionally than any other single group of women across the North or South.[32]

Perhaps even more nuns would have served if bishops had not been reluctant to let them go to the front because the need for them back home was still so great. Certainly the government's refusal to appoint additional chaplains in 1862 made it extremely difficult for nuns serving as nurses to go to Mass on Sundays, and this policy made bishops such as Kenrick and Hughes reluctant to send any more nuns than they already had. Many church leaders nonetheless recognized the important work the sisters could do on behalf of the faith and consented to their work among the suffering men.[33]

Although he could never provide as many chaplains or nuns as he would have liked to, Archbishop Purcell was a firm believer in the good they did, and when he could not send additional priests to be with Rosecrans's army he sent eight Sisters of Charity. Holy Cross priests at Notre Dame credited their sisters with more than seven hundred baptisms in 1862, an "edifying" fact that proved the "devotedness" of Catholic sisters and the truth of their faith in contrast to "the coldness and the helplessness of Protestantism." The deaths of two nuns who were serving in hospitals staffed by the order—Sisters Elise O'Brien and Fidelis Lawlor—while tragic, served as a "consecration" of the Holy Cross order that "must surround it with a happy prestige in the midst of the New World."[34]

Despite the fact that many nuns had more nursing experience than did most American women, many in the medical establishment did not greet them with open arms. First, they were women; second, they were Catholics; and finally, they were nuns. Before the war, they had been vilified in anti-Catholic literature such as the best-selling albeit utterly false tale of convent promiscuity and vice, *Maria Monk* (1836). For their own protection, many nuns refrained from wearing their religious habits and garb outside their convents for fear of being physically and verbally harassed. Like other women of their time nuns were expected to keep a low profile in public life, which was an overwhelmingly masculine world in the mid-nineteenth century. Not only were nuns often misunderstood or vilified by anti-Catholic Americans, but nursing work was still a questionable occupation for single women in American society. Dr. John Baxter Upham, who accompanied a contingent of Sisters of Mercy to a hospital on the North Carolina coast, initially gave them the cold shoulder due to his "supreme horror of 'lady nurses.'"[35]

Hospitals staffed or controlled by Dorothea Dix turned away Mother Angela Gillespie's Holy Cross nuns even though Indiana's Governor Morton had personally requested them. Only through the personal intercession of an Illinois Catholic priest and General Grant were some of the sisters able to find work in hospitals at Mound City and Cairo, Illinois. Henceforth, Mother Angela often relied on her cousin, General Sherman, to help secure employment for her nuns in the face of opposition. Likewise, the Sisters of Charity of New York relied on the endorsement of the prominent pro-war New Yorker Edwards Pierpont to get the government to employ them as nurses. Even after assigned, a sister nurse's ability to serve her wards was often undermined by prejudice. Daughters of Charity serving at a U.S. military hospital in Frederick, Maryland, complained that local Protestant ladies treated them poorly and "embittered" the wounded men against them. Only slowly did these nuns win the trust and gratitude of the hospital's doctors and patients.[36]

Nursing in Civil War hospitals was often exhausting, dirty, and dangerous work. Nurses routinely worked long hours performing such tasks as changing bandages, giving medicine, assisting in surgeries, and cleaning hospital wards. Even the journey to hospitals near the front lines could be perilous. Sisters of the Holy Cross traveling on a Union mail boat on the Mississippi River came under fire from Confederates, with a shot passing through one nun's veil. Nuns did not work in clean or sterile environments and they were daily exposed to men with horrific wounds and the deadly diseases that killed many more soldiers than did bullets. The Battle of Fort Donelson in February 1862 brought more than one thousand casualties to the hospital in Mound City. With only a handful of sisters, it was all the nuns could do to attend to their needs. "It was nothing but dressing wounds from morning till night," recalled one nun. "On an average there were seven or eight deaths every day, but what a consolation to us to know that scarcely any of them died without baptism." Another was particularly horrified to find insects crawling in men's open wounds and disturbed by the men who had been permanently blinded in battle. Sisters were not immune to disease and many times their fellow nuns had to take on additional work when another was laid low by some ailment. One nun working in a hospital in Tennessee begged her superior to send another nun, stating, "I could not do more than I do: for it requires unceasing exertions." Illness sometimes cut short the nursing careers of nuns as well. Sister Elizabeth Callnan, an Irish immigrant, became so sick with "brain-fever" within six weeks of leaving for a hospital in Beaufort, North Carolina, that she was forced to return home. Sister Fidelis, who became ill while working among the men at Mound City, died in mid-April 1862. By the time she had died, the hospital was so flooded with water from the nearby Mississippi River that her body had to be taken out on a skiff.[37]

Above all else, Catholic sisters sought to care for the souls of their patients, not just their bodies. Service in the hospitals allowed nuns to perform corporal acts of mercy that they hoped would allow them to serve their God by serving others and thus promote their own spiritual growth and holiness. The surest sign that they were doing God's will was through bringing wayward Catholics back to the faith, or, perhaps even more tellingly, by converting formerly anti-Catholic Protestants. Although impossible to verify, many nuns later claimed that hundreds of conversions, "inspired by the supernatural charity of these dedicated women," had taken place in their hospitals. When queried after the war about her experiences as a Civil War nurse, one nun said, "All that I can remember there was three hundred Baptized, [and] all I hope [are] in Heaven praying for us now." Likewise, a Daughter of Charity claimed that seven hundred baptisms and five hundred "conversions" of Catholics soldiers "who had neglected their faith" took place in one St. Louis military hospital alone.[38]

Although such numbers were impressive to Catholic bishops, stories of individuals' conversions were just as powerful. Post-war accounts of successful conversions are remarkably similar regardless of geography and among different women's religious communities. In many stories, a man converted or changed his ways to lead a model life only after encountering the nuns serving in his hospital. With the encouragement of sister nurses at the U.S. hospital in Philadelphia, a non-Catholic patient, James Cook, literally read himself into conversion. The nuns held him up as a "model for some of the [other] Catholics [in the ward], many of whom alas, forget to practice the religion of their fathers." In other accounts, soldiers converted just in time to ensure their salvation. A Holy Cross

nun remembered one dying soldier, a former seminary student who had married a preacher's daughter and became an anti-Catholic orator, who repented
and gave a good confession: "Father C[arrier] anointed him and before the sun
had risen his soul was in eternity." In another case in Philadelphia, a Daughter
of Charity baptized a man as he was bleeding to death from an open wound.
Crying out for God to have mercy on his soul so that he might see his parents
in heaven, the man "immediately expired." In an unusual case, a female soldier
and her child were brought to the Sisters of the Holy Cross, who convinced her
to allow them to baptize her and her child, both of whom died shortly thereafter.
These accounts of last-minute redemption showed that nuns cared not just about
their patients' bodily health, but also about preparing their patients for life after
death by providing them with the sacraments that ensured they died in a proper
state of grace.[39]

Though they often served only Union troops, northern nuns, like their counterparts in the South, prided themselves in being above politics and being willing
to help men of both sides. As a Sister of Charity from Cincinnati remembered
after the war, "We cared for Unionists and Confederates alike. We knew no difference and made no difference." In the highly politically charged atmosphere of
the Civil War, such neutrality was not always appreciated and was instead taken
as a sign of sympathy with the enemy. Thus Daughters of Charity from Emmitsburg, who regularly crossed lines to serve wounded soldiers, were accused by
some officers of being spies. The new warden of a prison in Alton, Illinois, was
warned in June 1864 by the Union Army's Commissary for Prisoners that nuns
were suspected of passing information and contraband goods to prisoners. The
following month he forbade the Daughters of Charity from visiting or caring for
Confederate prisoners. Regardless of whether these federal officers' accusations
were true, they showed that not everyone appreciated the sisters' commitment to
serving everyone regardless of their political and national affiliation.[40]

Both during and after the war, nuns steadfastly believed that their service
helped overcome powerful prejudices against their faith. Initially many Protestant leaders were wary of the nuns, believing they used their positions to force
conversions out of unsuspecting Protestant boys. While the nuns hoped their
wards would become Catholic, repeated testimony from Protestant chaplains
shows that they believed the nuns were primarily devoted to alleviating physical
suffering. Sent on an inspection tour by concerned New Englanders, a Unitarian
minister from Boston left the Sisters of Mercy's resort–hospital in North Carolina
well satisfied that they were "carry[ing] out the example of their divine Master,
who went about doing good." In another instance, a Protestant chaplain was said

to have asked specifically for Daughters of Charity to staff a field hospital outside of Gettysburg, for the nuns had made a strong impression on him by their work in several local Protestant churches turned into hospitals. At the same time, a Protestant general told a sister that even "Presbyterian ministers" admitted the good work the nuns did on behalf of religion during the war, "and you know they are not very profuse in your praise." General Benjamin Butler praised the Sisters of Charity of New Orleans for their "holy" and "self-sacrificing" labors on behalf of his men, and Pennsylvania Governor Andrew Curtin similarly praised other nuns for their work among soldiers at Camp Curtin. Nuns often reciprocated this kindness. Mother Angela called two Protestant chaplains working at hospitals staffed by nuns "very worthy men." She got along so well with the "zealous" Methodist minister that he allegedly asked for her help whenever he came upon a "hardened sinner" on whom he could make no impression.[41]

U.S. Surgeon General William A. Hammond became one of the nuns' strongest advocates, defending them against pressure from evangelicals to force Lincoln to hire more Protestant nurses. Hammond, a Protestant himself, told Lincoln that non-Catholic women "will not submit to the same discipline, nor undergo the same hardships." Praising the nuns as a "corps of faithful, devoted and trained nurses," he argued that their "obedience" and "irrepro[a]chable moral character" meant that Catholic sisters would naturally "predominate" among the ranks of nurses. This willingness to submit themselves to male authority, probably due to their experience in working under the all-male Catholic hierarchy, made sisters in demand among male surgeons who valued their work. Unfortunately, it probably also caused the jealousy and resentment among Protestant women, who more easily chafed at such restraints of the "privileged male authority and leadership" of Union hospitals. Lincoln himself came to appreciate the nuns' work, for he personally issued orders on behalf of the Sisters of Mercy working in Union hospitals in Washington and Chicago.[42]

Some Protestant ladies and nurses relented in their hostility to the nuns when they saw how much they truly cared for their patients and how well their hospitals were run. When a doctor's wife attending the Mound City hospital reproved Mother Angela for helping a man beyond saving, Angela replied, "What you do to the least of mine, you do unto me." This woman became a strong advocate and defender of the nuns years after that incident. Lew Wallace's Protestant wife, who observed the Sisters of the Holy Cross working in a hospital in Paducah, Kentucky, praised them for their "devotion" to their patients. When Protestant women became "tired," they went home. But the sisters, she claimed, remained at their posts even in the face of "infected places" or "contagion." Mrs. Wallace was particularly impressed with one nun, Sister Beatrice, who despite her young age and "delicate and refined features" did all she could to help her charges. Though not all women were completely won over by the nuns, even former critics had to admit, as did the "Ladies of the Union Aid Society" of St. Louis, that the kindness and hard work of the nuns gave them great influence over their grateful patients. One of Dix's own nurses, Sophia Bucklin, praised sisters at Point Lookout, Maryland, for being "ceaseless in the work of mercy amongst those poor suffering soldiers." Letters collected after the war for a book on the nuns showed that Protestant officers from General George B. McClellan to General Robert E. Lee uniformly agreed that the nuns had performed admirable service on behalf of their patients with no regard to their political affiliation.[43]

The perseverance of the nuns despite awful working conditions and constant prejudice changed non-Catholic Americans' perceptions of them and their faith. The ignorant images of Maria Monk were replaced by those of hardworking women, totally dedicated to their wounded and sick patients. *Harper's Weekly* positively depicted Holy Cross nuns in a May 1863 engraving of the *Red Rover* hospital ship. Mother Angela and her nuns indeed made good impressions wherever they went. The federal government gave the Holy Cross sisters two broken Confederate cannons captured in early 1862, known as the "Lady Polk" and "Lady Davis," to be melted down into a religious statute as a token of its gratitude. Though never so transformed, the cannons remained on display at the front entrance of Saint Mary's College until 1942, when they were donated as part of a scrap metal drive to aid the war effort against Germany and Japan.[44]

The ultimate tribute to nuns' hospital services came in 1874 when two Dominican sisters were invited to unveil the new Lincoln monument built over his tomb in Springfield, Illinois. According to one of the two sisters who pulled the "silken cords" holding an American flag over the image of the late president, Generals William Sherman and Ulysses S. Grant had personally requested their presence. This honor, bestowed on these two women in the place of all those sisters who had served during the war, was the greatest tribute the federal government ever paid to Catholics for what they had done to help preserve the Union.[45]

The devoted wartime service of chaplain priests and especially the sister nurses, so they themselves believed, changed the minds of many Protestant Americans they met in the Union Army. The German-born bishop of Fort Wayne, Indiana, John H. Luers, happily reported as late as 1864 that the service of priests and nuns in Union armies and hospitals had greatly reduced local prejudices against the Catholic faith in his diocese.[46] Yet the northern hierarchy and clergy never wholeheartedly embraced the conflict as did the majority of Protestant ministers. On the one hand, the fact that so many nuns left their convents to care for the sick while some priests served prominently as chaplains shows that some church leaders themselves strongly believed that Catholics should support the war effort, or at least the Catholic men fighting in it. On the other hand, the complete lack of coordination among U.S. Catholic bishops to provide for *all* the army's Catholics spoke to the larger faith community's disagreement over the war and Lincoln's handling of it.

5 Slavery Divides the Church

P resident Lincoln issued his preliminary Emancipation Proclamation on September 22, 1862. Lincoln justified the measure on the basis of military necessity, for he believed the he had to attack slavery in the rebellious states directly in order to save the nation. While many Republicans applauded the measure, the controversial measure drew the ire of many citizens of the North and Border States who despised abolitionism and feared the measure might prolong the rebellion. Catholic Americans were likewise divided over emancipation. While many northern Catholic leaders stated their dislike for the slavery during the antebellum era, they did not call for its immediate abolition. They knew it was a divisive issue that had damaged the cause of Irish repeal and split the major Protestant denominations before the war, and they hoped to avoid it if possible. They were further wary of joining the cause of antislaveryism because it was often touted by the same northerners who also attacked Catholicism as an inimical influence on American society. Father Boniface Wimmer, a German Benedictine monk who oversaw a monastery in rural Pennsylvania, made this clear in a letter he wrote shortly after Lincoln's election. "Catholics are naturally strong and sincere supporters of the abolition of slavery," he claimed, but they could not be expected to side with the Republicans, whose supporters included "the 1848 revolutionaries" and "secret societies" who hated Catholicism.[1]

After the war began, the overwhelming majority of Catholic leaders, bishops, and editors still hoped to avoid the slavery issue as a strictly political one that did not directly concern the church. Only a minority of the clergy and laypeople came to support emancipation as the means to end the war. This became very clear during debates over abolition and the church's teachings on slavery between anti-slavery Catholics, such as Brownson and the Purcell brothers, and anti-abolitionist Catholics, represented by McMaster and Bishop Spalding. Most Catholics sided with the latter, vehemently criticizing the wartime abolition of slavery as a dangerously unwise and unconstitutional measure. Many were starting to have second thoughts about a conflict that seemed to be growing both more radical in its aims and more destructive to human life with each passing month. Some Catholics feared that once Republicans had eliminated slavery they would then come after the church. Their lack of enthusiasm for emancipation matched their growing dislike of the war itself, a fact that did not go unnoticed by their critics in the Republican Party and Protestant establishment.[2]

The debate over slavery had played a decisive factor in shaping Catholics' political beliefs well before the American Civil War. Both slaveholding and non-slaveholding Catholics in the South and Border States had vested interests in slavery and were as proslavery as their Protestant neighbors. Catholic northerners of all classes, like most white Americans of that time, readily accepted common racial stereotypes that depicted blacks as inferior. Northern Catholics' allegiance to the Democratic Party also greatly shaped their view of the slavery question. However, the great majority of northern Catholics did not oppose abolitionism simply because they were proslavery or Democrats. They did so because they saw antislavery agitation as a threat to social order, the Constitution, and thus the Catholic Church.[3]

Irish Catholics in particular had already witnessed firsthand how slavery could divide them against themselves despite their common nationality and religion. In the 1840s slavery had helped to fracture the repeal movement that tried to dissolve the Acts of Union of 1801 between Ireland and Great Britain. Irish Catholics were appalled that their hero and leader of the movement, Daniel O'Connell, had been duped by abolitionist fanatics led by William Lloyd Garrison into tying together the two separate and unrelated issues of repeal and abolition. Having seen the destructive influence that abolitionism had on their hopes for Irish independence, many, regardless of how they felt about slavery personally, refused to have anything to do with antislavery agitation and castigated abolitionists as enemies of law and order. The Pilot's editor strongly denounced the "treasonable" abolitionist mob that had tried to free Anthony Burns in violation of the Fugitive Slave Law. "Freesoilism has begotten secular and ministerial threats affecting the safety of the Union,—it has begotten riots, robbery and murder," argued its editor, Donahoe. "We are thankful to have it in our power to say that we do not know a Catholic who, throughout this freesoil agitation, has not been on the side of the Union and the Constitution." At a time when their own loyalty was being questioned by nativists, Irish Catholics refused to join abolitionists, who were a tiny minority and hated by many in the North and South. Irish Catholics' rejections of abolitionism, in the words of one historian, were part of the plan of their community's leaders of "becoming more ardent in their statements of loyalty to the United States and in their emphasis on their support for republican institutions."[4]

Though Catholic opinion was largely tolerant of slavery where it existed, many northern Catholic commentators criticized abolitionist and proslavery zealots alike. On the one hand, the *Freeman's Journal* contrasted its support for the "compromises" that had preserved sectional peace on the slavery question with that of the *New York Tribune* and its abolitionist readers, "a band of noisy, treasonable fanatics" who advocated abolition to the nation's detriment. On the other hand, it equally condemned southern states such as Louisiana that promoted attempts to invade and conquer Spanish Cuba. Though he opposed the spread of slavery into new territories, Orestes Brownson himself voted for Buchanan in 1856 because of his opposition to both the Know-Nothings and the abolitionists, "the two most threatening dangers" to the nation. Brownson equally opposed efforts to abolish slavery in the South and defended the Fugitive Slave Law as a constitutional measure. American Catholics' dislike of abolitionism and tolerance of southern slavery was symptomatic of their desire to uphold law, order, and stability in American society. This desire reflected a conservative theological position shared by a majority of Catholics across the Western world in the mid-nineteenth century.[5]

Northern Catholic support for the Constitution as a bulwark to preserve stability in American society against the threat of antislavery chaos explains why they overwhelmingly supported the decision rendered in the case of *Dred Scott* (1857). The decision had particular significance for the Roman Catholic community because the author of the wide-sweeping decision, Supreme Court Chief Justice Roger B. Taney, was a fervent Roman Catholic Marylander. Though he had manumitted his own slaves, Taney saw the new Republican Party and abolitionists alike as threats to the South. Thus he sought to use the Court to end the slavery debate once and for all. Taney authored the Court's decision that denied the right of Dred Scott, an enslaved black man who was suing for his freedom on the basis of his prior residence in the free North, to sue in a state court because blacks could not be citizens. Furthermore the Court ruled that Congress could not outlaw slavery from federal territories, thus giving slave owners access to areas that previously had been rendered free by the Missouri Compromise. Instead of ending the debate, however, Taney's opinion touched off a political firestorm that only made sectional tensions worse.[6]

Although many Catholics apparently refrained from commenting on the decision, in keeping with their disdain for discussing politics, the few who did generally criticized abolitionism and supported Taney. Brownson, however, objected strongly to the idea that blacks could not be citizens and accused Taney of forgetting that Catholicism taught "the unity of the race, [and] that all men by the natural law are equal." Blacks were men just as much as whites and thus were capable of being citizens of the United States. Such an open dispute between two prominent members of the church drew the attention of non-Catholic editors, including those of abolitionist William Lloyd Garrison's *Liberator*. The paper commented that Brownson's comments were "remarkable" given his religion and that his paper had previously been "ultra pro-slavery." *The Pilot* called Brownson's accusations "wild" and unfortunate, for once again he had foolishly sown division and discord for no good reason. Like Donahoe, most northern Catholics were loyal conservative Democrats who opposed any criticism of the Chief Justice's decision, especially that of Brownson.[7]

Finally, for Catholics who prized sectional harmony and national stability over the humanitarianism of the abolitionists, John Brown's failed attempt to foment a slave rebellion by attacking Harper's Ferry, Virginia, in 1859 seemed to offer the ultimate proof of abolitionism's violent and destructive tendencies. *The Pilot* blamed the whole affair on the "Black Republican Party" and lamented the bad feelings it stirred up in the South against the North. A Catholic editor from Baltimore condemned the raid as the work of a "reckless and desperate madman." The *Louisville Guardian* saw Brown's use of scripture to justify his actions as no different from that of thousands of northern preachers who preached sermons advocating abolition by "all means" necessary. Yet Catholic condemnation of the raid should not simply be seen as evidence of proslavery sentiment. Some discerning Catholics blamed both North and South for the sectional strife that had come to a head in the wake of the raid. Brownson, just as committed to constitutional order but less committed to the Democratic Party than many of his coreligionists, denounced both southern invasions of Latin America and John Brown's raid as equally destructive of the Union. He reasoned that if the South saw fit to trample on the rights of foreign nations to enslave their citizens then southerners should have no objection to John Brown's invading southern states to free their citizens. McMaster similarly assigned equal blame for the sectional tensions that led to the raid on "Northern fanaticism" and "Southern ultraism." Thus Catholic leaders implied that their community, by staying out of the controversy, had laudably done nothing to endanger national harmony between the free and slave states.[8]

In 1861 the great majority of northern Catholics, like other conservative northerners, wanted a limited war to restore the Union. Such a conflict would be short and leave alone the social institutions of the South. Realistic northern politicians realized that moving against slavery would anger pro-war Democrats and the slaveholding Border States that had remained in the United States. After all, argued McMaster, this was not a "vindictive" war "intended to damage the South," but a war simply to "protect the *Union*, and to carry out the provisions of the *Constitution*—nothing more." With restoring the Union their paramount goal, many loyal northern and Border State citizens saw little need to worry about the fate of slavery and continued to reject the pleas of radical abolitionists. While it is certainly true that many Republicans and their political leaders were eager to move against slavery even before the war began, they still acted rather cautiously in the war's first year compared to the measures they would advocate in 1862 and beyond. Catholics who supported the Union but not emancipation thus shared a common position with many of their non-Catholic neighbors.[9]

Apart from their loyalty to the Democratic Party, their admitted racism, and their social conservatism, the history and moral teachings of their faith had an important impact on how Catholics thought about slavery. First, the church refused to take sides on the slavery debate in the United States, in order to avoid the institutional divisions that that occurred among Baptists and Methodists in the 1840s. Second, the Roman Catholic Church historically had never condemned slavery outright as a moral wrong and continued to tolerate it through the mid-nineteenth century. The church had a long tradition of reforming and eventually eliminating slavery in Europe through gradual emancipation. As the Jesuit Bernard O'Reilly told Charles and Maria Daly, "The Church has forbidden any Catholic to hold or to teach that slavery is an institution ordained by God, or that the slave trade was lawful." Still, throughout its larger history, the church had only condemned certain kinds of slavery, for example, Catholics owning other Catholics, abuses of the system, and, finally, the slave trade such as that between Africa and the New World that Pope Gregory XVI forbade in 1839. Since the founding of colonial Maryland, some American Catholic priests and laypeople alike had owned slaves and continued to do so at the start of the Civil War. A number of southern Catholic thinkers had further approved of the institution as a means of converting non-Christian slaves to Christianity. But many Catholics in the North and even in the Border States criticized the institution's moral failings while simultaneously rejecting immediate abolition as a solution to the problem.[10]

Thus Catholic critics of slavery or abolitionists could take diametrically opposed views on emancipation and be technically correct at the same time. On one side, Catholic opponents of slavery could rightfully argue that historically the church had actively emancipated some slaves and condemned certain abuses of slavery. On the other, the majority of Catholic Americans who hated abolitionists even more than slavery were correct that the church had never pronounced slavery an unequivocal moral evil and had always acted gradually to alleviate or eliminate the institution. Whereas American Protestants argued over various interpretations of the Bible when debating slavery, the Catholic debate was largely shaped by individual Catholics' interpretation of church dogma and history. Before the war, even those Catholic Americans who hoped for gradual emancipation agreed that slavery was a political issue, not a religious one that concerned the church, its leaders, or its press.

By October 1861, however, Orestes Brownson had joined northern radicals in openly advocating immediate emancipation as a means to win the war. In doing so, he made the issue of slavery's fate at the end of the war one that Catholic Americans could no longer avoid. After the federal defeat at Bull Run, Brownson suggested a harsher form of war was necessary to save the Union, one that was well in advance of Catholic and the larger public's opinion at that time. He advocated the suppression and imprisonment of anti-war northerners who undermined the country's military effort. He did so at the same time that his fellow Catholic editor, McMaster, had been thrown in jail for criticizing the war. Additionally, though he did praise the patriotism of many lay Catholics, Brownson strongly censured certain Catholic leaders for their lack of patriotism. Save a handful of loyal Catholic papers, all of the rest were "really secession sheets." Brownson also doubted the patriotism of some of the clergy, pointing out that many of them were foreign-born. Finally, he suggested emancipating the slaves as a possible means to win the war.[11]

Slavery, Brownson argued, was nothing but a "great moral, social, and political wrong," and attacking it might help the North achieve victory. Christianity and the fathers of the church taught that "God never gave to man the dominion [over] man." The Catholic Church had only "tolerated" slavery while always seeking its peaceful and gradual abolition. Furthermore the northern states were in an unprecedented war with a great rebellion, and they could not win if they continued to restrain themselves while the South came at them with no holds barred. A "just war" required the North to fight war not for its own sake but for peace, or, in Brownson's turn of phrase, "the removal of the causes which have rendered it necessary." If the enemy had a "weak spot" that the nation could exploit, then the North was bound by "common prudence and common humanity" to "strike our heaviest and deadliest blow" and thus end the war as quickly as possible. This

weakest spot, he argued, was obviously slavery. Because southerners had for-
feited their rights to federal protection of slavery by their rebellion and because
emancipation would deprive them of labor, fill the ranks of Union armies, win
support in Europe, and force the South to keep large armies at home for fear of
rebellion, the North was fully justified in emancipating southern slaves as a war
measure.[12]

While some Catholic leaders initially tried to ignore him, Brownson became
a reference point by which they would define themselves in terms of just how
much they were willing to support the war effort. One editor from Pennsylvania,
while stopping short of defending Brownson on abolition, nonetheless hailed his
article as a "vigorous defense of the cause of the Union" and called on Catholics to continue to support the *Quarterly Review*. Brownson's uncompromising
tone predictably angered more anti-abolitionist Catholics who were lukewarm
in their support of the war. The *Catholic Mirror* wrote that Brownson had lost
his status as an "authority" in the Catholic Church and was merely championing "his own individual opinions" on political and theological issues. Its editor
denounced him for having become an "ultra-abolitionist" and for advocating the
arming of slaves against their masters. Such a "savage" proposition would be the
end of the black race in the country, said the editor, and it was "in the highest
degree disgraceful" to the reviewer for having suggested it.[13]

Even a pro-war leader like Archbishop Hughes joined in the criticism of
Brownson. Writing anonymously for his diocesan newspaper, the *Metropolitan
Record*, the powerful archbishop blasted the article as "untimely and mischievous," alleging that Catholics had earned "great credit" for themselves by avoid-
ing the slavery debate. "We Catholics," the paper continued, were fighting a war
for the Union and Constitution, not one to "gratify a clique of abolitionists in the
North." No "true patriots" could ever advocate such a war, for an abolition war
would be unconstitutional, and it would be a disgrace to the men who had already
fought and died for the Union. Widely reprinted in other like-minded Catholic
newspapers, the letter denied slavery was the cause of the war, said the church
had no power to end it where it already existed, and described it as an institution
that had existed since "the earliest annals of the human race." Because Africa was
"a country of savages," Hughes claimed, enslaved people sent to the United States
had actually been saved by slave traders from a more wretched life under "barbarous" African leaders. In a remarkable statement for a Christian prelate, Hughes
played down the immorality of slave sales that led to the frequent separation of
families by comparing the institution favorably to the "degraded condition of

thousands of females in our large cities in the free States." "We have only now to say," wrote Hughes, "that we despise in the name of all Catholics the 'Idea' of making this war subservient to the philanthropic nonsense of abolitionism."[14]

Later, Hughes explained to government officials that his opposition to Brownson was meant to keep Catholics from turning against the Union war effort. Hughes informed Seward that he had written the letter out of fear that Brownson would have confused the minds of Catholic Americans about the reasons for the war, declaring that there would be "time enough" to deal with slavery after the war. The archbishop also told Secretary of War Simon Cameron that though the Irish were willing to fight for the Union they would "turn away in disgust" from fighting an abolition war. Brownson's response to this letter in January was a mock defense of Hughes's position that reaffirmed his own antislavery opinions even more strongly while criticizing Hughes's position as un-Catholic. Given subsequent Catholic reactions to the Emancipation Proclamation, however, Hughes clearly had a better sense of the laity's deep-seated anti-abolitionism than did Brownson.[15]

It was at this point that the first battle lines were drawn between the few Catholics like Brownson who supported emancipation and those who sided with Hughes. The editors of the *Catholic Mirror, Metropolitan Record*, and *New York Freeman's Journal* attacked Brownson's antislavery opinions and Lincoln's emancipation policy repeatedly throughout the rest of the war.[16] Some Catholics did come to support emancipation later in the war, but it was remarkable how little opinions changed for the most part after the initial Brownson–Hughes feud. Positions on the debate within the church reflected long-standing fears that abolition would cause social unrest, bring unwanted competition for jobs between blacks and immigrants, and was part of an ultimately anti-Catholic reform program. This helps to explain why positions on emancipation at this early date were not simply a matter of one's position on the war. As in Archbishop Hughes's case, one could be pro-war and yet anti-emancipation, a common position held by many War Democrats.

With regard to these debates over how to conduct the war, pro-war Catholics did not automatically side with Brownson. Many considered Brownson's later response to the archbishop to be disrespectful on the one hand and a symptom of his anti-Irish prejudice on the other. The *New York Tablet*, whose publisher was in fact Brownson's as well, blasted him for praising "New England" at the expense of Maryland and foreign-born Catholics. In a similar vein, Donahoe, who had already made clear his lack of sympathy for abolition, declined to comment on Brownson's views but did allow a letter to be published attacking Brownson for being anti-Irish. *The Catholic* was not as harsh; while it did not discount that "only by the most resolute measures" could victory be won, it merely declared that the decision should be left to the president. They would support Lincoln if he decided to use abolition as a war measure. Now was not the time to attack slavery, however, and any such discussion of it was merely a distraction from the war effort. The *Catholic Telegraph*, too, while not referencing Brownson directly, was not ready for abolition and criticized the idea that some slaves could be freed while others belonging to loyal masters left alone.[17] Even if Brownson had moderated his tone, few Catholic leaders would have joined him in proclaiming emancipation as early as the war's first winter.

Brownson's bid for leadership in the Catholic community on the question of emancipation was a failure and earned him the especial ire of ethnic Catholic opponents of the war. When he stood for election in New Jersey in 1862 as a Republican candidate for the House of Representatives, his Democratic rival, William G. Steele, soundly defeated him. Republican leaders' hopes that Brownson would capture the Catholic vote proved totally naïve. Many conservative or foreign-born Catholics, especially the Irish, resented his criticism of them for not doing enough to win the war. In 1863 Brownson erased any doubts that the hatred was not mutual when he blasted the loyalty of foreign-born Catholics and accused them and other anti-war members of the church of having "identif[ied] the [Catholic] Church with slavery and rebellion." "It is undeniable," Brownson told his fellow Catholic northerners, "that no religious body in the country stands so generally committed to slavery and the Rebellion, or as a body have shown so little sympathy with the effort of the government to save the unity and life of the nation as the Catholic." One astonished pro-war Catholic voice responded, "We scarcely know what to think of the writer, who at this crisis, comes forward unasked to furnish unfounded calumnies against Catholics to the enemies of our holy religion." The *Quarterly Review*'s Catholic readership continued to dwindle throughout the war, leading Brownson in 1864 to try to reinvent his newspaper as one primarily for a radical Republican and pro-Union audience.[18]

Despite Brownson's defeat in the arena of Catholic public opinion, Catholics could not avoid the nationwide debate over slavery that became even more heated in 1862. By the summer and fall of that year, a few prominent members of the Catholic Church gradually came to criticize slavery and its role in bringing on the war. At a funeral oration for a fallen Catholic soldier, German-speaking Bishop Martin Henni publicly encouraged men to enlist to save the Union in order to show their "gratitude to a Government, which by its Constitution and laws has secured you every civil right and temporal blessing, and dearest of all, perfect liberty of conscience." He went on to argue that Catholics should enlist immediately in order to "put an end to the existence" of slavery, "that great and crying shame upon all Christendom." Bishop Josue Young of Erie also spoke out in favor of the Union publicly and strongly criticized slavery in private. His influence was small, however, and was barely worth the trouble that Bishop Spalding took to appeal to Rome to silence him. While it might have been expected that another Catholic New Englander would join Brownson in championing the antislavery cause, it was actually farther to the west where the most effective and important antislavery Catholic voices were heard. Young's mentor, Archbishop Purcell, and the editors of the Cincinnati *Catholic Telegraph* probably made as great a contribution as Brownson did in convincing Catholic northerners to support emancipation.[19]

At the beginning of the war, Catholic Ohioans opposed abolitionism just as strongly as any other Catholics in the loyal states. The *Catholic Telegraph* clearly reflected that fact, though it was not as violently or openly anti-abolitionist as were the New York papers and officials. Certainly there was little evidence during the war's first year that the Purcell brothers and Bishop Rosecrans would become the most prominent clerics in favor of abolition in the entire American Catholic Church. Neither of the Purcells was very close to Brownson, having sparred with him in the 1850s over the Know-Nothings and later accusing him of promoting unorthodox and even Protestant views. In early 1862 the editors denounced emancipation, even if only a "war measure," as both "incendiary and stupid," predicting that it would unleash a slave insurrection that would ruin both the North and South. "Do the American people believe that we could be a nation with four millions of free negroes in our midst?" The clear implication was that it would be better to leave them enslaved. Such attitudes seemed to be typical of lay Catholics as well. Even before the infamous draft riots of New York City, Catholic workers rioted in 1862 in protest over the use of black laborers in Cincinnati's river shipping industry. Catholic Ohioans and their leaders, just like other Catholics across the North, thus continued to oppose abolition as an evil that would not aid the war effort and, above all, as a threat to their livelihood.[20]

Archbishop Purcell's conversion to emancipation seems to have resulted from his liberal tendencies, from the fact that the war was dragging on with no end in sight, and from a meeting in Rome with Bishop Felix Dupanloup. The bishop of Orleans, France, Dupanloup was famous for his liberal views and had just issued an antislavery pastoral prior to meeting Purcell. After returning from Europe to Ohio in August 1862, Purcell delivered a public address before a packed house of Cincinnati citizens, Catholics and Protestants, Republicans and Democrats, at Pike's Opera House. He was supposed to give a lecture primarily on his experiences in Rome for the benefit of St. John's Hospital and its efforts to heal sick and wounded Union soldiers. Though notified in advance that he would also talk about "this distracted country," probably no one in the audience could have predicted the direction the speech ultimately took. Joined by the 10th Ohio's chaplain, Father William O'Higgins, the archbishop cast most of the blame for the war on the South, blasting the institution of slavery for interfering with marriage and for fostering ignorance among the slaves. The South could have averted war, he continued, by proposing the simple compromise of gradual emancipation and promising to educate blacks "to be men" as the North had done. Instead, the South had resisted, and only the "sentiments of humanity" had kept the North from already proclaiming emancipation, enrolling "negroes . . . in our armies," and thereby having ended the war in only three months' time. While the speech was not a wholesale endorsement of emancipation, it was arguably the most antislavery public speech ever delivered by an American Catholic bishop. That conservative laymen criticized the speech did not deter him, for such attacks merely reaffirmed Purcell's status as a "Catholic Union prelate."[21]

A few days after the battle of Antietam in September 1862, Lincoln issued his preliminary Emancipation Proclamation. It immediately led to a contentious debate within the Catholic community, just as it did throughout the North as a whole. Brownson urged Catholics to accept emancipation as a war measure that was now a "military and a political necessity" without which the conflict could not be won. He also did his best to defend his church against the charge of being proslavery by emphasizing the historical role of Catholicism in eliminating European slavery. Catholics' anti-abolitionism, he argued, was due to their Democratic Party affiliations rather than a desire to perpetuate the practice. General William Rosecrans became the most prominent Catholic in the Union Army to support emancipation, first privately and later publicly. So well-known was Rosecrans's support of abolition that his future chief of staff, the anti-abolitionist Catholic Colonel Julius Garesché, had considerable misgivings about serving with his old army friend.[22]

Other northern Catholics reacted with the same unease about the new war aim that Garesché did. The editor of the Pittsburgh *Catholic* reproved those who questioned the loyalty of other Union men "because his sober sense disapproves of your hobby on the right way of ending the war." John Mullay thought the proclamation was totally out of character for the previously "conservative" Lincoln, and predicted bloodshed worse than Santo Domingo. For McMaster, the "unconstitutional" proclamation was the work of radical abolitionists and would backfire. Not only would it not help save the Union, but it was "lawless—barbarous—and dishonest." Even the pro-war Donahoe savaged the proclamation, declaring that any advantage obtained by it was more than made up for by an increase in southern resolve and hatred of the North. Not only would "nineteen out of twenty" slaves not accept it, for "they love their masters, as dogs do," but the proclamation, his paper opined, made it that much more evident that only the victory of the Democratic Party in upcoming elections could save the nation. Of those who did comment directly on Lincoln's measure, only Purcell and Rosecrans defended the president's right to issue the proclamation as a war measure. They did criticize, however, the manner in which it was proclaimed and doubted that it would actually free the slaves in the future.[23]

Most Catholics probably agreed that the government's new emancipation policy was wrongheaded at best and potentially devastating to the Union's chances for victory at worst. It received absolutely no support from anti-war Catholic voices either in the North or in the Border States. Bishop Spalding, for one, became even more anti-Lincoln after September 22. The bishop, like other conservatives, believed it an unjustifiable escalation of the war's already considerable horrors, opening the door to a new kind of conflict founded on the barbaric principles of "confiscation, colonization, and extermination." Spalding, already upset about having had to listen silently to General Rosecrans talk about abolition at dinner, attacked the "pretense of philanthropy" in the final version of the proclamation, which he asserted would only incite "three to four millions of half-civilized Africans to murder their Masters & Mistresses!" Spalding's intense dislike of abolition, however, still did not lead him to renounce the Union and openly support the Confederate cause like Bishops Richard Whelan or Patrick Lynch. Rather he, like other conservatives, vaguely wished for the restoration of the Union, but at the same time could not see how violence and "desolation spread around" was likely to achieve it. Colonel Garesché, remembering "family traditions" of the horrors of Santo Domingo, likewise feared that emancipation would promote "negro insurrection." He promised to resign should Lincoln carry out his threat and actually issue a final proclamation on January 1, 1863. His son, Louis Garesché, found it to be providential that his father was killed in battle on December 31, "the *very day* before the issuing of such a decree."[24]

By the spring of 1863, the *Catholic Telegraph* finally joined Brownson in advocating abolition. It did so not purposefully but only after a fierce intra-Catholic controversy over the historical role of the church in the elimination of slavery in the Western world. It began in March 1863 after the *Telegraph* lauded the Russian emperor for ending serfdom earlier that month. Rev. Purcell declared it to be a step that would help the progress of Catholicism in Russia because "our Church and slavery have never gone well together." McMaster immediately criticized this rather innocuous statement, attempting to demonstrate from church history that it had tolerated slavery and had never issued any condemnation of the institution. He declared that not only was slavery not a "sin" and thus the church could not interfere, but also that black slaves were members of a "semi-savage race" best suited for bondage. The *Telegraph*'s misguided statement, McMaster continued, could be used to justify the radical goal of immediate emancipation and was therefore guilty of "pandering to the infidel radicalism of the times." Though both men were technically correct, their different positions on the war ensured that they would be unable to find common ground on the issue.[25]

Father Purcell and Bishop Rosecrans, at first having no wish to get in a fight with McMaster, reacted to his criticism by becoming more openly abolitionist. They wrote another article, citing a number of church fathers and popes as authorities against the institution, insisting that the church had always been opposed to human bondage and that it was "no lover of slavery." They especially condemned slavery's "disregard for marriage" and opined that the institution had been dying even before Lincoln's proclamation. Slavery was "gone forever" and no Catholic should try to save it. They portrayed the church as the protector of human liberty and the oppressed, and ultimately criticized McMaster as an "advocate of slavery." In addition, the *Telegraph*'s editors went further than their historical argument and directly appealed to "the generous impulse of the Irish Catholic, [with] his sympathy with the downtrodden of our race, [and with] his generosity to the poor" to take a similar pity on the oppressed slaves. Father Purcell went beyond debating emancipation to openly advocating it as a moral cause that all Catholics should unhesitatingly support.[26]

To what extent did this newspaper debate change Catholic opinion on slavery and emancipation? Precisely quantifying lay support for either position is impossible, but there are signs that a few Catholics came to side with Purcell against McMaster. Even before the exchange, Sergeant Peter Welsh had already come to support emancipation as a war measure. "If slavery is in the way of the proper administration of the laws and the integrity and perpetuety of this nation," reasoned Welsh, "then i say away with both slaves and slavery[.] sweep both from the land forever rather then the freedom and prosperity of a great nation such as this should be destroyed." Brownson was so happy to see the *Catholic Telegraph* attack slavery that he was willing to forgive his past disputes with them to work together "in the battle for truth, freedom, and justice." "His voice can penetrate

where ours cannot, and will be listened to with respect, where ours will be unheeded," he said of Archbishop Purcell. General Rosecrans wrote a public letter to
Father Purcell at the end of April, assuring him that slavery "with its horrors, bar-
barities, and base immoralities . . . is dead," and added pointedly that "those who
would now uphold it, will be held up in a very short time to public odium and
execration." Father O'Higgins wrote Archbishop Purcell a congratulatory note
for his brother's "vindication of our dear old Mother Church from the damning
blotch of slavery." The *Telegraph* printed numerous letters from Catholics who
opposed slavery throughout the rest of the war. In addition, Purcell's bold stance
in favor of emancipation as well as the Union won him praise from abolitionists
as well as Republicans.[27]

Still, Purcell's *Telegraph* did not convince the country's other Catholic bishops
and editors to embrace emancipation. Of the approximately sixteen major Catholic newspapers published in 1863, only three of them supported emancipation
at some point during the war. The *Telegraph* spent the rest of the war defending
itself from anti-abolitionist Catholic newspapers. Criticism came from all the
usual quarters, with Spalding privately accusing Purcell and Rosecrans of having
given into "the abominable & almost Satanic fanaticism of its worst enemies!"
Unsurprisingly, he similarly criticized Brownson for his "mischievous & wicked"
portrayal of Catholics as "disloyal, because they will not in a body run mad with
this insane abolitionism." Spalding later claimed that the *Telegraph* had taken the
position it did to help secure a promotion for General Rosecrans. Nor did Archbishop Francis Kenrick approve of the "abolition" articles in the *Telegraph*. With
his blessing, Spalding wrote a stinging criticism of the Republicans and Purcell
to church authorities in Rome that was later published in the Vatican's official
newspaper, *L'Osservatore Romano*.[28]

In this anonymously published dissertation, Spalding did admit that slavery
was a "great social evil." He emphasized, however, the undesirability of immediately freeing the slaves due to the Protestant culture of the country, the lack of
good solutions to deal with freed slaves, and the likelihood that they would turn
to lives of drunkenness, dissipation, and crime. He argued that African Americans needed to be prepared properly for freedom through a gradual process of
emancipation combined with education, thus keeping with the Catholic "practice in times past" of gradual emancipation. In no uncertain terms he denounced
the "atrocious proclamation" of the president and declared that the war had become one no longer for the Union but for "the abolitionist party, for its particular
interests and not for the public welfare." Specifically referring to Purcell as one
who had inappropriately taken sides in the war, he argued that the church must

stay out of the conflict or lose "prestige" by engaging in secular matters. Further-more, many of the preachers and men who led the northern war effort held a "satanic hate" for the Catholic Church and would attack Catholics as soon as the conflict finished.[29]

Meanwhile, anti-abolition Catholic editors publicly attacked the Purcells for supporting emancipation. McMaster called Father Purcell the "Catholic Aboli-tionist," a nickname that was not meant to be a compliment. McMaster openly sneered at Purcell's pretensions of influencing Catholics within and outside his own diocese to oppose slavery. "Does not the Very Rev. editor *know* that, in the very diocese of which he is Vicar-General, we have more readers than he? Does he not know that, outside that diocese, we have ten readers to his one?" Donahoe undoubtedly spoke for many when he criticized both parties: "Cincinnati is a rabid Abolition city, and it is undoubted that the Editor of the *Telegraph* has be-come, of late, quite impregnated with that *ism*." Both men, he argued, had become fanatical in upholding their respective positions, and he hoped that "for the sake of decency and patriotism let them desist." Still, he was most critical of the *Tele-graph*, labeling Father Purcell a "confirmed negrophilist" who did not care about white laborers. "Slavery is an evil," Donahoe admitted, "but the *Greeleyizing* of our priests would be a greater evil." Bishop Hughes's *Metropolitan Record* like-wise accused the *Telegraph* of an "excess of . . . zeal in the cause of Abolitionism." Even in Cincinnati itself, James Farran, the Irish Catholic editor of the Demo-cratic newspaper the *Cincinnati Enquirer*, opposed Purcell's views, as did many nonelite Irish Catholics. Thus the Purcells and Bishop Rosecrans came to share the wrath of anti-abolitionist Catholics that had previously been directed solely at Brownson. Despite such criticism, however, the *Telegraph* hoped that when victory finally came, northerners "will insist on the total abolition of slavery."[30]

German Catholic editors held a similar but shorter-lived debate over the church and slavery. The Cincinnati-published *Der Wahrheits Freund* clearly iden-tified slavery as one of the main causes of the war. At first, *Der Wahrheits Freund* predicted that the Emancipation Proclamation would only make Confederates "yet more persevering in their opposition" and "cool" the patriotism of those who had volunteered originally to put down the rebellion. Perhaps influenced by Father Purcell's opposition to slavery, however, the paper changed its posi-tion in 1863. It strongly refuted the common contention of anti-war Catholics that antislavery sentiment equaled anti-popery prejudice. It argued that "many of the most eager Know-Nothings are now the most eager defenders of slavery." By contrast, "the Catholic Church, however, was always and is still today the most eager friend of freedom, the protectress of the besieged and the suppressor of the difference of color, all the same whether in Europe, Asia, Africa, Australia or America, in Poland, Italy or in the United States." *Der Wahrheits Freund* soon became the most prominent German Catholic voice to support emancipation.[31]

Despite his Democratic Party affiliation, *Der Wahrheits Freund's* editor stated that "the teachings of Christ in any case did not favor slavery" and that Catholics had more to fear from southern Know-Nothings than from northern abolitionists like Charles Sumner or Henry Ward Beecher. *Der Wahrheits Freund's* antislavery stance was rather moderate when compared to that of the *Catholic Telegraph*. Still, a rival German Catholic paper in Baltimore denounced *Der Wahrheits Freund's* editor as an abolitionist. Eventually such criticism caused the paper to abandon its support of emancipation altogether. By July 1864 it insisted that its "publisher and editor are neither Abolitionist nor Secessionist," and that "in the spirit of the Catholic Church [the paper was] for an early, honorable peace and for the reestablishment of the Union." *Der Wahrheits Freund* remained neutral during the 1864 elections, merely encouraging its readers to vote and "fulfill their holy responsibilities to the father land."[32]

Oertel's *Katholische Kirchen-Zeitung* of New York was decidedly more skeptical about the war effort and strongly opposed emancipation. In this regard, Oertel was the German Catholic version of McMaster. Like the *Freeman's Journal*, the *Kirchen-Zeitung* defended slavery as a biblical institution. It also mocked "present-day abolitionists and pseudo-humanitarians" for their deficient understanding of Christian teachings on slavery. After Lincoln announced his final Emancipation Proclamation in January 1863, the paper attacked the measure, stating, "By the same logic the president could decree a proclamation that all the slaves in Turkey are free and, in particular that all the harems should close." The *Kirchen-Zeitung*, like other anti-war Catholic periodicals, stated that the Know-Nothings of the past should be "renamed" the abolitionists of the present. Another German Catholic newspaper, *Die Katholische Volkszeitung* of Baltimore, promoted the view common in the English-language Catholic press that abolitionists were anti-Catholic. Its editor was just as critical of the abolitionists as were the editors of the *Kirchen-Zeitung*, *Freeman's Journal*, and *Catholic Mirror*. Oertel's constant opposition to the Lincoln administration and especially to emancipation made his weekly a more typical reflection of German Catholic opinion than *Der Wahrheits Freund*.[33]

Most Catholic Americans, even those opposed to slavery, showed little concern for the fate of freed slaves during the war. Catholics' lack of enthusiasm for emancipation was mirrored by their failure to help support missions to Mississippi freedmen after the fall of Vicksburg in July 1863. Brownson's friend, Dr. Henry S.

Hewit, who had been with Grant at the battle, wrote to the American-born bishop of Natchez, William H. Elder, to seek his help in getting priests for local blacks, who were dying in large numbers of malnourishment and disease. Elder, who answered the call for priests himself along with one of his diocesan colleagues, was appalled to find "the negroes dying in the streets of Vicksburg" and personally ministered to hospitals for African Americans throughout the late summer and fall. Realizing he could not handle the situation alone, Elder appealed to Purcell for additional help in baptizing and catechizing freedmen. Purcell immediately asked his fellow bishops for help and even contemplated asking the Society for the Propagation of the Faith, a French organization that helped to fund Catholic missions across the world, for money to help support such a mission. Even Bishop Spalding initially offered to allow any priest that could be spared to go and suggested that Purcell ask Father Sorin for help.[34]

And yet the effort ultimately came to naught. Spalding quickly found that he had no priests to spare. Archbishop Peter R. Kenrick of St. Louis, the archbishop of Baltimore's brother, snidely remarked that any priests or sisters sent should come from Cincinnati given the pro-emancipation stance of "those who write for the Telegraph." Almost as dismissive was Philadelphia's Pennsylvania-born bishop, James Wood, who wished Elder luck but doubted that his "negro Converts" would remain Catholic if they were anything like northern blacks. By the end of the year, it was clear the project was dead. "I am sorry indeed," wrote Elder that December, "that the poor negroes after all find so few friends who are willing to labor for their true welfare." Elder's gratitude for Purcell's efforts, however, did not prevent him from lecturing his northern fellow bishop about the necessity of clergy praying for peace and remaining politically neutral. Despite his sincere concern for Vicksburg's African American population, Elder believed that abolition meant the continuation of the war and its sufferings.[35]

Even with the conclusion of the 1864 presidential election, repeated Confederate defeats, and the crumbling of slavery throughout large parts of the South, Catholics still remained bitterly divided over emancipation and the war. Archbishop Purcell delivered a patriotic sermon on Thanksgiving 1864 urging Catholics to rally behind the "constitutional authorities" to preserve the Union and its laws, except "those defects which Christian civilization and our own experience have shown us the Constitution contained." And yet, even at this late date and in the years after the war, anti-abolition sentiment remained so strong that many could not bring themselves to support emancipation. Predictably, McMaster's *Freeman's Journal* savaged the Thirteenth Amendment and insisted on portraying slavery as "the natural and happy lot of the negro." He just as strongly opposed black suffrage in the years after the war. In 1865 Father Purcell was the lone Catholic voice that spoke out publicly in favor of the amendment. There were limits to how far pro-emancipation Catholics would go after the war when it came to supporting freedmen's civil rights. Even Brownson, who believed African American's civil and natural rights should be protected, thought it best to leave black suffrage to the states and had little confidence in the "perfectibility" of freedmen.[36]

Church leaders had no coherent plan to deal with the end of slavery, even in the last days of the war. Their failure to take care of the freed slaves mirrored their lackluster response to Bishop William Elder's humanitarian appeal on behalf of black refugees around Vicksburg in 1863. In the case of some Maryland Jesuits, they retained their slaves until the very end. In October 1864, with statewide emancipation looming, Father Basil Pacciarini, a prison chaplain at Point Lookout, Maryland, asked his superiors for directions about what to do with the community's slaves at St. Inigoes. It was this kind of procrastination and lack of enthusiasm for emancipation that led the *New York Tribune* to accuse Catholic authorities in Maryland and Missouri of resisting—or at least of doing nothing—to support efforts to pass abolition laws at the end of the war.[37]

At the close of the war, the church made little effort on behalf of African Americans in terms of humanitarian relief or evangelization. Shortly before the Thirteenth Amendment was passed that December, the *Catholic Mirror* argued that the church alone could elevate African Americans "to a standard of comparative equality with the white race. . . . [to] qualify him to fulfil [sic] the onerous responsibilities of his new position." In the editor's eagerness to criticize abolitionists for not providing for freed slaves, he implicitly acknowledged how little the church had done to end American slavery.[38]

In 1866 Catholic bishops from the reunited sections of the country met to discuss important matters facing the Catholic Church in the wake of the war. Gathered at the Second Plenary Council of Baltimore, the bishops called for greater attention to the freedmen and the welfare of their souls. They followed this appeal, however, with an indictment of the means by which African Americans had been given their newly found freedom. "We could have wished," began the council's short section on the freedmen, "that in accordance with the action of the Catholic Church in past ages, in regard to the serfs of Europe, a more gradual system of emancipation could have been adopted." Such a course could have "in some measure prepared [them] to make a better use of their freedom, than they are likely to do now." Deploring "the evils which must necessarily attend upon the sudden liberation of so large a multitude, with their peculiar dispositions and habits," the bishops agreed that such problems "only make the appeal to our Christian charity and zeal, presented by their forlorn condition, the more forcible and imperative." In the end, the council's appeal had no real effect in promoting Catholic relief or missionary efforts on behalf of African Americans in the nineteenth century. If anything, the appeal served primarily to promote intra-church unity by placating southern and anti-Republican bishops. The clergy and laity's lackluster response to the council's call to help the freedmen perfectly mirrored most Catholic leaders' opposition to emancipation during the war itself.[39]

Father Francis Weninger, a refugee of the European upheavals of 1848 who served as a Jesuit missionary to German Catholics in the Midwest, summed up the Catholic position in his post-war memoirs. He denounced the South for acting "ignobly and rashly" by seceding, stating that the cause of the North was "just" during the war while the Confederacy's was "utterly unjustifiable." Although he opposed secession, he agreed with men like McMaster and Donahoe that southerners "were by no means as great fanatics as the Republicans." While he criticized secession he more strongly denounced the influence of "bigoted Puritans," "savage Know-Nothings," and the "Germans of '48" in the Republican Party. He praised the "conservative" stance of the northern Democrats, whom he claimed "disapprove[d] of slavery" while rightly holding themselves "aloof" from abolition. He argued that the church had "frequently raised her voice to say that, when [Catholics] can emancipate [their slaves] without detriment to the temporal and eternal weal of these servants, they can no longer delay," and that southern racial justifications of the institution had "been proved by experience to be false." Still he could not bring himself to support the Republicans as Brownson and Purcell did. "Their war cry is 'No slaves and priests,'" he later wrote of the extreme element of the Radical Republicans, "hence the danger which hung over the church." Such fears kept many Catholics from embracing the war, eventually leading some to oppose it outright.[40]

6

Catholics' Opposition to the War

B y the beginning of 1863 northern Catholic support for the Republican-led war effort had already starting to decline. For pro-war Republican and Protestant leaders, the strength of Catholics' opposition to emancipation was what first raised questions of their loyalty. In addition, Irish Catholics' large role in the New York City draft riots in July 1863 seemed to confirm these northerners' worst suspicions. Not all Catholics were Copperheads, a derisive term that Republicans used for anti-war Democrats, but certainly many prominent anti-war Democratic Catholics such as McMaster strongly supported an immediate peace. The prominence of such anti-war Catholic leaders and their rhetoric, pro-war northerner's tendency to see the peace movement as sympathy with the enemy, and the draft riots all combined to paint Catholics across the Union as disloyal and unpatriotic.[1] As more and more Catholics opposed Lincoln and the war because of increasingly horrendous casualties or because of wartime policies such as emancipation, so, too, did they unknowingly reinforce the antebellum belief that Roman Catholicism was inimical to the republican institutions of the United States.

Catholic opponents of the war, however, saw themselves and other anti-war northerners as the true patriots in the conflict. They cared about defending the Constitution and seeking an end to the war short of implementing the particular program of one party. They were not religious pacifists,[2] but they could not stand idly by while the lives of countless white soldiers and their families were being wrecked for seemingly no purpose. Furthermore, Lincoln's government had stifled legitimate dissent and trampled on Catholics' religious rights, and soldiers had destroyed church property in the South. Such were the fruits of an unholy conflict that seemed to benefit the radical abolitionist party and no one else. As Maria Lydig Daly noted in her diary, "The Irish believe the abolitionists hate both Irish and Catholic and want to kill them off. The abolitionists always, the Irish say, put them in front of the battle." For these reasons, many Catholic newspapers and leaders continued to vote for the Democratic Party, even when it supported peace at the expense of the Union. Even though they were often racist and backed the "wrong" side in the war from a modern point of view, it would be a mistake to characterize Catholics' opposition as unprincipled obstructionism. Anti-war Catholics hoped to save their families, their civil liberties, and their religious freedom by opposing a war they believed could be easily ended through negotiation, were it not for the radical goals of Lincoln's administration. Even though such a position allowed them to be painted as traitors after the war, Catholic editors like John Mullay never believed that Catholics would get any credit for serving in the federal army anyway.[3]

Opposition to the war in the North grew in 1863 in large part due to Democrats' unhappiness with the Emancipation Proclamation and a series of Union defeats from late 1862 to the spring of the following year. Even General Rosecrans's victory at Stones River proved costly, adding to the manpower shortage already plaguing federal commanders. With volunteering rapidly slowing down and terms of enlistment running out, Congress passed a national conscription act in March 1863. Like other northerners who had stayed away from the fighting, many working-class Catholics feared being forced to fight in a war that had already killed so many men and wrecked so many poor families. They found such a prospect even more odious now that Lincoln had made emancipation federal policy. Although hiring a substitute or paying a commutation fee provided a means for these men to avoid service, the $300 fee was well beyond their means to pay, for the sum was as much as many working men made in a single year. Democratic politicians and editors, attempting to appeal to such disaffected men, denounced both measures with a heated "rhetoric [that] inflamed smoldering tensions." Thus anger at emancipation, combined with resentment over conscription, fueled discontent among many working-class northerners, especially Irish Catholics. These two unpopular policies set the stage for a summertime wave of anti-draft unrest that afflicted several northern cities. Nowhere was the violence more horrible than in New York City.[4]

No single aspect of Catholics' experiences in the Civil War left a more indelible impression on their fellow northerners than the New York City draft riots in July 1863. For those who already believed that Catholics were proslavery and unpatriotic, this event served to symbolize all that was wrong with Catholicism and its influence on American society. The heavy participation of Irish Catholics in the event called into question their willingness to serve their country in times of crisis and served as further proof to liberal Americans that Catholics would violently oppose attempts to reform American society. In all, the riots left just over one hundred people dead, many of them innocent African Americans, and there was widespread property destruction across the city. Though some historians discount the long-term effects of the riot for Catholics in New York or the North, the combination of the riots and the papal peace letters that arrived shortly thereafter from Rome greatly upset many pro-war northerners.[5]

While the negative reaction and outright condemnation of the riots by Republicans, Protestants, and anti-immigrant northerners has been well examined by previous scholars, surprisingly little attention has been devoted to understanding how Catholic leaders and editors interpreted the riots during the war. Damage control began even before the fires had stopped burning. It was not limited to just Irish Catholics, for German- and American-born Catholics felt the need to defend their church as well. They largely disavowed the riots and believed that the entire Catholic community, particularly the Irish Catholic population, had been unfairly attacked for the actions of anti-war New Yorkers. But before the riots and their fallout can be examined, they must be put into a larger context of patriotism, disaffection, ethnicity, class, and racism.[6]

From the beginning of the war to early 1862, some working-class Catholics, especially foreign laborers, already suffered greatly from wartime inflation and economic disruption. The difficulty of caring for families in these conditions led some to enlist and others to become very protective of whatever job they had. Rumors that the government had discharged non-native workers in a Boston naval yard in the war's first fall infuriated even Father Purcell, who went so far as to counsel foreign Catholics not to enlist until the government instituted fairer hiring practices. Many bishops wrote to Europe seeking money for their impoverished dioceses and to help those who relied on the church's charity for income. Certainly the disruption of the war hit workers differently in various industries and regions of the North, but many lower-class Catholics became especially wary of anything or anyone that might steal their livelihood from them. Opposition was not limited to the cities, either. The Germans of St. Mary's, Pennsylvania, a small community in the Appalachian highlands, became "notorious" for their opposition to federal recruitment efforts. From his rural monastery in western Pennsylvania, Father Wimmer complained in early 1863 that the war would soon "cause universal bankruptcy" if it continued. Fortunately, he noted, the Democrats were too powerful for Protestant and radical "instigators of the war" to openly attack northern Catholics. As these examples show, many urban and especially rural Catholics across the East and Midwest recoiled and became alienated from an increasingly activist federal government seemingly bent on disrupting their lives and infringing on their civil liberties, religious freedoms, and local ways of life.[7]

It was in this context that opposition to abolition and the threat of cheap African American labor became not just a moral question but one of economic survival. This dynamic reinforced already-existing racism and embittered lower-class Catholics against "philanthropists" who cared only for southern slaves but not the indigent northern poor. Labor competition, then, was even more immediate for many Catholics than were Lincoln's abrogation of certain civil liberties. In the summer of 1862, riots along the levees in Cincinnati broke out over the use of black laborers in the shipping industry. The Republican *Cincinnati Gazette* and some national Republican leaders identified the Irish and their hatred of blacks as the primary culprits, while Catholic apologists like McMaster and Father Purcell contended that all laborers had much to fear from competition with blacks. "It is a question of bread and butter or starvation to thousands, and nothing is more easily understood than jealousy in such a vital matter," wrote Purcell. The *Catholic Telegraph*, while regretting the violence done to "inoffensive colored people," nevertheless blamed native-born Americans for much of the destruction of black property. Purcell also accused the *Cincinnati Gazette* of stirring up old prejudices from the Know-Nothing era with the result that an Irishman was shot down in cold blood in the wake of the unrest. These riots and the anti-Irish commentary that accompanied them were further proof for McMaster and like-minded Catholics that "a more general emancipation" would cause even greater instability in American society. As soon as the war was over, he warned, antislavery forces would turn their guns on the hated "Papists."[8]

If competition for labor with blacks was already seen as an issue of starvation versus survival for some Catholics, the passage of conscription legislation in March 1863 seemed only a further assault on lower-class men and their families. Rising death tolls made enlisting in the army, even with the high bounties being offered, unappealing to many Catholic laborers. Archbishop Hughes's opinion that a draft would make military service fairer for Catholics was a case where his leadership and voice went unheeded by many of his flock. New York City, with its plethora of anti-war Catholic and Democratic papers and politicians, was unprepared to enforce the new legislation in July when the Battle of Gettysburg forced many state troops to hurry off to southern Pennsylvania to meet General Lee's invading forces. Even the twin victories of Vicksburg and Gettysburg in early July did nothing to appease anti-war laborers, who began rioting on July 13. In horrible violence that lasted for five days, the rioters attacked symbols of federal authority, the homes of Republican leaders, and the dwellings and charitable institutions devoted to poor blacks. White laborers killed many innocent African Americans and raged out of control until police forces and military units from Gettysburg finally put down the unrest. Perhaps most shocking of all, women were prominent among the rioters. Seen through the lens of the "cult of domesticity" as the keepers of family morals and faith, some lower-class women shocked native-born Americans' gender sensibilities by actively goading their male relatives into ever-greater acts of violence. Even though Irish policemen and Irish Catholic soldiers helped put down the violence, and even though many different individuals took part in the epic violence, contemporaries believed that the Irish played a larger role for a longer period of time than did either German or American laborers. Whether a completely accurate picture or not, the riot quickly became defined as an Irish Catholic one. As one New York editor commented, "No one . . . can have been an eye-witness of the unparalleled, fiendish outrages which were committed by a mob, almost exclusively consisting of Irish Catholics, without coming to the conclusion that such beings will never be fit to be citizens of a republic."[9]

The city's Catholic clergy did not sit idly during the violence and there were numerous stories of the heroic role that parish priests played in trying to calm Catholic rioters. The founding members of the Paulist Society, Fathers Isaac Hecker and Augustine Hewit, personally intervened with parishioners they found among the rioters. A blow to his head injured Hewit when he tried to take an anti-draft banner from the hands of one man. Shocked by this assault on a Catholic priest, many of the rioters calmed down and finally listened to Hecker's plea that they leave. Hecker continued to roam the streets to disperse any other Catholic rioters he could find. The *New York Tablet* reported many other such incidents showing priests' power over even the "nominal Catholics" who had participated in the rioting; the good ones, presumably, were at home or at church. Sister Ulrica O'Reilly likewise is said to have faced down rioters hoping to plunder her order's hospital in Central Park. Even the normally anti-Catholic *Harper's Weekly* praised Irishmen who had fought the riots, declaring "that the Roman Catholic priesthood to a man used their influence on the side of the law."[10]

Bishop Hughes, despite suffering from a fatal illness, intervened as well, but not quickly enough for many critics. Republican editor Horace Greeley, whose newspaper offices had been attacked during the violence, scolded Bishop Hughes to "control 'his people,'" causing Hughes to lash back, calling Greeley prejudiced. Nevertheless, Hughes wrote two open letters during and after the riots urging Catholics to refrain from violence and to return home as quickly as possible. He also invited the city's Irish to visit him at his residence on July 17. After the riots were over, Hughes gave a speech to a crowd of five thousand men from the balcony of his home. He urged them to obey the laws and redress any injustices of the government through the ballot, not violence. The speech was warmly received by his audience though not by his non-Catholic critics. They recognized his good intent but at the same time accused him of making light of his audience's misdeeds. *The Liberator* was among those who found the speech "very reprehensible." Another hostile Boston paper cited his speech as proof of the inadvisability of religious freedom in the face of "the agents of the Romish establishment [striving] for the murder of peoples and republics." Brownson thought it showed that Hughes, who had supported the draft, was afraid of the mob and so sought to placate it. "His address shows that he felt his impotence to control his people except by diverting their wrath from the draft to the English, the hated 'Anglo-Saxons,'" claimed Brownson. Such open criticism of Hughes showed that the riots had, rightly or wrongly, tarnished the image of the church in the minds of many northerners.[11]

A number of Catholic leaders strongly denounced the violence. During the riots, *The Catholic* proclaimed that violent resistance to the draft was unjustifiable, while Bishop John Timon of Buffalo urged restraint in an open letter to members of his diocese. Captain Edward Brownson, writing from his post with the victorious Army of the Potomac in Pennsylvania, hoped the administration "will have the nerve to put down the New York riot as it should be put down." Even the *Catholic Mirror*, despite its strong opposition to the draft, spoke out against the use of violence to stop it, applauded Hughes's role in calming the rioters, and warned Irish Catholics to stay away from mobs to avoid cause for the return of prejudices against them. The *Metropolitan Record* likewise strongly condemned violence against blacks, who were merely innocent political "footballs" poorly used by the real enemies of the people, the "Abolitionists who drag them [blacks] out of their proper sphere, and in the day of trouble abandon them to their fate." *Der Wahrheits Freund* was an unusual exception in that it published news about the riots without any editorial comment.[12]

Anecdotal evidence suggests that Irishmen in the Union Army were ashamed of their countrymen for the part they played in the rioting. Colonel Guiney was particularly angered that the "souless ruffians of New York and Boston . . . are making trouble in the very hour of victory." "I hope the artillery will exempt them from the Draft forever," he wrote. Sergeant Peter Welsh labeled them "disgracefull." Welsh believed the rioters were "agents of jef davis" who had timed their actions to coincide with Lee's invasion of Pennsylvania. For this treason, he suggested that their leaders should be "hung like dogs" while hoping that the "authorities will use canister freely" on the crowds to "bring the bloody cutthroats to their censes." "God help the Irish," said Welsh. "They are to easily led into such snares which gives their enemys an opportunity to malighn and abuse them." Coming from a man who had experienced the horror of artillery bombardments in person, this was incredibly strong language. Although he eventually relented, saying that perhaps many in the crowd had been misled by "jeffs agents," Welsh strongly regretted that the violence had occurred when "one unanimous efort might finish up this acursed war in a few weeks." James Denny of the 78th Pennsylvania likewise blasted the anti-war "demagogues" who led the political opposition at home that he blamed for the riots. Likening them to the "Tories of the Revolution," he thought their political futures would be finished after the North's coming victory.[13]

While the vast majority of Catholics deplored and denounced the riots' violence, apologists also sought to prove that the rioters were not all Catholics or that some other reason than the rioters' religion or ethnicity was to blame for the destruction. McMaster and Mullay emphasized that Americans and Germans had been involved, not just Irishmen. Oertel, while regretting the "abominable excesses" of the rioters, seemed to blame the violence on "bad Catholics" who never went to church. He could not refrain from writing an inflammatory editorial in the wake of the riots criticizing the war effort, abolition, and the draft as "unpractical." This was also the tactic adopted by the *New York Tablet*, which claimed that only "nominal Catholics" had been involved in the violence. Brownson admitted that "nearly nine-tenths of the active rioters were Irishmen and Catholics" whom the clergy had "neglected" to teach properly. Nonetheless, he argued that Catholic Irishmen were "among the bravest and most efficient" in quelling the riots, thus proving that the riots were not "Catholic" in nature or origin. It was in fact a "Democratic mob." Father Purcell similarly blamed Democratic "demagogues" such as McMaster who spread their political agenda of sedition and treason by appealing to men as Catholics while themselves refusing to pay heed to church authorities. For these two leading antislavery men, Catholics' association with the Democrats, rather than an alleged violence or vice inherent to Catholicism itself, was ultimately to blame.[14]

Many Catholic editors joined Brownson in acknowledging the role the Irish had played in the riots but also tried to highlight the role of church figures in quelling the violence. *The Catholic* correctly acknowledged the "humiliating fact" that most of the rioters were Catholics, but it blamed the rioting on the vice of the city itself and the bad influence of politicians. That ministers of the church worked to quell the riot showed that the Catholic faith was not to blame for the unrest. To its credit, the *New York Tablet* strongly condemned the riots and violence against blacks, declaring "Shame!" on any Irishman who so quickly forgot his own "persecution and oppression" in Europe as to become in the United States "the foremost persecutors, the murderers, the tormentors of a poor, hapless, despised race!" The Sadlier brothers argued that the Irish participation in the riots was mitigated somewhat by the fact that they were being overly blamed for the trouble and that there were "numberless instances" of priests quelling local rioters and saving lives and property. Brownson argued that because many Catholics had enlisted at the beginning of the war and because no group had "fought more bravely" or sacrificed more than they had, Catholics as a group were not disloyal.[15]

Catholics also apologized for the riots by arguing that secular and Protestant newspaper coverage of them reflected traditional prejudices against foreigners and Catholics. They also blamed the violence not on the rioters, but, ultimately, on the administration for treating Catholic laborers unfairly. Father Purcell reminded a fellow Cincinnati editor of the many Protestant-led mobs in English and American history, including the one that burned down the Ursuline Convent in Massachusetts in 1834, to refute the charge that "in nearly all the mobs in the large cities, and indeed everywhere, Roman Catholics have been the controlling element." McMaster, amid the riots, printed columns declaring that the draft was a "palpable and perilous infraction of the Constitution," defended the rioters for opposing it, and denounced what he saw as a crime wave committed by "semi-savage" blacks for whom freedom meant doing "whatever their brutal passions prompt them to do." The military's crime in killing innocent white men was worse in his view than Irish Catholic laborers killing "innocent" black men— innocent because they were not in favor of abolition. Mullay agreed, denouncing Lincoln's government as the "Washington Despotism." Lincoln's unprecedented draft, he argued, had reduced "American freemen" to the status of "the veriest slave of the most crushing European despotism." Philadelphia's diocesan editor, despite his pro-Union position, also warned that criticism of Catholics after the draft riots was part of "moves in the grand game" to undermine the church in the United States.[16]

Catholics also reacted with chagrin and anger to press coverage of the riots, particularly because it seemed to completely ignore their soldiers' considerable sacrifices. Donahoe, always the champion of Irish patriotism in the face of prejudice, was incensed by unfavorable comparisons of black and Irish sacrifices during the war by *Harper's Weekly*. Rather than applaud "these wretched [black] people" for their bravery, Donahoe churlishly discredited reports of their heroism coming from such a source as the "Know-nothing, abolitionist bigots" who ran *Harper's Weekly*. Anti-Catholics' reaction to the riots was not surprising, argued John Mullay, for only a "simpleton" could believe that the sacrifices of the Irish on behalf of the Union would have any effect on public prejudices against them. Donahoe, however, shrugged off the ravings and plotting of "bigots" against the Irish and Catholics as more than counterbalanced by the many "gallant Catholic chiefs" serving in the army whose devotion "the Nation is never likely to forget." The press coverage of the riot was merely the opportunity for "unreclaimed Know-Nothings" to once again attack the Irish while ignoring the much greater sacrifices they had made in "Abolition battles" that the "originators of the war have shirked" themselves. "This is Abolition chivalry, and Puritan gratitude," complained McMaster.[17]

The draft continued to be a source of controversy among Catholics throughout the war. Even though many non-Catholics increasingly resisted the war effort in the summers of 1863 and 1864, resistance to the draft and other anti-war activities was more probable in states such as Wisconsin, Massachusetts, and New York that had higher numbers of immigrants and Catholics. Not only did the draft seem to target the poor, but many Catholics also despised it because there was no exception for clergymen. The Benedictine Father Wimmer was one of many church leaders who had to repeatedly appeal for an exemption for his priests. "I have no money" to pay for substitutes, Wimmer complained to Lincoln in the summer of 1863. Arguing that his men had taken an oath to a "mission of peace," he recommended that Lincoln adopt Bavarian laws exempting clergy from the draft, for "such a thing" as forcing clergymen to fight is "unheard of in the annals of Christians nations." This was an ominous sign for many and seemed a poor reward for the patriotism of northern clergy such as Purcell and Hughes. "Until the passage of the Conscription bill, America had exercised no tyranny on the Church. There can be no doubt that Heaven blessed it for such justice," wrote Donahoe. But now the U.S. government had allegedly done something unparalleled in history, rendering it "odious to Christendom." In short, the editor of *The Pilot* said what even the clergy were too afraid to say in public, that drafting clergymen was the work of "a parcel of infidels" in the government. "The only satisfaction in this matter is, that there will be soon a Presidential election," Donahoe finished. The failure to exempt the Catholic clergy, while married Protestant ministers with other careers were often exempted, was a strong argument in the arsenal of anti-war Catholics against the Lincoln administration.[18]

While historians must be careful not to ascribe Catholic opposition to the war solely to their Democratic politics, it is certainly accurate to classify James Mc-Master as the most prolific of all Catholic Copperheads. Having opposed the Republicans and Lincoln's presidential campaign in 1860, McMaster continued to attack the president and Secretary of State Seward repeatedly throughout the war. McMaster was not only a member of the anti-war Democratic group the "Sons of Liberty," but he was also a member of the Order of American Knights. He spoke out in favor of the famous anti-war politician Clement Vallandigham of Ohio, and even met with him while he was in exile in Canada. Although he would later testify of his opposition to the violent measures of these groups, such as shooting provost marshals enforcing the draft, McMaster was also linked briefly with Confederate agents who tried to burn down New York City in late 1864.[19]

In addition to political reasons, McMaster based much of his opposition to the war on his own understanding of the Catholic Church's moral teachings and history. While he readily recognized the role of political strife in bringing about the Civil War, he ultimately saw its basic causes and its possible peaceful resolution in religious terms. For McMaster, Protestantism was "doomed to perish in the social and political ruin it has wrought" in bringing on the war. "May it not be," he asked rhetorically, "that a grand salvation for the country, even in this crisis, will be found in the Catholic Church?" Such an argument, as has been seen already, was a common one among conservative Catholic leaders during the secession crisis and the war itself. Only the church could remind the two sides they were "brothers" and should stop the increasingly pointless violence. Deploring the war's destruction, McMaster called on his Catholic readers to help restore peace on "Christian" terms. He advised Americans to turn their back on radical, pro-war preachers like Henry Ward Beecher and to embrace true Christianity— that is, Roman Catholicism—as the only means of saving the country.[20]

In continuing to argue for peace, McMaster cited no less an authority than Pope Pius IX to argue that Catholics should work for an end to the unnecessary slaughter of the Civil War. McMaster was alluding to the fact that the pope had written letters to both Archbishop Hughes and Archbishop Jean Odin of New Orleans prior to the draft riots in 1863 asking them to work for a peaceful resolution to the war. The original letters, written in October 1862, appear to have been lost, and duplicates did not arrive in New York until July 1863 shortly after the draft riots. One Protestant editor, who was upset that more Americans were not alarmed by the pope's intervention, saw the letters as evidence of a return to the papal policies of medieval times when the pope claimed the ability to "regulate all things on earth, if not in heaven." The editor criticized the pope's idea of having Hughes serve as a peace "commissioner" given his poor handling of the draft riots. Furthermore, continued the Protestant writer, though some Catholic priests had acted to stop the violence, the fact that they did not teach their flocks to refrain from such violence in the first place was a damning mark against the Catholic faith. The riots demonstrated Catholics' ingratitude to their adopted nation, which had given them the "largest blessings and the most liberal favors," as well as their basic ignorance "of their duties as citizens."[21]

The fact that the Roman pontiff, the symbol of all that was wrong with Catholicism for anti-Catholics of that time, had called for peace without regard to the fate of the Union or emancipation unnerved many American Protestants. It lent credence to the old argument that Catholics were under the control of a foreign ruler and thus posed a threat to American society. *The Independent*, a Congregational paper that was perhaps the most important Protestant publication printed during the war, characterized it as Pius IX's boldest attempt to assert "his public assumption of authority over us," in line with the constant meddling of Catholic clergymen in American politics and education. Assuring its readers that he would "miserably fail," it called them to "piety and patriotism [which] will preserve us from Papal and all kindred interventions." Probably prompted by Bishop Spalding's request that Rome take a stand against pro-war bishops, the peace letters were followed by an unpublished papal missive in November to Purcell, admonishing him for not doing enough to promote peace. The pope's December 3 letter to Confederate President Jefferson Davis, which politely but unwisely referred to him as the "illustrious President" of the Confederacy, promised Davis that he would "not cease with most fervent prayers to beseech and pray God . . . to pour out the spirit of Christian charity and peace upon all those people of America and deliver them from the evils so great with which they are afflicted." The letter further incensed anti-Catholic northerners. Though McMaster implied that this letter did not mean recognition of the Confederacy, it was still interpreted as such by the influential *Independent*. Taken together, the four letters provided seemingly overwhelming evidence that the pope secretly sympathized with the Confederacy.[22]

These papal letters posed a problem for pro-war Catholics while giving a considerable boost to those who sought peace. Pro-war Catholics like Brownson and Father Purcell were left to explain away the letters in an effort to save northern Catholics from accusations of being unpatriotic by complying with their spiritual leader's instructions to work for peace. The *Catholic Telegraph* chose to deal with the letter to Purcell by not mentioning it in August even once, though later in March of the following year it denounced an Irish printer for including the letter in an anti-war pamphlet to convince Irishmen that the pope favored the South. Purcell's paper also took pains to assure its readers that the pope's letter to Jefferson Davis meant only that Pius IX "like everyone else is anxious for peace, but is *no advocate of rebellion at home or abroad*." Bishop Spalding was appalled at Purcell's verbal sleight of hand and stubborn refusal to support any Catholic peace movement even at the behest of the pope himself. A Pittsburgh Catholic editor promoted perhaps the most novel interpretation of all. The pope, "always the friend of liberal institutions" and the United States in particular, had sent the letter precisely to forestall the possibility of foreign intervention. The editor mused that one of those foreign powers had probably suppressed the letter in the first place.[23]

Like the editor of the *American Quarterly Church Review*, Brownson also realized the important temporal connection between the pope's peace letters and the draft riots. Though normally it would be appropriate for the pope to make such a plea for peace, in the case of the American war Brownson argued that there were certain principles involved that simply could not be sacrificed and that required the war to continue until the Union was restored. The federal government could no more consent to the dismemberment of the Union than the pope could consent to give up "temporal sovereignty" over the Papal States. Both the pope and the Lincoln administration, despite their differences, were in fact struggling to maintain their national borders through military force. The pope's call for peace could be justified by Catholic "just war" theology if the goals of the federal government were "without any reasonable hope of success," but this was not the case in either the fall of 1862 or 1863 Brownson argued. The rebels were carrying on a hopeless, unjust war, one which they had no hope of winning without help from foreign nations and northern Democrats. Given these "facts," Brownson said the pope's "well-meant" letters were only likely to satisfy the Copperheads by turning Catholics against the war. Unfortunately, they showed that the pope was "wholly deceived" about the American situation. In effect, Brownson tried to show that devout Catholics could appreciate the pope's intent while patriotically rejecting the letter for both temporal and theological reasons consistent with church teaching on just war.[24]

As Brownson predicted, the letters were a long-overdue godsend for anti-war Catholic leaders and lent considerable strength to their calls for peace. Answering the criticism of the *Washington Chronicle*, the *Catholic Mirror* defended the pope's neutrality in the conflict as a sign of his "character as spiritual Father of all christendom." Pius IX recognized that there were now "two Powers" governing where there had been one, argued the editor, and so he offered his prayers for an end to the war's devastation. Clearly the *Mirror's* willingness to purchase peace at the price of disunion influenced its interpretation, which nonetheless was accurate. In New York, Mullay accused the War Department of "suppressing" the letters for fear of their influence on the public, hoping this latest outrage would "rouse the indignation of every Catholic in the country." To him and like-minded anti-war Catholics, the incident was further proof that the Lincoln administration was not simply content to crush civil liberties but was now attacking religious freedom as well. The editor hoped that "every patriot, North or South, whether Catholic or Protestant," would offer an "Amen" to the pope's prayer. Citing the papal letters written to Hughes and Davis in an article in early 1864, the *Freeman's Journal* claimed that they were proof that the pope saw the "great moral question" of the war not as slavery but as one concerning "the right of States to domineer and dictate laws to other states." Noting that Catholic theology respected everyone's "right to live under their own institutions and laws," McMaster drew the only possible conclusion in his mind that the South was right, for it was fighting only for peace, while the North and "the Puritan Brownson" were clearly in the wrong for prolonging the war and attacking slavery. Such interpretations of the document surely fostered and multiplied suspicions about Catholic loyalty among Americans already upset about the riots and the letters themselves.[25]

As for Pius IX, conflicting evidence exists regarding the strength of his preference for one side or the other. On the one hand, he and his chief adviser, Cardinal Giacomo Antonelli, reportedly expressed their sympathy for the North and antipathy for slavery to Rufus King, the U.S. minister in Rome. On the other hand, he also granted an audience to an unofficial Confederate emissary, A. Dudley Mann, and was apparently angered over reports accusing the Union Army of using the Irish as cannon fodder. Ultimately Pius IX was probably more influenced by the pro-southern and anti-war version of events that reached him in Rome. Like other Europeans, the pope and many at the Vatican were disgusted by Union General Benjamin Butler's infamous "woman order," which had threatened to treat any woman in New Orleans who insulted Union soldiers as a prostitute. Probably speaking for the pope as well, Cardinal Barnabo of the Congregation of Propaganda Fide questioned the sincerity of the United States' friendship with the Papal States after Lincoln's administration recognized the Kingdom of Italy in 1862. This act was especially upsetting to the pope because the kingdom's leader, Victor Emmanuel II, hoped to conquer the Papal States in order to make Italy a unified nation.[26]

In the end, despite Pius IX's consistent support for an immediate peace, the Vatican never officially recognized the independence of the Confederacy, nor did it take any further steps to intervene in the conflict. Even Charleston's Bishop Patrick Lynch, who personally went to Rome to plead the South's case, argued after the war that Pius had never recognized the Confederacy. Preoccupied by events in Europe of a much more immediate concern, the papal court viewed the American war as a minor issue. Catholics on both sides tried to argue for analogies between their cause and that of the Holy See in Italy, but in the end it is likely that Pius IX simply saw the American war as needlessly costly and sincerely wished for its quick end. In the summer of 1864, he instructed Bishop Timon of Buffalo to spend $1,000 in the pope's name on behalf of wounded soldiers. Pius directed that the money was to be split evenly in the care of both Union and Confederate casualties. Such a laudable action strongly suggested that Pius IX's interest in the American Civil War was mostly humanitarian.[27]

By early 1864 many pro-war Catholics had new reasons for optimism, especially after Grant, the hero of Vicksburg and Chattanooga, was called east to direct the war effort. Brownson praised the government's recent military moves and expressed "great confidence" in Grant. Colonel Guiney likewise praised Grant for his determination to drive onward to Richmond. Even after Guiney was wounded in the Overland Campaign, he declared, "The Enemy is now driven to the wall and I hope Grant will press him to it until a rebel throat is unable to shout for 'Quarters!'" Donahoe rejected calls for an armistice in early May, arguing that "the only method by which a permanent peace may be obtained is by the overthrow of those who have made, and are still making, superhuman efforts to destroy the integrity of the Union." Continuing the war was thus necessary even if it meant fighting the Confederate armies "to the death." Similarly, Philadelphia's Catholic Herald declared the Confederacy dead and opined that "in mercy to its citizens it should give up." A homesick Irish Catholic private, Joe Duff, likewise hoped that the "Union [will] be preserved," while his bitter anger toward stay-at-home Copperheads only grew stronger.[28]

The horrific casualties of General Grant's Overland Campaign that summer, however, put to the test pro-war Catholics' insistence that the country must be preserved. Just as war weariness had set in during the latter stages of the Mexican War, many pro-war Catholic newspapers grew to deplore the Civil War as casualties mounted and hardships for Catholic families increased. One Catholic editor from Pittsburgh, who had hoped and wished for Grant's success, grew increasingly dismayed about the bloodshed and large debt the country seemed to rack up with little end in sight. By the end of July, the Catholic Herald's editor criticized pro-administration papers for stating that the country welcomed a new draft when it clearly did not, going so far as to suggest that General George B. McClellan be recalled to restore the country's confidence. Even Donahoe, who had argued for fighting the war "to the death" at the beginning of May, deplored the "unnecessary and frightful slaughter" and began to talk of peace and a re-newed commitment to the restoration of the "old Union." This thinly veiled refer-ence to emancipation implied that only Lincoln's insistence on the policy stood in the way of such a reunion.[29]

With the war's turn for the worse, a number of Catholic editors had to choose between their traditional abstention from American politics and open partisan advocacy in the presidential campaign of 1864. Once again, as during the slavery debate, divisive intra-Catholic squabbling was the result. Father Purcell, who re-mained committed to the "utter annihilation" of slavery as a boon to both white and black, publicly criticized all but four Catholic journals as not truly Catholic but merely in the service of "private or party interests to the disregard of truth." In a certain sense this was true, for many pro- and anti-war Catholic newspaper-men openly endorsed the Democrats and General McClellan's candidacy. By the summer of 1864, speaking not as "Catholic journalists" but as American citizens, the Sadliers recommended that "all true lovers of their country" should vote for McClellan as the most able candidate in the field and a moderate between the extremes of abolitionism and the Copperheads.[30]

The Sadliers were in good company among Catholics who had lost all faith in Lincoln. *Der Wahrheits Freund* backed away from its outspoken pro-emancipation position and refused to take sides over the upcoming presidential election. Do-nahoe justified supporting the Democrats because Republicans were merely the successors of the anti-Catholic Know-Nothings and because peace was only pos-sible if the constitutional rights of all white American citizens were respected, including those of slaveholders. Only McMaster outdid Donahoe in vigorously campaigning for the Democrats in 1864. In particular, McMaster sought to use Bishop William Elder's arrest and expulsion from Natchez in the summer of 1864 (for refusing to say the traditional prayer for the president) as a means to remind voters of Republicans' religious biases. Even though Elder was eventually allowed to return to his city, McMaster argued that the whole affair was proof that the "Puritan" fanatics were plotting to dispose of American Catholicism as soon as the war on slavery was finished. Mullay also campaigned strongly on behalf of the Democrats in the 1864 elections. He even urged Democrats "to arm without delay" in case Lincoln refused to give up power. Brownson, who never wavered in his support for the war, nevertheless initially campaigned on behalf of the radical Republican John Frémont against President Lincoln, whom he consid-ered totally incapable of saving the Union. "We have tried him," said the reviewer of the president, "[and] found him wanting." It was only with the withdrawal of

Frémont from the election that he reluctantly once again favored Lincoln as a superior choice to McClellan and the Democrats.[31]

By the end of 1864, the Catholic community's support for the war effort nonetheless seemed to have dropped to its lowest point. This fact stood out clearly in the Catholic religious press, which came out more forcefully in favor of the Democrats and peace than ever before. Only Brownson's and Purcell's papers still openly supported the Republicans, while McMaster, Mullay, and Donahoe all openly campaigned for the Democrats. Of those who remained neutral, many of them almost certainly hoped for a Democratic victory that would reverse the Republican policies of conscription and abolition that they so despised. As far as many Republican and Protestant northerners were concerned, the way many Catholics voted in November was simply the latest proof of Catholic disloyalty to the imperiled Union. Catholics reacted with chagrin to such accusations but had little success in fighting off attacks on their patriotism, even with many Catholic soldiers, priests, and nuns still in the army. McMaster, who blamed War Democrats for the party's presidential defeat, saw nothing but dark times ahead for his coreligionists and the nation at large. Once again he argued that only the Catholic Church could restore true representative government and undo the harm caused by Lincoln's "Puritan Commonwealth."[32]

Nonetheless, from Lincoln's re-election until the end of the conflict, a few Catholic editors continued to support the war effort despite the country's Republican leaders. The *Catholic Herald*'s editor rejected any compromise short of total Union victory. "Poor rebellion! Where now are thy boasts?" he mocked. "Under the heel of right, justice and power." Father Purcell's *Catholic Telegraph* continued its fierce advocacy of the war and emancipation. To the very end, he tried to convince Catholics to support abolition, in one instance citing the *Catholic Almanac* of 1865, the first released since the start of the war, as proof that Catholicism did better in free rather than slave states. The *New York Tablet* was more cautious, but the Sadliers' paper preferred war to a dishonorable peace and even counseled Catholic acquiescence to the Thirteenth Amendment for the good of the country. Pro-war and pro-emancipation Catholics lost their strongest voice, however, when Orestes Brownson ceased publishing his quarterly review at the end of 1864 after the deaths of his sons Edward and William. Edward had been killed at the Battle of Ream's Station in August, and William had died in a stagecoach accident in the West on his way to enlist in the Union Army. Between these deaths, his failing health, and some of his Catholic critics' attacks on his personal faith, Brownson could not carry on any longer. Unlike Purcell, Brownson no longer had the heart or strength to keep expressing his pro-war, pro-emancipation views to an audience who refused to listen.[33]

At the same time, the anti-war Catholic press continued to oppose both the abolition of slavery and the conflict with little regard to better news coming from southern battlefields. Oertel slightly tempered his criticism but nonetheless regretted the influence of abolitionists, Puritans, and other fanatics over Lincoln. Although at the end of the war he finally acquiesced to slavery's demise, he still suggested a path of gradual emancipation that would allow the South to retain its slaves with the understanding that all newborn children would be free. The *Catholic Mirror*'s editors kept quiet on the war for the most part in 1865, undoubtedly remembering their earlier incarceration. In early 1865, Mullay continued to oppose abolition while likening the Confederates to the patriots of 1776, fighting for the right of self-government. Not only did he label the Thirteenth Amendment "unconstitutional," he praised Confederate troops protecting Richmond for their "gallant and skillfull defence" of the city. Likewise, McMaster continued to attack Lincoln, the abolitionists, and the ongoing conflict. Even as late as March 4, McMaster warned the northern public not to give in to the "delusion" that the South was about to surrender. In keeping with his unalterable belief that only a compromise could bring peace, he resorted to making wild, uninformed, and always dire predictions about the likelihood of the imminent defeat of Union Armies, such as General Sherman's in the Carolinas. Such defeats, he argued, and the new resolve of the southern people, would ensure that the war "will go on" indefinitely.[34]

Regardless of whether they approved of the war, most Catholic leaders came to reject such pessimism as news of an avalanche of Union victories reached the North in the spring of 1865. By the beginning of March, Donahoe was so cheered by news of victories at Charleston and Wilmington, and of Sherman's march through the Carolinas that he declared that the end of the war and its bloodshed was not far off. The Sadliers, too, approved of Lincoln's insistence on reunion at a peace conference at Hampton Roads, Virginia, and praised the capture of Richmond. Even as the editors hoped for an imminent peace and a speedy reconstruction of the nation, they maintained the justness of the Union cause over that of "our brave but sadly misguided brethren." General Lee's surrender at Appomattox on April 9 mercifully ended all doubts of Union victory. *Der Wahrheits Freund* uncharacteristically but enthusiastically printed the news of Lee's surrender prominently in its editorial section and predicted that the rest of the Confederacy would soon follow his lead. When news of Richmond's fall reached Pittsburgh, the local Catholic editor was so happy that he promised he would even greet a local Protestant editor, with whom he had been sparring over Pius IX's *Syllabus of Errors*, with "an embrace more cordial than any he has received since he left his mother's arms." Father Purcell, faithful to the cause of emancipation and the slaves to the very end, highlighted the fact that it was "colored men" who had finally liberated the city.[35]

Despite their differences over the war, Roman Catholics across the North and Border States joined their fellow Americans in lamenting Lincoln's assassination after John Wilkes Booth, a popular stage actor and Confederate sympathizer, shot the president in Ford's Theater on Good Friday. Lincoln expired the next day. Donahoe, almost at a loss for words, found enough to denounce Booth's act as "cowardly," to praise Lincoln for saving the Union, and to assure his readers that the newly restored nation would continue on even after Lincoln's death. *Der Wahrheits Freund* declared Lincoln's assassination at the end of four years of war a "terrible blow" to the nation, while even the anti-war *Katholische Kirchen-Zeitung* proclaimed it a "terrible calamity for our country" and denounced Booth as a "devil in human form."[36]

Pro-war and anti-war Catholics, like Democrats and Republicans, were united in their denunciation of the heinous crime. They considered Booth's actions an attack on national stability and social order. Father Purcell denounced the assassination as "the most atrocious of all" of the "wicked deeds" in the nation's history. "Though the liberty of the press allowed the most unmeasured abuse of his administration, though his motives were misrepresented and his person abused, and he was denounced as a tyrant, yet no one thought that any hand would be raised to shed his blood." While not apologizing for his own attacks on the president, McMaster criticized the assassination as a "fiendish atrocity . . . [and] an act of *frenzied madness*." Joining with Archbishop John McCloskey and the Sadliers' *New York Tablet* in denouncing the act, McMaster even praised the martyred president for the moderate and reasonable terms he gave to defeated Confederates. Spalding, now the archbishop of Baltimore, deplored the deed in the strongest of terms. He instructed his flock that it was their "duty" to join with their non-Catholic neighbors to denounce the crime and show sympathy for their fallen president. Similarly, Bishop Domenec of Pittsburgh lamented the president's death while imploring the Catholics of his city to pray for the new president, Andrew Johnson, and his government. The city's Catholic paper called the assassination a "national calamity" and, like McMaster, praised Lincoln for the "generous terms which he was disposed to concede to the conquered rebels."

Thus Catholics of all political persuasions joined the rest of the North in lamenting Lincoln's loss as a threat to the quick and peaceful end of the war and restoration of the Union.[37]

Catholic remorse over the death of Lincoln, though sincere, did little to mitigate their reputation for opposition to the war and to the president personally. Upon hearing of the assassination, a pro-war mob ransacked the offices of the *San Francisco Monitor*, the West Coast's only Catholic paper, in addition to a number of Democratic offices. Catholics' loyalty came into question yet again during the trial of Mary Surratt, a Maryland Catholic widow whose boardinghouse in Washington, D.C., had been used by the Lincoln assassination conspirators.[38] Purcell, Donahoe, and others were enraged by reports that insisted all of the conspirators were Catholics or criticized the church in connection with the assassination. The subsequent hanging of Mary Surratt was an extremely controversial event that some Catholics like McMaster denounced as "murder." In addition, shortly after her execution on July 7, a story circulated that a priest had attempted to see her on several occasions to give her the sacrament of penance but was denied by the War Department. Only when he promised to maintain his silence about his belief in her innocence was he given a pass to see her the day before her execution. The obvious implication of all this was that the government was silencing free speech and possibly discriminating against Mrs. Surratt because of her religion. General James A. Hardie, a Catholic himself who was in charge of approving the pass, flatly denied this, but the damage had been done. The later discovery that one of the leading conspirators, Surratt's son John, was hiding in the papal army did little to alleviate suspicion of the church and its members. Predictably, McMaster criticized the 1867 trial of Surratt's son as an enormous waste of money and one that would only serve to prove his mother's innocence. Criticism of the role that Catholics had played in the assassination was closely related to attacks on the Catholic Church, its priests, and laypeople for their lack of enthusiasm for the war.[39]

Some Catholics interpreted such criticism as confirmation of the fundamental anti-Catholicism of Republicans and Protestant Americans. Now that the war was over—so some Catholics argued, as they had done since 1861—their enemies would shift their sights from slavery to popery. In particular, Catholic editors like the Sadliers lashed out at Horace Greeley for the following statement that appeared in his *New York Tribune* on December 20, 1864: "Whereas all the Catholic clergy within the rebel lines are active rebels, we know of scarcely one under the Union flag who is any more loyal than the law requires him to be. As a body, their influence discourages enlistments in our armies, and tends to enfeeble and paralyze the prosecution of the war." Given Catholics' affinity for the anti-abolitionist Democrats, their involvement in the draft riots, and Pius IX's peace letters, it is likely that many pro-war northerners agreed with Greeley's statements.[40]

Northern Catholic leaders, who knew all too well about the tremendous sacrifices their soldiers had made on behalf of the Union, were outraged by Greeley's accusations. Donahoe seemed particularly sensitive on this issue, which he saw as an attack on all Catholics. Such criticisms as Greeley's article were products of a "virulent insanity" on the part of those who were inexplicably trying to alienate loyal Catholics from the war effort. In this sense, the editor of *The Pilot* proclaimed, Greeley and his ilk were the true "national foe," not Catholics. At the war's end, Donahoe continued to complain about the lingering "religious animosities" of many Americans toward Catholicism despite Irish Catholics' substantial wartime sacrifices. He was dismayed by the lack of appreciation for what Catholics had done on behalf of the Union. The *New York Tablet* labeled such criticism along with attacks on public funding for Catholic institutions as part of an "Anti-Popery Crusade." Criticizing the Republicans' efforts to make the country a "Puritan Commonwealth," McMaster suggested that Catholics should immigrate to Mexico to avoid a coming persecution of the church that would happen as soon as slavery was abolished. Maybe then, when deprived of their labor, he mused, the "Yankees" would finally be forced to acknowledge the value of Catholics and Irishmen to the United States.[41]

Other editors were just as enraged but believed that their community's contributions to victory would prevent a third wave of nativism from sweeping the country after the war's end. *The Catholic* had much more faith in the "common sense" of the northern people than to fear that they would willingly and wholeheartedly join "fanatics" in a "crusade" against Catholicism. Similarly, the *Catholic Telegraph* refuted Greeley's charges that Catholics were disloyal and proslavery, while also assuring its readers that the time was long gone when such charges would have "swept like a whirlwind over the land . . . [for] Catholics have shown their devotion to the country and flag." Refuting Greeley's claims that the Catholics of Maryland and Missouri had done nothing to end slavery in those two states, Father Purcell warned Greeley that attacking Catholics on the slavery question was both "criminal and injuring the cause of emancipation." Even though the issue of a "crusade" against Catholicism was periodically raised after the war, the *Katholische Kirchen-Zeitung* assured its readers that it was only a "minority" of such "twisted heads" that supported attacking the church, not the majority of non-Catholic Americans. Even Donahoe eventually came to reject the idea as "absurd," because the American people had begun to rely on their own judgment rather than that of a "political and sectarian [Protestant] ministry."[42]

Though some had dismissed the threat of a new anti-Catholic movement, the fact that *The Pilot* and other newspapers even discussed the possibility of a war on Catholicism was both significant and troubling. At the end of the Civil War, Greeley's attacks on the loyalty of the Catholic clergy and laypeople proved the continued strength of anti-Catholicism in American society and politics. The service of Catholics alongside their Protestant neighbors during the war had not united Catholic and non-Catholic alike in "the same baptism of precious blood." Perhaps the soldiers were now "brothers in patriotism and love of country," as Donahoe claimed, but the war proved an alienating experience for many Catholic civilians. Trumped-up prosecutions of Catholic priests and nuns in Missouri after the war for refusal to take loyalty oaths worried even the most optimistic Catholic leaders. The missionary Belgian priest, Father Pierre-Jean De Smet, a Missouri resident who had strongly supported the Union cause, denounced the law mandating the oath as "iniquitous." When a Republican-dominated Congress recalled the American minister at the Court of St. Peter's in 1867, the move was a tacit rebuke to both the Vatican's actions during the war and the U.S. Catholic Church and its growing influence in American society. Continued post-war criticism of Catholics' un-American religion and lack of wartime patriotism only further drove them to create their own separate institutions and subculture in order to protect the faith and their ethnic traditions from seemingly ever more hostile forces in mainstream American society.[43]

7

D uring Reconstruction, nativism and anti-Catholicism in national politics and society remained as strong as ever. Republican attacks on the
Democrats as the party of "Rum, Revolution, and Romanism" and a
resurgence of post-war nativism far outweighed any instances of religious tolerance resulting from the patriotism of Catholic soldiers. In fact, most evidence
suggests that tolerance was somewhat more common in the Democratic South,
where Catholics were few in number compared to the Republican-dominated
North. Prominent northern Protestant and Republican leaders, for religious and
political reasons, emphasized Catholic opposition to the war. Catholics, likewise,
continued to see the Republicans as religious bigots well into Reconstruction. "As
they caused the four-year civil war over slavery," argued Father Boniface Wimmer in 1876, "so they would also have gladly conjured up a religious war and
would have suppressed immigrant Germans and Irish."[1]

In the last half of the nineteenth century, a number of events at home and
abroad served to reinforce old religious prejudices from before the war. Events in
Europe, such as the promulgation of the *Syllabus of Errors*, the post-war declaration of the dogma of papal infallibility, and the struggle for Italian unification
caused many Republican and Protestant leaders to empathize with European
liberals seeking to curb the power of the Catholic Church. In the United States,
efforts to recruit Catholic veterans to liberate Ireland or defend Pius IX's lands
raised questions about the ultimate loyalties of American Catholics. Most important, the renewed debate over American public education made Catholics
targets for Republicans seeking a campaign issue in the 1870s. When Catholic
leaders perceived that the war had done little to change outsiders' views of their
faith community, prominent bishops and laymen moved ever more forcefully to
create a separate subculture where they and their faith could be protected from
hostile outside forces.

Since Catholicism was an international religion headed by a European, events
in Europe greatly influenced the perception of Catholics in the 1860s and 1870s.

Memories of the draft riots, the Lincoln assassination, and anti-war Catholic voices were thus not the only factors shaping Protestant Americans' opinions of Catholicism in the immediate aftermath of the war. Even as Catholic editors attacked Greeley for impugning Catholic loyalty, European events once again cast their religion in a bad light. Pius IX's apparently reactionary policies, the cause of Irish nationalism, the "Roman Question" (which was the debate over the papacy's political claims to the Papal States), and European nationalist movements all had large and negative influences on many Americans' perceptions of the U.S. Catholic Church and its followers.

Before the end of the Civil War, the Vatican issued a pronouncement that seemed to question the church's willingness to embrace progress and democracy. In an attempt to combat the spread of liberalism in theology and European politics, Pope Pius IX issued the *Syllabus of Errors* in 1864. The syllabus sharply criticized many of the tenets of mid-nineteenth-century liberalism as incompatible with orthodox Roman Catholicism. The pope's refusal to "reconcile himself and agree with progress, liberalism and modern civilization," confirmed the fear of many Republican and Protestant Americans that Catholicism was inherently backward and un-American. A number of liberal Catholics on both sides of the Atlantic tried to interpret the document as positively as possible, arguing that it had been badly mistranslated in some cases and misunderstood in the others. Their efforts, however, were generally unsuccessful in reducing fears of an increasingly reactionary Vatican. American Protestants' criticism of the *Syllabus* brought together American Catholics, such as Brownson and Spalding, who had been divided over the war. It helped to reinforce their shared feeling of religious oppression especially when taken in context with anti-Catholic editorials such as Greeley's in December 1864.[2]

At the First Vatican Council (1869–70), Catholic bishops from around the world met to define papal infallibility as a dogmatic teaching of the universal church. Issued while Pius XI still clung to what remained of the Papal States, the dogma had only a very limited application to the doctrinal teaching function of the Roman pontiff. Anti-Catholic American critics, however, interpreted infallibility in the widest possible sense, seeing it as a threat to the United States because of its growing Catholic population, who would now be faith-bound to do whatever the pope instructed. No amount of rationalizations from Catholics, even from those with such impeccable patriotic credentials as Brownson, had any positive effect. Infallibility both raised the question of the pope's relationship to secular governments across the world while also seeming to cast serious doubt on the loyalty of Catholic citizens. In Germany the proclamation became a convenient excuse for Chancellor Otto von Bismarck and his liberal allies to wage a Kulturkampf against Catholicism to shore up nascent German nationalism.[3]

Immigrant Catholics' refusal to turn their backs on their ethnic cultures and homelands also brought into question where their ultimate loyalty lay. Thousands of Irish Catholics belonged to the Fenian Brotherhood with the hopes of using their Civil War military experience to liberate their native land. At first there were signs of support from some native-born politicians and editors, including the former Know-Nothing-turned-Republican Nathaniel Banks. Fenianism, however, quickly became unpopular after its followers launched several ill-fated invasions of Canada in 1866 and the early 1870s. Venting his disgust at the Fenians to his friend General Oliver O. Howard, General William Sherman spoke for many Americans when he advocated dealing with the Irish "harshly" if they were caught threatening the "peace" of the country by invading Canada. "No matter what the alleged cause of Grievance it is not for them to embroil us in [a] quarrel," Sherman stated. Both Presidents Andrew Johnson and Ulysses S. Grant intervened to thwart Fenian plans. Neither man wanted a conflict with Britain, even if the North was still upset over British sympathy for the Confederacy during the war. The Fenian invasions not only caused many to wonder how truly American the Irish immigrants were, it also forced the government to step in to vouch for their citizenship to get American Fenians out of British prisons.[4]

Ironically, by condemning its secretive and violent ways, the American Catholic Church helped the U.S. and British governments put down Fenianism. Many church leaders supported their Irish Catholic parishioners' desire for Irish independence, but they did not believe that violent means justified this end. During the Civil War the Fenians quickly and often ran afoul of American church authorities, who distrusted them because their proceedings resembled secret societies that laymen were forbidden to join. Some bishops, such as the Irish American James Duggan of Chicago and the American-born James Wood of Philadelphia, actively opposed the Fenians, announcing that the sacraments would be denied to members of the organization. Duggan pronounced the movement a "delusion" and a scheme for some men to get rich at the expense of other gullible Irish immigrants.[5]

Despite such clerical hostility to the Fenian Brotherhood, many Irish Catholics remained in the organization. Acting too aggressively against Fenians ran the risk of driving committed Irish nationalists out of the church. The Republican *Chicago Tribune*, noting that the Fenians had resolved to ignore any interference from the clergy, implied that if forced to choose between love of country and church the Fenians would choose the former. Fenians' dislike of episcopal meddling did not mean that they did not care about their religion. One Fenian

in Peoria, Illinois, attacked Duggan's announcement as that of a "selfish unpatriotic clergymen." "[Fenians] know that Catholicity is not inconsistent with love of
country, and they cannot, nor shall they, be alienated from either, by the misrep-
resentations or assaults of those [who] would be much better—and more profit-
ably engaged in the performance of their ecclesiastical duties." The man's anger
should not be construed simply as choosing nationalism over religion. Rather, it
was a desperate plea for the two to be reconciled. As late as 1869, John P. Brophy,
a leading member of the Fenians in New York, assured Archbishop Spalding that
he was a "dutiful child of our holy Church" and promised that the Fenian leadership was willing to change "anything" about their organization if it was in conflict
with church doctrine.[6]

Fenianism was not some "remarkable intellectual awakening" by which the
Irish Catholic working class threw off the shackles of the church in favor of labor
solidarity. The church was already beginning to take a progressive stand in favor
of labor and greater social responsibility on behalf of the poor and industrial
working class. Support for Ireland, the working class, and the church were not
necessarily incompatible, and were in many cases simply three different but related parts of Irish Catholic Americans' daily lives. Union Colonel James Mulligan refused to allow Illinois Fenians to use his name to counteract church hostility to the organization. "Whoever places me in hostility to the church misplaces
me," he wrote in a public letter to his good friend Fr. Dennis Dunne, a prominent
priest in Chicago. Mulligan emphatically denied that his recent letter in support
of a local "Irish Nationalist Fair," whose goal was to raise money and support for
Irish independence, in fact constituted support for the Fenians.[7]

On the one hand, conflicts between the church and Irish Catholic Fenians
were real and did lead some Irishmen away from the church. On the other hand,
pronouncements from anti-Fenian clergymen may have caused many Irish
Catholics to avoid the organization altogether. An Irish Catholic soldier serving
in the West refused to join the organization despite the fact nearly all the Irishmen he knew in the U.S. Army belonged to it. He saw the group as a scheme of
unprincipled Irishmen for "picking the pockets of their foolish countrymen" and
denounced it for leading men away from the church. Historians have quoted this
letter to show the strength of the Fenians in the army, but this particular soldier's
hatred of the movement should not be dismissed so easily. The percentage of
Irish Catholic civilians who were Fenians was certainly much smaller than it was
among those in the U.S. Army. Many Irish men and women chose the Catholic
Church over Fenianism. The rather small numbers of Fenians who gathered to
invade Canada is the best evidence of this fact.[8]

Over time, a number of bishops, even those who had initially denounced the Fenians, came to realize that the best way to handle them was to ignore them. The movement, they predicted, would die a natural death. Archbishop Spalding's newspaper purposefully gave little notice to the Fenians in the post-war years, issuing only a mild rebuke of the raids that took place in June 1866. By refusing to comment on the Fenians' activities, most American bishops skillfully avoided pitting Irish Catholic immigrants' ethnic and religious loyalties against each other. The vast majority of Irish immigrants remained within the Catholic Church largely unaffected by this latest incarnation of a failed Irish independence movement. In the wake of the raids of June 1866, one Catholic newspaper gently reminded Irish Catholics to avoid "lending themselves to Quixotic attempts for the liberation of Ireland." Such an admonishment was barely necessary for, despite its large membership rolls, very few Irish Catholic Americans took part in the raids. By the mid-1870s, the Fenian movement effectively died from dwindling membership, poor finances, and its inability to achieve its goal of a free Ireland.[9]

The year following the first unsuccessful Fenian raid witnessed another foreign recruiting drive aimed at all American Catholics, North and South. During the Civil War, a number of Irishmen had brought their valuable military experience gained in the papal army to the federal army. Now that the American war was over, some in the Vatican hoped that American Catholics would return the favor. In late 1867, Italian forces besieged Rome, hoping to conquer the Papal States and thus create a united Italy for the first time since the fall of the Roman Empire. Pius IX, who clung to power only because of the presence of French troops supporting his regime, insisted that possession of his territory was essential to his ability to act independently as the spiritual head of Roman Catholicism and thus resisted all pleas to surrender his territory. The vast majority of American Catholics strongly denounced the pope's enemies and supported his right to continue his rule of the Papal States.[10]

The pope's plight had been a special cause of concern for American Catholics ever since the late 1840s. The fierceness of their support for Pius's political sovereignty over Rome dismayed many secular and Protestant Americans. In 1867, after learning of a plan to send the pope French Canadian volunteers, James McMaster proposed sending a company of young American Catholic men "of the very highest type," physically fit, and whose morals and Catholic piety were beyond reproach, to aid the pope in his plight. "One hundred Irish Americans, good Catholics, of our best fighting material . . . would make short work of several square acres full of the cowardly Italian monkeys that gather round the braggart Garibaldi," crowed McMaster. By January 1868 he reported that he had received "a great many letters" from men across the country in support of the plan, including from those who had "served with distinction in the civil war, on one side and on the other." Meanwhile, *The Pilot* received a letter claiming that American college students in Canada were eager to enlist if only an American equivalent of the Canadian papal troops was formed. Archbishop John McCloskey's effusive praise for the Canadian troops as they left from New York for Rome in February 1868 suggested that perhaps the American bishops would support sending the pope a similar group of American volunteers.[11]

Charles Carroll Tevis, a former Union officer and Fenian now serving in the papal army in Rome, tried to turn McMaster's plans into reality. Initially Tevis, writing as a Roman correspondent for the *Freeman's Journal*, asked only for money for the papal defense fund and not for men. In response, McMaster launched a campaign to raise money for the pope and encouraged men who could pay their own way to write to him about enlisting. After several months, however, Tevis seems to have successfully lobbied his superiors in Rome for permission to visit the United States to recruit men for the papal army. By early May, McMaster learned of the plan and threw his journal enthusiastically behind the cause of raising an American battalion. Tevis declared that veterans of the Civil War, "whether North or South," would be preferred. While other nations' volunteers were simply lumped into the papal army without national distinction, it would be different for any Americans who volunteered. "The military prestige gained in America, during the long and bloody civil war, has obtained for our countrymen the proud privilege of forming a separate battalion for the defense of their spiritual chief," he wrote. Tevis estimated that if all the Catholic parishes in the United States subscribed $100 in gold per year, American Catholics could easily equip and send to Rome a battalion of one thousand men. A number of Catholic editors from both the North and South endorsed the project, including, most importantly, the influential owner of *The Pilot*, Patrick Donahoe.[12]

Although the support of many American Catholics for sending monetary aid to the pope was sincere, the bishops were indignant at the idea of sending American volunteers. Archbishop Purcell, far from approving it, declared, "We have reached a crisis of affairs." He asked Archbishop Spalding to convene a conference of nearby bishops to deal with the issue, which he feared would hurt Catholics in the eyes of non-Catholic Americans. Spalding had already written a long letter to the Vatican in May protesting the call for American troops. His trusted Catholic contact in the War Department, General James Hardie, told Spalding of Tevis's suspect wartime career. Accused of being "inefficient and insubordinate," deserting his men in combat, filling out false request forms, and allowing his junior officers to engage in horse trading during the war, Hardie reported that Tevis's resignation from the army had been accepted "for the good of the service." "He may be sincere in his present desire to serve His Holiness," wrote Hardie, "but I fear he will eventually be the cause of more harm than good." Moreover, Hardie feared that Tevis's plan might violate neutrality laws that banned foreign enlistment on American soil and would anger American public opinion against Catholics. "No act could be more unpopular in this country, more unfortunate for the interests of religion and the welfare of our Catholic citizens, than the endeavor to raise recruits for the Papal military service," he wrote. Hardie, Purcell, and Spalding clearly understood that a proposed battalion would confirm old prejudices that Catholics held a greater loyalty to the pope than to their own country. By this time, however, the story had hit the mainstream press, to the great dismay of those opposed to Tevis's plan.[13]

Learning that Tevis was on his way to the United States, Spalding acted quickly: he suppressed a packet of circulars outlining regulations for enlisting American troops, and he hosted a secret meeting at Mount St. Mary's in Emmitsburg with Archbishops John McCloskey of New York and Purcell. Soon the three men had worked out a firm refusal to the pope's request, which they later published in the *Catholic Mirror* in early July. The plan to enlist American volunteers, they declared, was unfeasible. They asserted their lack of confidence in "Lieutenant-Colonel" Tevis, strongly denied that they had anything to do with the idea, and politely offered instead to continue raising money for the pope's defense fund. When Tevis arrived in New York in late June, armed with a commission and benediction signed by Pius IX, McCloskey received him coldly and sent him away empty-handed.[14]

The bishops' refusal to back the plan ensured its failure. Understandably, Pius IX and his American supporters were upset with the plan's rejection. Angered by the bishops' refusal, Pius nevertheless quickly gave up on recruiting Americans for his army. The affair was even more embarrassing for its American supporters. A chastened Donahoe still defended the project as legal and denounced the "bigotry" of one American newspaper's coverage of the story, while McMaster tried unconvincingly to deny his leadership of the project. As for General Tevis, he returned to Rome defeated and humiliated, his reputation having been attacked and tarnished in the American press. McMaster quietly closed up subscriptions for the pope's defense in August. In the end, the few American Catholics who did serve in the papal army were not enough to save Pius IX's kingdom. Catholics such as Brownson angrily watched as many of their non-Catholic countrymen celebrated the downfall of the Papal States in 1870.[15]

The nationalist movement in Italy was only one of a number of similar attempts by Western European states to foster an increased sense of national pride and unity among their citizens at the expense of institutions that threatened to compromise their loyalty to the state. The Catholic Church, the greatest such international institution, repeatedly fell under suspicion from European nationalists, from Chancellor Bismarck of Prussia to liberal French and Italian politicians. Bismarck's Kulturkampf, in which he tried to reign in and even suppress the church and its adherents in the newly united German Empire, was only the most famous attempt to curtail the power of the church in Europe during the latter half of the nineteenth century. While Bismarck's Germany exiled resisting Catholic bishops, priests, and some religious orders, French and Italian liberals passed laws to limit the church's influence over education. In the United States, a number of prominent Republicans followed closely and applauded these efforts, hoping to achieve similar results during Reconstruction.[16]

While these European issues damaged the image of American Catholicism, events in the United States ultimately proved more important to the continued vitality of anti-Catholicism. The battle over the common school fund and the presence of the Bible in public schools reignited in the wake of the Civil War. During the latter half of the nineteenth century, Catholics continued to build their parochial school system to protect their children's faith from Protestant or secularizing influences in the public schools. The school controversy was a relic of antebellum feuds between Catholics and Protestants over the nature of education in the United States. More than any other issue, the fight over public education in antebellum America reinforced many Protestant's fears of what would happen to the nation's institutions and values should the tiny Catholic minority become the majority. Many American educators such as Horace Mann and Protestant leaders such as Theodore Parker believed that the purpose of public schools "was to produce citizens worthy of a democratic republic." Catholics worried that religious and moral teaching in the common schools were Protestant in nature and they protested against textbooks that openly attacked Catholicism. Catholic leaders campaigned against religious teaching in the schools or actively promoted separate but ideally government-funded parochial schools that would safeguard the faith of their children. Non-Catholic Americans saw such protests as more evidence of Catholics' long-standing opposition to education and thus the democratic values of the American republic. As Horace Mann once said, in "a Protestant and Republican country" such as the United States, both education and "private judgment" were essential and the "birthright" of

Thomas Nast's depiction of Catholics' attacks on public education as analogous to that of the Confederates at Fort Sumter (American Antiquarian Society).

all. Catholic apologists, who were often just as anti-Protestant as their detractors were anti-Catholic, in turn argued that American democracy was founded on Catholic principles and values.[17]

Though largely unsuccessful in their efforts to appropriate funds for their schools before the war, Catholics continued to press their case. In Cincinnati the Purcell brothers tried to take a different route by agreeing to a union between the public and parochial schools in 1869 as long as Protestant practices (such as the reading of the King James Bible) ceased. The local school board agreed, but the Protestant and Republican press immediately attacked its decision.[18]

The debate in Ohio soon unleashed a new wave of anti-Catholicism across the North. In 1870 Thomas Nast, a prominent Republican cartoonist who worked for *Harper's Weekly*, depicted a fictional version of Fort Sumter that spelled out the Catholic threat to the nation. Instead of the Confederates firing on the beleaguered fort, he depicted Catholic bishops and Jesuit priests firing on the White House, which had the words "Public Education" written across it. Equating Catholicism with the Confederacy demonstrated how the Civil War, and the alleged disloyalty of many Northern Catholics symbolized by the New York City draft rioters, directly shaped post-war anti-Catholicism. But Nast's cartoons and criticism from Republican and Protestants leaders could not keep the Bible in Cincinnati's public school rooms. Such determined opposition ensured that a legal battle dragged on for years, but, ultimately, in 1873 the Ohio State Supreme Court upheld the decision to remove the Bible from the state's public schools.[19]

Because of the school debate, anti-Catholicism in American politics became nearly as prominent as it had been in the days of the Know-Nothing Party. Seemingly unceasing Catholic attacks on the public schools only strengthened many northerners' resolve to defend the nation against an "international Jesuit conspiracy." In the same year the so-called Bible War began, the infamous Tammany Ring, led by the Democrat Boss William Tweed, pushed through a bill to help fund large private schools in New York, almost all of which were Catholic. Several years later, New York Democrats passed the "Gray Nuns Act" allowing nuns to continue teaching in public schools without the usual "certification tests." Some Protestant and Republican New Yorkers saw the law as yet another Catholic grab for power over the public education system. Ignoring their service to the Union Army, an anti-Catholic cartoon from 1872 portrayed Irish Catholics as aligned with the Ku Klux Klan and ex-Confederates against President Grant and Catholics' former comrades in the Union Army. After the economic crisis of 1873 threatened Republicans with political defeat, many turned to education and anti-Catholicism as issues with which they could win the 1876 presidential election. Future presidential candidate Rutherford B. Hayes, a former Union general, successfully exploited the issue to win the Ohio gubernatorial election in 1875. The Sadliers' *New York Tablet* commented sadly that the election proved that Know-Nothing bigotry was still alive and well in American society.[20]

If for some German Catholics the war and its aftermath were a "functional equivalent of their homeland's Kulturkampf," many Irish and American Catholic leaders and editors equally shared this sense of alienation during the school debates. It was symbolic that when the American Catholic bishops protested the German Kulturkampf they did so from Cincinnati, the city that was also the center of the school debates. Republican opponents of parochial schools often commented favorably on Bismarck's attack on Catholicism and hoped to implement a similar nationalizing program in the United States. Because Catholics believed their requests were fair and practical, they found such statements to be both troubling and frightening. Catholic leaders publicly rallied behind parochial schools and pointed to state-supported denominational schools in parts of Europe and Canada as models. If European nations financially supported both public and denominational schools, then why could the United States not do the same? In response to

Republicans' open embrace of nativist rhetoric, Catholics sought protection in the Democratic Party and in the creation of their own separate institutions.[21]

The memory of the American Civil War was never far from the school debate. A number of "self-ordained super-champions of public education" consciously called on memories of the "Roman Catholic lackluster commitment to the Union during the Civil War" to bolster their case as well as to question the loyalty of their Catholic opponents. President Grant, who was considering the idea of running for a third term, linked the Union's struggle from 1861 to 1865 to the debate over education in the 1870s. In October 1875, before a reunion of several thousand Union veterans in Des Moines, Iowa, the president called on Americans to resist Catholic efforts to obtain public money for parochial schools. "If we are to have another contest in the near future of our national existence, I predict that the dividing line will not be Mason and Dixon's but between patriotism and intelligence on the one side, and superstition, ambition and ignorance on the other." By "superstition" everyone in his audience knew he meant Roman Catholicism. By choosing to deliver his speech in front of a reunion of Union veterans, Grant had in the most powerful way possible linked the struggle for the Union to the struggle against Catholic influence in American society. In short, even the president joined the rest of his party in reviving anti-Catholicism for political gain.[22]

Catholics recognized that Grant's speech had escalated the conflict over public versus parochial education. One St. Louis Catholic editor sharply criticized Grant for making education a national issue, whereas since the foundation of the nation it had been left up to the states. He saw Grant's later proposal to tax church property as the desperate and hypocritical measure of a man seeking a third term, and called on Catholics across the country to defeat Grant's "cry against Popery" at the ballot box. A St. Louis priest also attacked "compulsory education" as part and parcel of the persecution of the church then taking place around the world. The Sadliers' *New York Tablet* blasted Grant's use of religious prejudice to seek a third term and revived the paper's predictions from 1865 of an imminent religious war against Catholicism. This was a particularly galling development, the editor wrote, given that "Catholic blood [had] flowed as freely as water" only ten years before in defense of the Union and that Washington himself had famously praised Catholic patriotism of the Revolutionary era. A Pittsburgh editor labeled Grant's speech a "bigoted tirade." He accused the president of being "ungrateful" and "unjust," reminding the president that his wartime successes were due "in a large and respectable measure . . . to the valor and support which a Catholic soldiery unhesitatingly gave him."[23] Both Grant's speech and Catholic outrage showed that the Civil War was still relevant to the question of Catholic loyalty and patriotism.

In addition to these Civil War allusions, Catholics across the country accused Grant of base political motives in his speech. McMaster echoed the Sadliers' warning of a coming "crusade against Catholics," but also thanked the "Methodistic ass," President Grant, for helping to reinforce the Catholic Church's unity by persecuting it. The *Catholic Mirror* likewise insinuated that the president was under the control of the Methodists. Comparing the American situation to Bismarck's Kulturkampf, its editor further denounced Grant as a "Caesar" bent on destroying American liberties by forcing compulsory education on the people. When the Chief Justice of the Supreme Court of the Arizona Territory, Edmund F. Dunne, spoke out in favor of the constitutionality of funding parochial schools, Grant swiftly replaced him. Donahoe's *Pilot* criticized the move as more proof that Grant was an "ignorant military President" who could only rely on Catholic-baiting to get a third term. General William Rosecrans's son, the Paulist priest Adrian Louis Rosecrans, mercilessly mocked Grant's Iowa speech in an unsigned editorial in the *Catholic World* which was so sarcastic that some obtuse observers mistook him for agreeing with Grant.[24]

Republican leaders brushed accusations of bigotry aside and determined to use the anti-Catholic issue to help win the election of 1876. Republican James G. Blaine proposed a constitutional amendment in December 1875 to forbid the use of public education funds for Catholic schools. In his annual address to Congress, Grant went even further, advocating the taxation of church property, forbidding religious instruction, and barring illiterate immigrants from voting. Ultimately the Republicans chose Ohio's governor, the Civil War veteran Rutherford Hayes, to run in 1876.[25] Aided by Nast's cartoons and the anti-Catholic editorials decrying the influence of the "foreign church" in the United States, Republican leaders hoped to appeal to Protestant voters by reviving all the standard antebellum fears of the Catholic Church. The Democrats, however, modified the amendment to make Congress powerless to enforce it and then overwhelmingly voted in favor it. This legislative sleight of hand, combined with Catholic restraint, helped cool the anti-Catholic issue and undermined its worth to Republicans in November. In the end the amendment was never ratified. Father Wimmer gave thanks, calling the results of the 1876 election "a victory of truth over deception and a victory of Catholics over the powerful sect of Methodists, to which belong[s] President Grant." Although Wimmer was mistaken in thinking that the Democrat Samuel Tilden had won, his palpable relief over the defeat of proposed anti-church laws was widely shared by other Catholic leaders.[26]

Though the education question had been temporarily defused, the debate's lesson for Catholic leaders was that political anti-Catholicism was still acceptable after the Civil War. Despite the amendment's defeat, the similarities of the movement to Bismarck's anti-Catholic reforms were very troubling for American Catholics. Both sides had invoked the memory of the Civil War to support their positions, making it clear that Catholic contributions to Union victory carried little weight with many non-Catholic northerners in the 1870s.

While the aforementioned events stirred up tremendous anti-Catholic prejudice, both contemporaries and historians could point to many instances of growing religious tolerance as well. Sometimes service in the war helped break down old ethnic and religious barriers. Irish Catholics made tangible advances in politics, and the Fenian movement forced the U.S. government to solidify Irish Americans' status as naturalized citizens. Nuns, who had been objects of scorn and resentment in the antebellum era, had won the praises of many soldiers and government officials for their services to Union soldiers. As mentioned previously, northern officials had shown their appreciation for sisters' service as nurses by inviting two Dominican nuns to take part in the unveiling of President Lincoln's tomb in 1874. Some Protestants also praised a former chaplain of the 18th Illinois, Father Louis A. Lambert, for attacking a mutual enemy, the prominent atheist Robert G. Ingersoll. Despite their religion, Catholic officers such as James Hardie, Philip Sheridan, and David Stanley successfully advanced in the post-war U.S. Army. A number of historians have argued that for Irish Catholics the war helped promote their assimilation. Similarly, one study of Catholic Virginians persuasively argued that post-war appreciation for Catholic service in the Confederate Army allowed many of them to advance in post-war Virginia society.[27]

Leaders from both religious traditions tackled common social issues related to intemperance, urban poverty, and harsh working conditions for industrial laborers. This desire to emphasize common goals above sectarian difference was symbolized by the post-war career of the former chaplain who became archbishop of St. Paul, John Ireland. Ireland became well-known after the war for his desire to reconcile the church with American institutions and values, so much so that he joined many of his former wartime comrades in the Grand Army of the Republic fraternal organization, actively supported the Republican Party, and spoke at veterans' reunions across Minnesota. He even supported compromises allowing Catholic children to attend public schools and criticized the close ties of the church to the Democratic Party, much to the chagrin of the New York clergy. Ireland and his wartime chaplain friend, Father Cooney, were so committed to the cause of temperance that they welcomed members of the Protestant Women's Christian Temperance Union into their national Catholic temperance meeting in

1894. In this instance, Protestant and Catholic Americans proved themselves able to work toward a common reform for the betterment of society. Perhaps shared sacrifice on behalf of the Union did soften ethnic and religious prejudices, thus helping Catholics like Ireland integrate more easily into northern society after the war. Throughout his post-war career, Ireland consistently supported measures to make the church more compatible with modern America.[28]

Still, the most influential and typical Catholic episcopal and lay leaders saw continuing anti-Catholicism as well as radical changes to the nation during the war as threats to the church. While Catholic thinkers, bishops, and newspapers celebrated devout Catholic men who had saved the Union, they also continued to create parallel Catholic institutions to those of Protestant Americans. At the Third Plenary Council of 1884, bishops mandated that all parishes should build Catholic schools to help safeguard the faith of Catholic children from the Protestant or godless common schools. Catholics resisted the new bureaucratic and scientific versions of social and civil reform that swept across the North in the post-war period in favor of a religiously conservative worldview that valued authority, unity, and stability. They feared Republican efforts to strengthen national power, in part because they were Democrats, but also due to their fears of state power being directed against the American church as it had been throughout Europe.[29]

In the latter half of the nineteenth century, bishops and prominent laymen faced with such a perceived threat took concrete steps to safeguard their community from Republican, Protestant, and nativist interference. Catholic leaders enlarged the parochial school system and founded more Catholic colleges and universities such as the Catholic University of America in 1887. They established more of their own religious newspapers and encouraged Catholic men to join their own fraternal organizations such as the Knights of Columbus or the Ancient Order of Hibernians. Certainly the Knights (one of whose first leaders, James Mullen, was a Civil War veteran) consciously tried to reconcile Catholicism and patriotism in their rituals and actions. But they also recognized that promoting greater piety among their members and respect for their faith required them to create their own fraternal organization separate from non-Catholics. They became essentially "an unofficial Catholic anti-defamation society" and were particularly devoted to highlighting Catholic contributions to American society, especially cherishing the fact that the European "discoverer" of America, Christopher Columbus, was Catholic. Lay Catholic women similarly could join auxiliary groups to those organizations, while the same orders of nuns who had served so selflessly in the war became the backbones of separate Catholic schools, orphanages, women's colleges, and hospitals. Catholic men and women built up a substantial subculture all the while refuting nativist attacks leveled now by the American Protective Association on their Americanness. Though some Catholic veterans did join the GAR, many others probably stayed away because of its secret rituals and alliance with the Republican Party. Additional waves of immigrants from southern and eastern Europe, who, like the Germans and Irish, settled into their own ethnic neighborhoods and founded their own ethnic churches, furthered the isolation of the church from mainstream America.[30]

The victory of conservative bishops over more liberal Catholic leaders in the Americanist crisis of the 1890s demonstrated how so-called modernizers and Americanizers such as Archbishop Ireland were in the minority. In fact, the victory of the anti-Americanists in this debate had already been foretold by the victory of anti-war conservatives over pro-emancipation voices during the Civil War. Thus, building on nineteenth-century nativism, the war and its immediate aftermath accelerated and strengthened Catholic thinkers' apologetic and separatist tone. It had reinforced their identity as *Catholic* Americans. Catholic thinkers of the era could not embrace the war and its radical changes to American society wholeheartedly. Their religious, social, and political conservatism proved to have a lasting impact on the church's leadership and Catholic life for years to come. Nonetheless, post-war apologists and veterans in particular would actively try to remind their Protestant neighbors of the courage, sacrifices, and patriotism of Catholic citizens during the late Civil War.[31]

8

Catholics Remember the Civil War

In the late nineteenth century Catholics were still seen as an anti-modern, anti-democratic, and alien threat to the nation's Protestant identity, its democratic government, and its society. Republicans' reliance on anti-Catholic rhetoric during elections in the 1870s and 1880s, including such slogans as "Rum, Romanism, and Rebellion," showed that Donahoe's call for "no more nativism" had failed. Editorials and cartoons critical of Catholicism continued to appear in leading national journals, while Mark Twain, the nation's preeminent literary voice, accused Catholicism of being allied to ignorance and slavery in *A Connecticut Yankee in King Arthur's Court* (1889). Also during the 1880s, former priest Charles Chiniquy, rivaling his fellow Canadian Maria Monk in his shrill attack of his former faith, denounced the Jesuits for planning the Lincoln assassination. He also wrote and spoke frequently about the danger that the Church of Rome posed for American institutions. In 1887 nativists in the Midwest founded the anti-Catholic American Protective Association (APA). Serving as a smaller but still influential late-nineteenth-century version of the Know-Nothings, the organization soon spread throughout the rest of the country.[1]

At the same time, the church itself experienced great change during the late nineteenth and early twentieth centuries. Immigrants continued to come from Ireland and Germany, but they were quickly outnumbered by even newer ones from Italy, Poland, southeastern Europe, and Mexico. No longer was the church simply divided into Irish, native-born, and German enclaves; rather, it started to resemble the larger national diversity of Catholicism formerly present only in Europe itself. New generations of Catholics descended from veterans and civilians who lived through the war were joined by those who had only recently come to the United States seeking a better life. These newer immigrants presumably had little understanding of the war, its importance in American history, or the contributions of Catholic soldiers to saving the Union.[2]

Despite the continued strength of nativism and anti-Catholicism throughout the nineteenth and early twentieth century, Catholic apologists and veterans believed that their wartime sacrifices could be publicized to promote religious tolerance. Their children and newer Catholic immigrants, too, needed to be taught about the valor of Catholic men in the late Civil War. Irish- and American-born Catholics embarked on an impressive but uncoordinated campaign to remind the country and their own growing and diversified community of their services in print, bronze, and stone. These efforts attempted to lionize Catholic soldiers such as those of the Irish Brigade, to celebrate the devotion of Catholic chaplains such as Fathers Cooney and Corby of Notre Dame, and to remember the contributions of prominent Catholic heroes such as General Rosecrans to the Union cause. Such accounts were apologetic in purpose and ignored wartime divisions over issues such as slavery or controversial episodes such as the draft riots. German Catholics were the exception, for they apparently neither wrote histories nor erected monuments commemorating their soldiers' service.

The patriotic memory that English-speaking Catholic northerners created was a message that generally only reached other Catholic Americans. Unlike the Irish in the former Confederacy, Catholic northerners' efforts apparently made only a small impression on most non-Catholic Americans. The plea for tolerance in Father Corby's *Memoirs* was nowhere near as influential or well received in the North as Father Abram Ryan's ode to the defeated Confederacy, "The Conquered Banner," was in the post-war South.[3] Despite their best efforts, northern apologists were unable to use the sacrifices of Catholic soldiers, priests, and nuns on behalf of the Union to defeat anti-Catholicism or convincingly demonstrate their religion's compatibility with the United States' democratic values and government.

Shortly after the end of the war, prominent English-speaking Catholic laymen and veterans started to commemorate their wartime services to the nation. Orestes Brownson argued as early as 1866 in the *American Republic* that Catholics should be accepted as equals into American society because of their Civil War service. Similarly, Louis Garesché, the dead colonel's son, memorialized his father's career by reminding his readers of his martyred father's devotion to "*his duty, his country,* and *his God.*" At the end of the century, George Barton's *Angels of the Battlefield* sought "to furnish for the first time a full and detailed story of the labors of the Catholic Sisterhoods in the Civil War." Such efforts praised Catholic patriotism while simultaneously offering a tacit rebuke to anti-Catholicism in American society. Historian Michael Hochgeschwender fittingly called the foregrounding of Catholic loyalty, bravery, and unity over divisions and negative aspects of the conflict in the memory of the war the "Catholic Civil War national-integration mythology."[4]

Irish veterans were the most prolific in the effort to create a positive memory of the Catholic Church's role during the Civil War. One way to remember and celebrate their shared sacrifices during the war with men of their own faith and also their non-Catholic comrades was to join veterans' organizations. There were significant and early barriers to them belonging to the Grand Army of the Republic, the most prominent Union veterans' organization, however, due to the GAR's middle-class, Protestant, and Republican leadership. In addition, church leaders distrusted it as a "quasi-Masonic secret society." In the face of such opposition, Catholic veterans founded their own groups such as the Irish Brigade Association. The creation of Catholic veterans' groups arguably paralleled the contemporaneous growth of separate Catholic schools, charities, and social organizations in the nineteenth century. Such veterans' groups were "parochial rather than national in vision," in contrast to the GAR. Over time, however, the GAR proved to be more appealing to Catholics as it became less partisan and more concerned with pensions and memorializing the Union that all veterans together had saved. More and more Catholics joined their fellow veterans in the GAR, especially after a committee of bishops in 1886 agreed that Catholics could become members of the organization in good conscience.[5]

Not only did Irish Catholic Union veterans join such organizations to share the comradeship of their old army friends, they also sought to leave behind lasting legacies of their heroism to remind future generations of what they had done as Irishmen and Catholics to save the Union. David Powers Conyngham's celebratory account, *The Irish Brigade and Its Campaigns,* appeared only two years after the conflict ended. Brevet General St. Clair Augustin Mulholland of the 116th Pennsylvania was even more important than Conyngham in his efforts to commemorate Irish and Catholic wartime service. He gave countless lectures and wrote extensively to extol Catholic patriotism. Mulholland's *The Story of the 116th Regiment, Pennsylvania Infantry* (1899), his crowning literary accomplishment, celebrated his former regiment's contributions to the Union cause. Irish Catholic veterans built lasting monuments to their bravery and sacrifice, such as the Irish Brigade memorial and the Father Corby statue at Gettysburg.[6]

Catholic apologists and veterans also suppressed memories of divisions within the community and completely ignored the issue of slavery. For example, Father William Corby did not discuss slavery or the draft riots at all in his *Memoirs of Chaplain Life.* Conyngham's *The Irish Brigade* and George Barton's *Angels of the Battlefield* also avoid these topics. Even in the case where Catholics broke from the majority of their peers and supported emancipation, post-war Catholic writers neither praised nor mentioned such instances of Catholic opposition to slavery. A small biography of General Rosecrans, which was written shortly after his death, completely neglected to mention his once famous abolitionist sentiments, while an official history of the Archdiocese of Cincinnati failed to mention the Purcell brothers' opposition to slavery. Instead, the writer included a long quotation about Purcell's successor, Bishop William Elder, which praised him for his vigorous defense of Catholics' First Amendment rights during the federal occupation of Natchez, Mississippi. One Catholic priest's wartime prediction that Purcell's attack on slavery would "render [his] name imperishable in history" proved to be utterly wrong, at least during the late nineteenth century.[7]

Recent scholarship has challenged the idea that white northerners forgot both slavery's role in bringing on the war and the rights of southern blacks in an attempt to reunify the white populations of the North and former Confederate states. Certainly Corby, Mulholland, and other veterans took great pride in Catholics' role in saving the Union and insisted that they had fought on the right side. They did not embrace the "Lost Cause" narrative of the war that glorified white Confederates' struggle for states' rights. Still, Catholic memorialists, influenced by faith and partisan affiliation with the Democrats, strongly believed that reconciliation was a supreme Christian virtue to be practiced alongside celebrating Union victory. In 1880, Rosecrans, who passionately hated both secessionists and slaveholders throughout his life, was prominent in the Blue-Gray Associations designed to convince veterans to vote for the Democratic candidate, former Major General Winfield Scott Hancock. Likewise, George Barton's study of nuns praised veterans of both sides as "chivalrous men . . . who caused American manhood and valor to be known and respected the world over." Proponents of erecting a monument to Father Corby at Gettysburg highlighted Corby's reconciliationist post-war claim that he had made his famous battlefield absolution "for all, North and South."[8]

With the exception of recent scholarship, twentieth-century Catholic writers and apologists either ignored slavery or apologized for the American church's position on emancipation. The foreword to Rev. Benjamin Blied's pioneering study *Catholics in the Civil War* (1945) defends the church's position on slavery while accusing Lincoln and other "Black Republicans" of political "opportunism" in their support for abolition. Blied tacitly approved of the church's gradualist approach to emancipation as the only one possible for it to take. Arguing that the radical and political nature of abolition precluded Catholics from joining ranks with northern abolitionists, Blied stated that Catholics "were too insignificant politically and socially to advance a program of their own." In the end, the abolition of slavery was simply not an important part of the Catholic memory of the war compared to the more pressing need to reunite the nation and to celebrate Catholic heroes as proof of the larger community's patriotism and respect for American democracy.[9]

The University of Notre Dame, more than any other Catholic institution, took an active role in shaping a positive memory of the church during the war. The university's contribution to the Civil War did not end with Lee's surrender in April 1865 and the return of the last of its chaplains from the battlefield. The university's post-war contribution to the Catholic memory of the war nearly equaled in importance its actual role during the conflict. Similar to Mulholland and Conyngham's post-war apologetic writings, the university constructed a memory of its Civil War past that emphasized Catholics' patriotism and loyalty rather than divisions and anti-war sentiment within the community. More than anyone else, Fathers Corby and Cooney contributed to creating a positive image of Notre Dame's wartime patriotism. They eagerly participated in the larger effort to commemorate Catholic Americans' sacrifices on behalf of the Union cause. While their activities took on various forms, their most important contribution was the GAR post they started together, which served to remind their fellow veterans and other Americans of Catholic patriotism and sacrifices on behalf of the nation.[10]

After the war, both Cooney and Corby returned to Notre Dame. Cooney worked closely with Archbishop Ireland and traveled widely on the temperance lecture circuit, continuing the dry crusade he had started during the war in his regiment. As for Corby, he became the university's third president after the death of Father Patrick Dillon in 1866. Corby served twice, from 1866 to 1872 and 1877 to 1881. Appointed the Holy Cross's Provincial General for the United States in 1886, Corby's post-war career was both eminently successful and very demanding. In the late 1870s when asked by an old soldier for an account of his absolution at Gettysburg, Corby admitted that he had kept no notes from the war and simply forwarded the man a copy of a rather modest sketch of the event he had made previously for General Mulholland. Neither Cooney nor Corby initially had much time or energy to dwell on their past service.[11]

By the 1880s, however, both men joined with fellow veterans to celebrate their wartime exploits. Cooney's success on the temperance circuit inspired him to lecture on what became his second favorite topic: Catholic patriotism. In 1887 Cooney responded to a Baptist minister's contention that "one of the greatest dangers to this country was Romanism" by lecturing on the role Catholics had played in the defense of the country in the Civil and Revolutionary Wars. Surrounded by a cheering and friendly crowd made up largely of former veterans of the 35th Indiana, he argued that the large number of Catholics in the Union Army proved that Catholic Americans were "the safest bulwark for [the nation's] preservation." In this speech and another given a few years later, Cooney implicitly criticized Protestantism as more dangerous to the welfare of the United States by blaming the war on men using their private judgment to interpret the Constitution, thereby causing secession. Furthermore, Cooney estimated that one-third of the veterans belonging to the GAR were Catholic, thus serving as a living testament to Catholic patriotism. The enthusiastic reception Cooney met on both occasions indicates that many Catholics believed in his version of history and were determined that the price they paid for their patriotism in the 1860s would be remembered. General Rosecrans wrote Cooney from Washington, D.C., to give his hearty approval.[12]

While Corby did not lecture publicly about Catholicism in the war, his efforts were ultimately even more important in shaping public opinion. As historian Lawrence Kohl noted, Father Corby seriously began to memorialize his service in the war only in 1888, when he attended the twenty-fifth anniversary of the Battle of Gettysburg. Assisted by his chaplain friend, Father Thomas Ouellet, S.J., Corby celebrated a special Mass and blessed the brigade's new monument near the end of the ceremony. The dedication ceremony as well as the statue itself combined a reverence for their common Irish ancestry, Catholic faith, and patriotic sacrifices that helped to inspire Corby to write about his own service. He intended the book not just to chronicle his experiences, but also to celebrate the patriotism of Catholic soldiers, the nuns, and other chaplains during the war. Addressing his reader "not as a foreigner but as a native-born American citizen," Corby hoped that his account would silence the "useless vituperation" of "bigots." Only when anti-Catholicism disappeared from the media and politics "can we call ourselves a free people, bound together by the most sacred ties that patriotic blood is able to cement." Praise for the book poured in from former chaplains and soldiers, priests, and Catholic newspapers across the country. A laywoman who edited a journal in San Francisco called it both "appropriate and pertinent." She told Corby that she hoped to use it to refute the arguments of the local APA. The *Memoirs* was a great success with many Catholic Americans and made Corby the most famous of all the Catholic chaplains to serve during the Civil War.[13]

Both Corby and Cooney eagerly drew attention to their service as a further reminder of the Catholic Church's positive role during the Civil War. About the same time that Corby published his book, Major William O'Grady, formerly of the Irish Brigade, wrote a letter in the *New York Herald* arguing that Corby should receive a Medal of Honor for performing absolution "under fire" on the second day of the Battle of Gettysburg. Such an honor, awarded for the performance of a Catholic ritual on the battlefield, would have been a powerful symbol of tolerance for Catholics in general and appreciation specifically for what Corby had done during the war. Mulholland and other Irish Brigade veterans sought to get him the award for that very reason. They were ultimately unsuccessful, however, mainly because the act did not properly fall under the "law authorizing issue of medals." "The memory of his noble deeds will be more enduring than a bronze medal," wrote the government official who turned down their request. Despite this disappointment, Corby began collecting Civil War relics, including the green flag of the 63rd New York Regiment, which was proudly displayed with other Irish Brigade artifacts at Notre Dame. The university's collection of Civil War relics eventually included the swords of the Catholic Generals Meagher, Shields, and Rosecrans. In addition to these artifacts, in 1891 Notre Dame commissioned a dramatic painting depicting Corby's absolution at Gettysburg that proudly hangs in the university today. Father Cooney also had a print made depicting his wartime activities in the Army of the Cumberland.[14]

On his fortieth year of priesthood in 1899, Cooney left one last important monument to his service in the Civil War. Taking the money his regiment had given him when he left the service in 1865, Cooney commissioned a chalice that was meant to depict a "synopsis of the ministrations or services of the Catholic Church in the army, during the war of the Rebellion." When finished, its base depicted nuns serving in the hospitals as well as a priest offering a Mass for the soldiers, helping the wounded, and distributing communion. At Cooney's anniversary Mass, Notre Dame's president, Father Andrew Morrissey, praised Cooney's service as a chaplain and his example to his fellow priests. Holy Cross priests, well-wishers, members of the university community, and Union veterans packed the church in honor of Cooney. It was a fitting tribute to his services during the war.[15]

Most important, Corby and Cooney sought membership in local Union veterans' organizations in the late 1890s so that they might be living reminders of Catholic participation in the war. For Corby, these veterans' groups included the Second Army Corps Association, the Military Order of the Loyal Legion, and the Irish Brigade Veterans Association, in the latter of which he served as chaplain. While his membership in all these organizations was impressive, the most important veterans' group at the time was the GAR. Some Catholic leaders looked unfavorably on the organization because of its affiliation with the Republican Party and its non-Catholic rituals. Many clergymen preferred that their

The Holy Cross priests and brothers of Notre Dame GAR Post 569 (University of Notre Dame Archives).

followers join Catholic societies instead. One priest refused to let GAR members wear their organization's badge during a funeral Mass for a Catholic veteran and fellow member. At first Corby was hesitant about joining the organization, even after learning that a Catholic priest, Rev. D. B. Tooney, had been the former commander of a nearby post named for James Mulligan. Putting his fears aside, Corby applied for membership in 1896, and, a year later he and Cooney founded the Notre Dame Post 569 of the GAR.[16]

The members of the Notre Dame GAR post, wrote Corby, would serve as "living examples of true Catholic & American sentiment." Father Corby became the unit's commander and Father Cooney served as its chaplain. This was not an ordinary GAR post, for it was comprised entirely of Catholic priests and brothers who had served in the Union Army during the Civil War. Prominent newspapers across the country reported the story and even printed engravings of its members. Fittingly, General Mulholland came out for the mustering-in ceremonies of the post and was one of several speakers at the event. Surrounded by the symbols of American patriotism and Roman Catholicism, the former general of the 116th Pennsylvania gave a fitting address that blended patriotism and religion together just as Post 569 did itself. For the rest of his life, Corby actively sought out other priests for the organization, stating, "There is absolutely nothing in the ritual or services of the Grand Army of the Republic to interfere with your duties as Priest or as a Catholic." Corby assured fellow priests that the hierarchy of the church had met with Catholic members of the GAR, such as General Rosecrans, and had come away assured that its rituals were not antithetical to Catholicism.[17]

When both men died, Corby in 1898 and Cooney in 1905, they were laid to rest with the rites of the church and the GAR. Not only was Corby's ceremony well attended by the school's religious community, but state and local GAR members also paid their respects. The editors of the *Notre Dame Scholastic* filled a special issue with loving tributes to Corby from the clergy, laity, and Catholic newspapers from across the United States. One Protestant veteran wrote that while he appreciated the church for its patriotism during the war, he was upset that many of his Catholic friends had apparently been forbidden to join the GAR. The *Scholastic*'s issue pointedly reminded its readers that the GAR was "under no ban" and that the church valued patriotism. Both the "laurels" won by Catholics during the war and the establishment of the Notre Dame GAR post were certainly proof enough. Though Cooney's death did not receive the national attention of Corby's, his funeral was nevertheless well attended by students and faculty of the university as well as members of the local GAR. The chalice used to celebrate the funeral Mass was none other than the Civil War one he had had made six years before. Cooney's fellow priests bore his coffin "enveloped in the national ensign" to its final resting place nearby Fathers Sorin and Corby. The *Scholastic* found it to be a "fitting" end for someone who had struggled for "national and temporal union" as well as the "universal and eternal union" that he now joined in death. Both funerals consciously blended patriotism and faith as a reaffirmation of the compatibility of Catholicism with American society.[18]

In the early twentieth century, some Catholics decided that a more lasting tribute to Catholic chaplains was necessary. Inspired by a speech that Mulholland had given about Corby's absolution at Gettysburg, the men of the Catholic Alumni Sodality of Philadelphia passed a unanimous resolution in favor of raising money to erect a monument in Corby's honor. Mulholland soon took charge of the effort, which immediately received a favorable response from Catholics across the country, with one newspaper portraying it as an answer to the "false pleadings of sectarian bigots." The contract fittingly went to a local sculptor, Samuel A. Murray, who had worked on both the colossal Pennsylvania Memorial at Gettysburg and a sculpture of a Catholic Revolutionary War hero, Commodore John Barry.[19]

Although Mulholland died in February 1910 before the monument was finished, the financial foundation had already been laid to see the project through to completion. Finally, in late October, the statue was ready to be unveiled. On October 28 speakers gave addresses in honor of Corby and a campfire was held in which local parochial school children sang patriotic songs. Gettysburg's local priest said Mass the following morning for the assembled crowd of sodality members, Notre Dame alumni and faculty, and other church figures. The school's president, Father John W. Cavanaugh, and Father Walter Elliott, a former Union soldier, both spoke. Despite poor weather, several hundred Catholics showed up for the event. After several more addresses, the ceremony ended with the benediction of the monument by Father Elliott. The Catholic Alumni Sodality's official history of the event closed with the admonition that the monument would be a lasting legacy of Catholic loyalty to the republic, "not unnecessary in this day and generation." The following May, an exact copy of the statue was dedicated at Notre Dame. Just as at Corby's funeral thirteen years before, GAR members attended and stirring addresses were given celebrating Corby's patriotism and faith. Later, in 1963, on the Battle of Gettysburg's centennial, Notre Dame held a special Mass near that statue and dedicated a new plaque in front of Corby's monument. Other university presidents and officials have attended commemorative Masses at the site since, including current university president Rev. John Jenkins, who celebrated Mass and gave a speech in honor of the sesquicentennial anniversary of the event. Notre Dame and American Catholics have since taken great pride in this bronze and stone tribute to the patriotism of the Catholic Church during the Civil War.[20]

Even before the war ended, Catholic leaders and writers lavishly praised high-ranking members of their faith as embodiments of the larger community's patriotism. Martyrs such as Whipple and Garesché, who had died heroically on the battlefield, were seen as paragons of Catholic piety who had made the ultimate sacrifice on behalf of the nation. Catholic leaders and apologists, seeking to refute lingering nativism and religious prejudice by showing the compatibility of their faith with being American, continued to praise their fighting men and soldiers throughout the nineteenth and twentieth centuries. Even if they could not defeat nativism with such arguments, it was important to remind future generations of Catholics in an increasingly diverse church about what their heroic ancestors had done to save the Union during the war.

Irish Catholics' willingness to make a hero of General Meagher, a man known more for his Irish nationalism than for his piety, meant that even the religiously lax Philip Sheridan might possibly become a Catholic hero. During the war and its immediate aftermath, Sheridan's status in the larger Catholic community was ambivalent. Pro- and anti-war Catholics were initially divided over him and his wartime and Reconstruction career. While he was raised Catholic, he controversially had arrested and jailed a priest serving as a Confederate chaplain on flimsy evidence and angered Irish Catholic Democrats like the editors of *The Pilot* by his support for Republicans' reconstruction policies after the war. Still, Sheridan's lukewarm faith was suspect to some Protestants who resented the idea of Catholic being in charge of the army. Thus he was criticized by one man, alongside Sherman and Rosecrans, as one of an alarmingly large number of "Romanists" in the army. Much to this critics' dismay, he gloomily added, "the Rank and file of the army is [also] papist."[21]

Although Sheridan did attend Mass with his wife and family, he was a nominal Catholic at best. Yet after his death a number of Catholics tried to turn Sheridan into a Catholic hero. When he passed away in 1888, he rightly received praise for his contributions to victory from Protestant and Republican newspapers as well as Catholic ones. The *Freeman's Journal* carried a front-page illustration of the general clutching a cross to his heart as angels lifted him up to heaven. This angered some Protestants who refused to admit that one of the three great heroes of the war had been even nominally Catholic. Some took pains to assure their readers that Sheridan was not Catholic, while another engaged in petty anti-Catholic commentary while describing Sheridan's funeral Mass. In the end, Sheridan's sterling career did little to promote tolerance for his family's faith among non-Catholic Americans.[22]

Despite his defeat at Chickamauga, General Rosecrans, rather than the less pious Sheridan, became the greatest Catholic Civil War hero of the nineteenth century. As the most prominent devout Catholic officer in the Union Army, "Old Rosy" naturally became a symbol of Catholic patriotism to his coreligionists across the West and North. In January 1889 Rosecrans received a letter from Georgetown University, the oldest and most prestigious Catholic school in the country at that time, awarding him an honorary degree in recognition of "your eminently successful and honorable career, your high position, and the invaluable services you have rendered your country" in the words of its president, Father Joseph Richards.[23]

An equally important recognition came from Notre Dame, where the general's son Louis had briefly attended school during the war. Notre Dame awarded

Rosecrans its prestigious Laetare Medal for his service during the Civil War. The accompanying certificate praised Rosecrans as "one of the greatest, of those noble chiefs who led our hosts to victory." Calling him a "Christian soldier," the university credited his strong faith with instilling in him and other American Catholics a "duty of patriotism and whole-hearted devotion to the public weal." Whenever the "camps of fanaticism" tried to slander the Catholic Church as "hostile to liberty and false to the principles of American government, [the church] finds her best response and her strongest vindication in the lives of men like you." The medal, which has since become the most prestigious award given to an American Catholic every year, is meant to call attention to the positive contributions of Catholics to American society. Catholic newspapers across the country reported the bestowing of the award on Rosecrans. Today the university remembers Rosecrans alongside other Laetare Medal winners on the first floor of the university's main building.[24]

On March 11, 1898, Rosecrans died at his home in California. Many, including one of his former soldiers, President William McKinley, honored his memory and paid their respects to his family. Local California officials, northerners and southerners, and even Republican newspapers that had fiercely criticized him during the war, all paid him tribute. Amid this praise for his wartime exploits, both his controversial relationship with Grant and his defeat at Chickamauga were largely forgotten. Government offices in Los Angeles closed for the funeral and thousands of people turned out to pay their last respects. Both the funeral Mass held in the city's cathedral and the burial afterward visibly celebrated Rosecrans's strong faith and praiseworthy patriotism. Los Angeles's American-born bishop, George T. Montgomery, presented Rosecrans as a model for others: "As a Catholic, as a soldier, as a true patriot and citizen, Gen. Rosecrans passed away. With how much justice may it be said of him: 'Well done, thou good and faithful servant.'" Confederate and Union veterans gave him one last salute as his body was temporarily laid to rest in a nearby cemetery. The Paulists in New York also celebrated a Mass in Rosecrans's honor, and the sermon was fittingly given by Rosecrans old friend from West Point, Father George Deshon. In 1902 Rosecrans was reburied in Arlington National Cemetery in another ceremony, attended by Union veterans and President Theodore Roosevelt, that similarly combined the Catholic faith with American patriotism.[25]

Catholics and their newspapers were unabashedly celebratory in their tributes to Rosecrans. In praising his career, Catholics were remembering their larger faith community's own service to the country during the war. To celebrate Rosecrans was to celebrate the role of the Catholic layman in preserving the Union.

The *Western Watchman* of St. Louis described him as not only one "of the greatest generals" but also "one of the purest and best men living," and praised him for his "uncompromising Catholicity." Both American and Irish Catholics celebrated his memory. The *Irish World and American Industrial Liberator* approvingly re-printed large parts of Father L. W. Mulhane's memorial tribute to Rosecrans. *The Pilot* also celebrated Rosecrans's victories and faith and credited him for having "dispelled the mists of prejudice from the minds of others." "He was as brave in the spiritual warfare as on the field of blood, and we may confidently hope, has won his place in that Heavenly Kingdom which is taken only by the valiant soldier of the Cross," wrote its editor. "May he rest in peace!" Notre Dame's *Scho-lastic* called Rosecrans "one of [America's] most distinguished and patriotic sons" and his death a great loss to the church and the country. Catholics across the country were united in remembering Rosecrans as a good general and a devout Catholic.[26]

After his death, a number of Catholic writers continued to laud Rosecrans as an example of a true Catholic patriot. Father Mulhane, the general's friend, wrote a celebratory memorial to Rosecrans that was published shortly after Rosecrans's death. The first tribute written in his honor, Mulhane hoped it would keep "green the remembrance of the Christian warrior's noble life." Joseph Taggart, a member of the Knights of Columbus in St. Louis, included Rosecrans in his 1907 book *Bi-ographical Sketches of the Eminent American Patriots*, which celebrated the roles of American Catholics in American history, including Charles Carroll, Commo-dore John Barry, Chief Justice Roger Taney, and General Philip Sheridan. Taggart summarized Rosecrans's career in this way: "He lived a pure and upright life, and left to his country an inheritance of honor, and the splendid example of an untarnished name. He was a soldier born of a heroic race, who knew no fear but the fear of God." Together these works sought to preserve Rosecrans's memory as an unquestionable example of Catholic patriotism for future generations of Americans.[27]

As time elapsed after Rosecrans's death, his wartime career became less prom-inent in the minds of Catholics and historians. William Lamers's *Edge of Glory*, released at the start of the Civil War centennial in 1961, was the only biography written about Rosecrans in the twentieth century. David Moore's *William Rose-crans and the Union Victory* (2014) is just the second book-length biography on the general, a remarkable fact given the plethora of biographies on Confederate generals of lesser rank and importance. Frank P. Varney's *General Grant and the Rewriting of History* (2013), which attempts to defend Rosecrans against Grant's criticisms, is perhaps an indication that Rosecrans may finally be starting to get his due from historians. None of these three studies, however, discusses in great detail Rosecrans's faith or his status as a Catholic hero.[28]

Compared with those of the Irish Brigade, the nurses, and Father Corby, physical monuments to Rosecrans's legacy have been, until recently, just as modest as the small number of books dedicated to his life. A major boulevard in Los Angeles is named in his honor, he has a modest tomb in Arlington, an Ohio elementary school bears his name, and a modest rock-mounted plaque marks his birthplace in Ohio. Rosecrans was not honored by an equestrian statue until September 28, 2013, when one was dedicated in Sunbury, Ohio, thanks to the effort of Tom Paul, a local Rosecrans enthusiast and re-enactor. Paul's group, which raised nearly $200,000 for the monument, emphasized on its "Rosecrans Headquarters" website that the general was a local hero, inventor, and congressman. Rosecrans's status as the highest-ranking devout Catholic, however, was not mentioned in promotional materials and seems not to have been a major motivating factor in the statue movement.[29]

Despite the efforts of Lamers, Varney, Paul, and Moore to memorialize his Civil War generalship, the legacy of General Rosecrans as a *Catholic* Civil War hero has continued to decline through the present day. This is largely because the story of the Catholic Church during the war has become an almost exclusively Irish Catholic one. While the Irish Brigade and Father Corby have remained at the center of Catholics' commemoration of the Civil War, Rosecrans has faded into relative obscurity. Even at Notre Dame, where a ceremonial sword belonging to Rosecrans resides in a prominent display at its visitor center, Eck Hall, the weapon is poorly labeled and its owner's significance is not explained. Ultimately, the neglect of Rosecrans in the Catholic narrative of the Civil War today reflects how the experiences of non-Irish Catholics during the conflict have been forgotten. Whether American-born and German Catholics will take a more prominent place in this narrative is yet to be seen.

In an era that saw rapid immigration, increasing diversity within the church, and struggles to adjust to a rapidly industrializing economy, commemorating Catholics' Civil War service was understandably not a priority for every Catholic in the North. A good example of this apparent apathy was German Catholics' nonexistent role in the creation of a positive Catholic memory of the Civil War. They apparently felt no need to commemorate their Civil War service. Scholars of German American history have yet to identify any significant German Catholic heroes or Union officers. Likewise, there are no monuments to German Catholic soldiers who served in the Civil War comparable to those erected to Irish and American Catholics after the war. Their remembrance of the Civil War, or lack thereof, highlights the unevenness of Catholic efforts to memorialize their role in the war.

German Catholics' apathy resulted from their community's greater degree of separation from American society both before and after the war. It also may be indicative of a weaker sense of German Catholic identity compared to its Irish counterpart. Kathleen Conzen's study of Stearns County, Minnesota, describes the typical experience of German American Catholics during the war as an overwhelmingly negative one. The predominant anti-war sentiment of the German Catholic press, from New York to St. Louis, speaks to the truth of her conclusions. The war disrupted their communities, and in some cases, Conzen argues, men who might have become local heroes became alienated from the larger anti-war community. With such dominant feelings of apathy toward the war, no efforts were made to memorialize the German Catholic community's service and contributions to the Union cause. In one sense, they shared this experience with other Germans who were alienated by nativist prejudice directed at the largely German 11th Corps after its rout during the Battle of Chancellorsville. Yet, after the war, Protestant Germans and the Forty-Eighters constructed battlefield monuments and erected statues, such as Franz Sigel's equestrian statue in St. Louis's Forest Park, while German Catholics did not.[30]

This fact becomes even more striking when German Catholics are compared to the Irish. The Irish were always eager to remind others of their service as a means to greater acceptance in the postbellum nation. The fact that German Catholics were unable to muster their own ethnically and religiously homogeneous regiments like the Irish probably affected their memory of the war in two important ways. First, it made it difficult for German-speaking Catholic priests to find regiments to serve in, which in turn probably discouraged devout German Catholics from serving. With no easy access to the sacraments necessary for their personal salvation, many devout Germans probably thought that military service was not worth the risk. Second, it meant that they had no regiments like the Irish Catholic 69th New York or 35th Indiana that they could celebrate as their own. The Catholic Encyclopedia, published in the United States in the first decade of the twentieth century, was filled with Catholic war heroes of American and Irish ancestry of all ranks. Significantly, the Encyclopedia does not contain a single reference to any German Catholic soldier who served in the Civil War, from either the North or South.

German Catholics' opposition or indifference to the war has all but obscured instances of their devotion to the Union. The patriotism of individual German

Catholic men like Peter Boffinger and Anton Bullenhaar has been almost completely forgotten due to the German Catholic community's neglect of its own history. Even with the tremendous post-war growth of the Central Verein, created before the war to help bring together local German Catholic societies into one larger organization with a national consciousness, a historian looks in vain in its meeting records for significant reference to the war or the conflict's meaning for German Catholics. Christian Keller has argued that many German Americans, reacting to negative press coverage of German soldiers' battlefield performances, increasingly withdrew from American society after the war. German Catholics also took umbrage at such criticism, but their isolation was probably even greater due to their Catholic faith which, when combined with their German culture, set them even further apart from most Americans.[31]

As more and more German Catholic immigrants came to the United States in the late nineteenth century, the fact that they had no connection to the war and thus had no reason to remember it merely reinforced their community's existing apathy about the conflict. Joseph Scheuermann was a devout German Catholic farmer who had immigrated to Kentucky in the early 1870s. Despite the fact that there would have been evidence of the late war all around him, he never once mentioned it in any of his letters to his family back in Germany. German Catholics' self-imposed isolation ran so deep that they cut themselves off from other Catholics after the war. They believed that only by preserving the German language could they keep their children Catholic. "Language saves the faith!" was their favorite rallying cry. They even requested their own German-speaking hierarchy from the Vatican so they could remain apart from the increasingly "Americanized" Irish. Given this strong separatist attitude, it is little wonder why most German Catholics showed so little desire to join their fellow American or Irish Catholics in celebrating the larger Catholic community's contributions to Union victory.[32]

Irish- and native-born Catholic commemorations of the Civil War and the Catholic role in it continued throughout the twentieth century and into the early twenty-first. Some of the more prominent memorial efforts included the Knights of Columbus funding the construction of a Civil War memorial facade to St. Francis Xavier Catholic Church in Gettysburg. Another was the construction of the "Nuns of the Battlefield" monument near St. Matthew's Catholic Cathedral in Washington, D.C., by the Ancient Order of the Hibernians. The laywoman who led the effort, Ellen Ryan Jolly, also authored an impressive history of the nuns during the war. She was even the driving force behind an earlier campaign to get special government markers placed on the headstones of every Civil War nun. Her activities made her the most important Catholic woman, lay or religious, in promoting Catholics' Civil War patriotism in the early twentieth century. Throughout the twentieth century, Catholic leaders gave numerous speeches, laid wreathes, or paid their respects before Catholic audiences at a number of monuments and sites dedicated to the memory of their ancestors' sacrifices and the church's patriotism during the Civil War. As the 150th anniversary of the war approaches its end, appreciative twenty-first-century Catholics still pay honor to these memorials, from Father Corby's famous statue at Gettysburg to the relatively unknown 9th Connecticut Statue in Bay View Park, Connecticut.[33]

Father Peter Guilday, an eminent historian at the Catholic University of America, delivered a fairly typical address before a meeting of the Knights of Columbus in 1934. In his speech he highlighted the "big three": (1) Archbishop Hughes, (2) the chaplains, and (3) the nuns. Guilday did not forget the laity either, listing the names of prominent generals on both sides, none of whom was German. Refraining from pronouncing judgment on either cause, and totally neglecting the issue of slavery, Guilday implicitly commemorated the sacrifice of Catholic men and women on both sides as equally praiseworthy. Whether they had been Confederates or federals, their patriotism was now equally useful in refuting charges of Catholic disloyalty still prevalent nearly seventy years after the war. Such reminders seemed as necessary as ever in the face of continuing anti-Catholicism, embodied in restrictive immigration policies of the late 1920s, the rise of a virulently anti-Catholic version of the Ku Klux Klan throughout the nation, and the anti-Catholic rhetoric of the 1928 presidential campaign between Herbert Hoover and the Catholic Democrat Al Smith. The emphasis Catholics put on how their service showed them to be true Americans in their post-war writings, monuments, and orations underscored their continued separation from American society. As the strength of such post-war and twentieth-century anti-Catholic nativism shows, apologists' efforts to remember the brave deeds of their ancestors were effective among other Catholics but were largely ineffective in changing other Americans' opinions.[34]

Conclusion

The Catholic Civil War story, or rather stories, were both similar to and yet different from those of other Americans. Like African Americans and Protestant or Jewish immigrants, some Catholic leaders seized the opportunity that the war provided to prove their loyalty. Like devout pro-Union Protestant Americans, pious pro-Union Catholics hoped the war would help promote the cause of true Christianity in the post-war nation. Like anti-war Democrats, anti-war Catholics resisted Lincoln's government and thought that peace and defending the Constitution was more important than military victory. Poor Catholic northerners shared many of the same political, family, and economic motivations of their neighbors leading them to resist the draft and avoid service in the army.

American Catholics' faith and their clash with antebellum anti-Catholic nativism set them apart and influenced their understanding of, and participation in, the American Civil War. For many pro-war Catholics the conflict was not just about preserving the Union, it was also about gaining tolerance for themselves and their religious faith in American society. A majority of Catholics and their leaders rallied behind the Union cause at the beginning of the war for a variety of other reasons, too, including economics, Irish Fenianism, and American patriotism. Initially there was widespread appreciation for Catholic service. During the first two years of the war, Catholic Americans had seemingly proved themselves just as interested in the defense of the republic as their Protestant neighbors.

This unity did not last long. At first, opposition to the war seemed to be limited to extremists like McMaster and those living in the Border States. As casualties mounted toward the end of 1862, however, many conservative and Democratic Catholics joined other members of their party in criticizing the war and Lincoln himself. One of the key factors in their dissent was slavery. Conservative Catholics opposed abolition as unconstitutional and because they believed the radical enemies of slavery were also anti-Catholic nativists. Whereas pro-war Catholics hoped to defeat nativism through service, anti-war Catholics hoped to avoid playing the role of cannon fodder for their Protestant or Republican enemies.

They prided themselves as the true patriots, upholding the Constitution, civil liberties, and local rights against radical policies they believed would undermine social stability. They did not want the Union to fail, but they thought that it could be saved only through negotiation and by turning away from Republican policies that were needlessly prolonging a horrifically bloody conflict.

The war and its aftermath ultimately accelerated the growth of a separate Catholic subculture in the United States. Although they were not the only northerners to oppose the war, Catholics' well-known opposition to the war and emancipation reinforced traditional prejudices in the minds of many Americans. Men like McMaster and events like the draft riots were primarily responsible for the failure of their pro-war coreligionists' attempts to use the war to defeat nativism and anti-Catholicism. The stridency of these anti-war Catholics enraged many pro-war Protestant and Republican Americans, and some of them responded by attacking Catholics as unpatriotic. For their part, anti-war and anti-Republican Catholics denounced their critics as Know-Nothings and as ungrateful for the service and sacrifices of thousands of Catholic men in the Union Army. Post-war events at home and abroad, such as the school debates, the Fenians, and the struggle for control of the Papal States, reinvigorated anti-Catholicism during Reconstruction, thereby further reinforcing the experience of alienation Catholics felt during the last half of the war. Certainly large numbers of Catholic soldiers joined the GAR and took part in public commemorations with other Americans, but officially the church promoted separate schools and institutions as a means to preserve American Catholics' faith.

Post-war Catholic apologists and former veterans nonetheless consciously promoted a positive memory of their community's wartime activities to defeat late-nineteenth-century nativism. Catholics erected a number of large monuments and wrote many books and essays extolling their wartime bravery, conveniently ignoring slavery, the draft riots, and the community's underrepresentation in the federal army. However, this heroic and sanitized version of their contributions to the war was directed at a receptive Catholic audience. On the one hand, Catholics remained a mainstay of the Democratic Party, increasingly joined labor unions with non-Catholic neighbors, and interacted peacefully with others despite religious differences. But on the other hand, acceptance of Catholic individuals did not mean a lessening of public prejudice against their ethnic or religious heritages. Donahoe's wartime plea for "no more nativism" in American society or politics was never realized in the nineteenth century or for much of the twentieth century.

As the decades wore on and the old veterans passed away, the church found new opportunities to demonstrate its loyalty in the two world wars. These conflicts created a new generation of heroes that could be celebrated by Catholics whose ancestors came to the United States as part of the antebellum or post–Civil War waves of immigrants. In 1917, in response to the U.S. declaration of war against Germany, Catholic bishops created the National Catholic War Council to present a united front during the First World War. This represented a major change from the divided stand of the hierarchy during the Civil War, and the NCWC was consequently better able to provide for Catholic men's spiritual welfare at the front in France as well as present a unified and patriotic image of Catholicism in America.[1]

Despite a strong resurgence of religious prejudice in the 1920s, anti-Catholicism notably declined in the United States because of the church's unequivocally patriotic response to the Second World War. Also important was the determination of many American soldiers to stamp out religious prejudice when they returned from the war. In 1955 the sociologist Will Herberg famously proclaimed Protestantism, Judaism, and Catholicism to be equally authentic American religious affiliations. The election of a Catholic hero of World War II, a Massachusetts Irish Catholic named John F. Kennedy, to the presidency in 1960 seemed in some minds to put the long history of American anti-Catholicism to rest. Still, the ongoing culture wars, ignited in part by Catholic leaders' resistance to abortion and changing sexual morals in the 1960s and 1970s, quickly revived fears of Catholic power in the minds of many American liberals.[2]

By the second half of the twentieth century, the Civil War was simply not as immediate to the descendants of native-born, Irish, German, or other ethnic Catholics. The church had already begun to shed much of its multi-ethnic character, for it had successfully helped to Americanize many of its adherents well before the end of the century. At the same time, overt prejudice against Catholics seemed to be lessening and the old fight against religious bigotry no longer seemed quite so pressing an issue. Now Catholic Americans could honor their ancestors without feeling the simultaneous need to prove their faith's compatibility with modern American society and the nation's democratic institutions.

At a sesquicentennial Mass held at the spot of Father Corby's absolution at the Battle of Gettysburg, Notre Dame President John Jenkins praised Corby's actions not for demonstrating Catholics' patriotism but for showing that the war possibly might have been avoided. Jenkins praised Corby for his "sacramental invocation of God's mercy for all," both North and South. "If others had Corby's moral imagination, I believe," stated Jenkins, "the brutal and bitter resolution of this conflict could have been avoided." By calling on modern-day political opponents to emulate Corby and resolve their conflicts peacefully, Jenkins unwittingly echoed the arguments of Spalding, McMaster, and the majority of anti-abolitionist Catholics who rejected what they saw as Republican extremism, consistently called for peace, and even came to advocate for talks with the Confederacy. Accused of being unpatriotic and un-American by pro-war northerners both during and after the conflict for holding such views, it is ironic that the very values Jenkins championed in his commemorative speech in fact led to discord and resentment between Catholics and other Americans living in the Civil War era. As for pro-war Catholics who joined their fellow northerners to save the Union or emancipate the slaves, their story, like that of African American soldiers in the Civil War, Japanese Americans who fought in World War II, or Muslim Americans who served in the Iraq and Afghanistan Wars, shows the limits of using military service to eradicate long-standing prejudices in American society.[3]

Acknowledgments

This manuscript would not have been possible without the help of many generous people and institutions. I thank the Cushwa Center of the University of Notre Dame; the German Historical Institute of Washington, D.C.; the Special Collections Library of the University of California–Los Angeles; the University of Erfurt, Germany; and the Corcoran Department of History of the University of Virginia for providing me with the funds necessary to conduct my research from California to New York to Ireland to Germany. I thank all the librarians and archivists I met during my research for their support of my project, for allowing me to visit, and for putting up with my innumerable requests for primary sources. In particular, a special thanks to the wonderful archivists of the Sisters of Mercy, N.Y.; the Sisters of Charity, N.Y.; and the Daughters of Charity, Emmitsburg, Md., for all the free photocopies and books.

A number of historians offered their advice during the research and writing of this book, including Father David Endres, Ryan Keating, Patrick Carey, Sister Betty Ann McNeil, Patrick Hayes, Susannah Ural, Randall Miller, and Father Gerald Fogarty. I am very grateful to friends and family who gave me feedback as I wrote and revised this book. Special thanks are also due to Kevin Whelan, director of the Notre Dame Dublin Program, who generously let me stay at his home while doing research in Ireland. Many of my undergraduate friends from Notre Dame allowed me to stay with them while I was researching this book, and I am extremely grateful to them for their hospitality.

In addition, I must thank all of my history professors at Notre Dame and at the University of Virginia for providing me with an excellent education and nurturing my passion for American history. I thank Dottie Pratt, now at the University of South Carolina, who advised me as an undergraduate to go to Virginia to pursue a Ph.D. on the American Civil War. I am also very grateful to a number of professors and mentors at Virginia, Professors Elizabeth Varon, Father Fogarty, and Joseph Kett, for reading and helping to improve my work. Finally, I owe an immense debt to Professor Gary Gallagher, whose support, generosity, and guidance helped me finish my Ph.D. and who was extremely helpful in suggesting improvements to my book throughout. I have been truly blessed to be his student, and I will always be thankful for everything he has done for me during graduate school and beyond.

The editorial staff at Fordham University Press has been amazing to work with on my first book. Fredric Nachbaur has provided support and been willing to push back deadlines, for which I am very grateful. My series editor, Andrew Slap, made many suggestions for revision that resulted in a much tighter and better-focused argument. I cannot thank Andy enough for believing in this project and for his patience as I juggled revising it with becoming a father and holding down a full-time position at the Virginia Foundation for the Humanities.

Finally, I thank my wife for all her love and support during my many research trips away from Virginia and for reading the manuscript countless times. She helped catch many mistakes, gave me her impressions as a general reader, and put up with my late-night editing. This book is dedicated to her with my love and appreciation for all that she has done to help and encourage me in my career as a historian.

Appendices

Appendix A.   Circulation of Catholic Newspapers in the Civil War Era

Title	Place of publication	Published during Mexican War	Circulation year: number
Brownson's Quarterly Review	Boston; New York	Yes	1853: 2,000; 1873: 1,700; 1875: 1,500
The Catholic	Pittsburgh	Yes	1844: 600; 1856: 1,894; 1868: 2,700
Catholic Herald, (later *The Universe*)	Philadelphia	Yes	Unknown
Catholic Mirror	Baltimore	No	1852: 1,500; 1875: 5,000
Catholic Telegraph	Cincinnati	Yes	1837: 700; 1852: 3,000; 1876: 6,000
Der Wahrheits Freund	Cincinnati	Yes	1838: 3,300; 1869: 20,000; 1876: 14,000
Die Katholische Kirchenzeitung-Zeitung	Baltimore; New York	Yes	1854: 4,000; 1869: 10,000; 1876: 2,500
Metropolitan Record	New York	No	1860: 15,000
New York Freeman's Journal	New York	Yes	1840: less than 300; 1853–54: 10,000; 1881: 15,000
The Pilot	Boston	Yes	1852: 15,000; 1855: 50,000; 1866: almost 100,000; 1872: 103,000

Source: Willging and Hatzfeld, *Catholic Serials of the Nineteenth Century*.

Appendix B.   List of Fifty-Three Known Priests Who Served as Union Chaplains

Name	Diocese	Regiment or Hospital
Bourget, Julian Prosper, C.S.C.	Fort Wayne	Hospital: Mound City, Ill.
Boyle, Francis Edward	Baltimore	Hospital: Washington, D.C.
Brady, Thomas M.	Detroit	15th Michigan
Bruehl, James, S.J.	New York	Hospital: Beaufort, S.C.
Butler, Thaddeus J.	Chicago	23rd Illinois
Carrier, Joseph C., C.S.C.	Fort Wayne	6th Missouri
Christy, Richard C.	Pittsburgh	78th Pennsylvania
Cooney, Peter Paul, C.S.C.	Fort Wayne	35th Indiana
Corby, William, C.S.C.	Fort Wayne	88th New York
Corcoran, Edward P.	Cleveland	61st Ohio
Dillon, James M., C.S.C.	Fort Wayne	63rd and 182nd New York
Doane, George Hobart	Newark	New Jersey (no unit specified)
Egan, Costney Louis, O.P.	Baltimore	9th Massachusetts; Hospital: City Point, Va.
Fusseder, Francis	Milwaukee	24th Wisconsin; 17th Wisconsin
Geselachowski, Alexander	Santa Fe	2nd New Mexico
Gillen, Paul E., C.S.C.	Fort Wayne	170th New York
Gombettelli, James, O.S.F.	Buffalo	13th Pennsylvania Cavalry
Ireland, John Benjamin	St. Paul	5th Minnesota
Kelly, Thomas F.	Chicago	90th Illinois
Lambert, Louis A.	Alton	18th Illinois
Lemagie, Charles L.	New Orleans	2nd Louisiana Cavalry
Leveque, Zepherin Joseph, C.S.C.	Fort Wayne	Unknown
Martin, Michael F.	Philadelphia	69th Pennsylvania
McAtee, Francis, S.J.	Boston	31st New York
McCarthy, Patrick Francis	Baltimore	Hospital: Washington, D.C.
McCollum, Bernard	Philadelphia	116th Pennsylvania
McCosker, John	Philadelphia	55th Pennsylvania
McGlynn, Edward	New York	Hospital: New York
McGrane, Peter	Philadelphia	Hospital: Philadelphia
McGrath, Matthew F.	Baltimore	Hospital: Georgetown, D.C.
McKee, Edward	Philadelphia	116th Pennsylvania
McMahon, Laurence Stephen	Boston	28th Massachusetts

Meittenger, Gustavus	Albany	2nd New York
Mignault, Napoleon	Milwaukee	17th Wisconsin
Mooney, Thomas F.	New York	69th New York State Militia
Mullen, Daniel	Hartford	9th Connecticut
Murphy, Patrick Joseph R.	Chicago	58th Illinois; Hospital service
Nash, Michael, S.J.	New York	6th New York
O'Brien, Edward	Chicago	17th Illinois Cavalry
O'Brien, Nicholas O.	Boston	28th Massachusetts
O'Hagan, Joseph B., S.J.	New York	73rd New York
O'Higgins, William T.	Cincinnati	10th Ohio
O'Reilly, Bernard, S.J.	New York	69th New York State Militia
Ouellet (Willet), Thomas, S.J.	New York	69th New York; Hospital: Newbern, N.C.
Quinn, Thomas	Hartford	1st Rhode Island State Militia Infantry; 1st Rhode Island Light Artillery
Rizzo da Saracena, Leo, O.S.F.	Buffalo	9th Connecticut
Scully, Thomas	Boston	9th Massachusetts
Stephan, Joseph Andrew	Fort Wayne	Hospital: Nashville
Taladrid, Damasio	Santa Fe	1st New Mexico; 1st New Mexico Cavalry
Tissot, Peter, S.J.	New York	37th New York
Trecy, Jeremiah F.	Mobile	Gen. Rosecrans's headquarters
Vahey, John	Chicago	Hospital: Alton, Ill.
Wiget, Bernadin F., S.J.	Baltimore	Hospital: Washington, D.C.

Note: This list excludes some men commonly listed as Catholic Union chaplains. Brinsfield et al., the editors of *Faith in the Fight*, claim that there may have been three additional chaplains, Joseph Fialon, Bernard McCrossin, and Joseph O'Callaghan, but I was not able to confirm that these priests were chaplains using other sources. Germain's "Catholic Military and Naval Chaplains" mistakenly identified Rev. William C. Meredith as a Catholic chaplain when he in fact was Episcopalian. *Sources*: Germain, "Catholic Military and Naval Chaplains"; *Metropolitan Catholic Almanac and Laity's Directory*; Corby, *Memoirs of Chaplain Life*; Blied, *Catholics and the Civil War*; Brinsfield et al., *Faith in the Fight*; Hope, *Notre Dame One Hundred Years*; Schmidt, *Notre Dame and Civil War*; Daly, *Diary of a Union Lady*; Conyngham, "Soldiers of the Cross."

Appendix C.   List of Female Religious Communities That Served as Union Nurses

Religious communities	Location	Diocese	Nuns who served in the war
Daughters of Charity[a]	St. Joseph's Central House, Emmitsburg, Md.	Baltimore	308[b]
Sisters of the Holy Cross	St. Mary's College, Notre Dame, Ind.	Fort Wayne	63
Sisters of Charity of Nazareth[a]	Motherhouse, Nazareth, Ky.	Louisville	37
Sisters of Charity of Cincinnati	Mount St. Joseph-on-Ohio, Cincinnati	Cincinnati	36
Sisters of Mercy of Pittsburgh	St. Mary's Convent, Pittsburgh	Pittsburgh	34
Sisters of Mercy of Baltimore	Mount Saint Agnes Convent, Baltimore	Baltimore	22
Sisters of Mercy of New York City	St. Catherine's Convent, New York	New York	15
Sisters of St. Joseph of Philadelphia	Mount St. Joseph, Chestnut Hill, Philadelphia	Philadelphia	14
Sisters of Charity of New York	Mount Saint Vincent-on-Hudson, New York	New York	13
Sisters of Mercy of Cincinnati	Convent of the Divine Will, Cincinnati	Cincinnati	11
Sisters of Providence	St. Mary-of-the-Woods, Ind.	Vincennes	11
Sisters of St. Joseph of Wheeling	Mount St. Joseph, Wheeling, W.V.	Wheeling	10
Sisters of Mercy of Chicago	Saint Francis Xavier Convent, Chicago	Chicago	10
Sisters of the Poor of St. Francis	St. Clare's Convent, Cincinnati	Cincinnati	10

Note: This list is limited to female religious communities based in the states that remained within the Union in 1861. A number of southern communities in Union-occupied cities, including Memphis and New Orleans, also sent sisters to visit Union hospitals on occasion.

[a] Some nuns from these communities also served in Confederate hospitals.

[b] This number comes from Sr. Betty Ann McNeil, former archivist of the Daughters of Charity, Emmitsburg, Md.

Sources: Jolly, *Nuns of the Battlefield*; Maher, *To Bind Up the Wounds*; *Metropolitan Catholic Almanac and Laity's Directory*.

Notes

Introduction

1. *Brownson's Quarterly Review* (Boston and New York) (hereafter *BQR*), July and October 1861.

2. *The Pilot* (Boston), October 19, 1861; *Der Wahrheits Freund* (Cincinnati), April 25, 1861, September 17, 1862; *Catholic Herald* (Philadelphia), July 19, 1862; *The Catholic* (Pittsburgh), July 18, 1863.

3. While some historians have recently debated and found wanting the term "republicanism" for understanding the ideology of the Revolutionary period and even the nineteenth century, it is clear that Protestants who feared the growth of Catholicism purposefully characterized it as antirepublican or undemocratic. Whether this was evidence of a coherent ideology of republicanism is beside the point: anti-Catholic preachers often highlighted their opponents' faith's hierarchical structure and insistence on dogmatic infallibility as antithetical to America's society and politics. For example, see Jon Gjerde, *Catholicism and the Shaping of Nineteenth-Century America*, ed. S. Deborah King (Cambridge, U.K.: Cambridge University, 2012), 7, 11, 20–60; Mark A. Noll, *America's God: From Jonathan Edwards to Abraham Lincoln* (New York: Oxford University Press, 2002), 240–44, 258; and Mark A. Noll, *The Civil War as a Theological Crisis* (Chapel Hill: University of North Carolina Press, 2006), 18. For some important examples of the historiographical discussion of republicanism's role (or lack thereof) in American society and politics, see Joyce Appleby, *Liberalism and Republicanism in the Historical Imagination* (Cambridge, Mass.: Harvard University Press, 1992); Daniel T. Rodgers, *Contested Truths: Keywords in American Politics since Independence* (New York: Basic Books, 1987); and J. G. A. Pocock, "Between Gog and Magog: The Republican Thesis and the Ideologia Americana," *Journal of the History of Ideas* 48 (April–June 1987): 325–46.

4. For examples of works that emphasize growing Catholic separatism during the mid-nineteenth century, see Jay P. Dolan, *The Immigrant Church: New York's Irish and German Catholics, 1815–1865* (Baltimore: John Hopkins University Press, 1975); Kathleen Conzen, "Immigrant Religion and the Republic: German Catholics in Nineteenth-Century America," *German Historical Institute Bulletin* 35 (Fall 2004): 43–56; and Gjerde, *Catholicism and the Shaping of Nineteenth-Century America*.

5. Ray Allen Billington, *The Protestant Crusade, 1800–1860* (New York: Macmillan, 1938), 1–18; James Hennesey, S.J., *American Catholics: A History of the Roman Catholic Community in the United States* (New York: Oxford University Press, 1981), 46–54, 56–57.

6. Hennesey, *American Catholics*, 57–68; Billington, *Protestant Crusade*, 24; George Washington, "From George Washington to Roman Catholics in America, March

1790," Founders Online, National Archives, http://founders.archives.gov/documents/ Washington/05-05-02-0193; Boston's Catholic newspaper, *The Pilot*, often considered the leading Irish American newspaper in the nineteenth century, quoted this letter from Washington on May 18, 1844, during the height of anti-Catholic violence in Philadelphia in May in order to refute the charges of nativists that Catholics were a threat to American society.

7. Philip Hamburger, *Separation of Church and State* (Cambridge, Mass.: Harvard University Press, 2002), 201–6; Billington, *Protestant Crusade*, 33–48.

8. In this context, Native American refers not to American Indians but to white, Anglo-Saxon, Protestant (WASP) Americans who were born in the United States. Also included in native Americans would have been many Protestants with Irish or non-English ancestors who had assimilated, leaving behind their past ethnic identities.

9. Tyler Anbinder, *Nativism and Slavery: The Northern Know Nothings and the Politics of the 1850s* (New York: Oxford University Press, 1992), 3–19.

10. Because the U.S. Census does not record religion and the American church did not accurately record the number of its members in 1860, historians can only guess at the total number of Catholics in the United States in 1860 or the Union states in 1861–65. The estimate here of 3.1 million Catholics comes from Gerald Shaughnessy's old but widely cited study on the growth of the church in America, *Has the Immigrant Kept the Faith? A Study of Immigration and Catholic Growth in the United States, 1790–1920* (New York: Macmillan, 1925), 262. According to the *Catholic Laity Directory* for 1861, there were 2,317 priests, 2,517 churches, and 43 dioceses and 3 vicariates in the United States in 1861. The latter number excludes the new Vicariate of Marysville, California, which was accidentally left out of the *Directory*. My estimate that about 90 percent of Catholics remained within the Union in 1861 is based on the fact that roughly 89 percent of all priests and 90 percent of all churches were located in the North, West, or the slaveholding Border States that did not join the Confederacy. *The Metropolitan Catholic Almanac and Laity's Directory* (Baltimore: John Murphy & Co., 1861), 229, 231. Historian Patrick W. Carey estimates that by 1860 nearly 63 percent of all Catholics in America were Irish. *Catholics in America: A History* (Westport, Conn.: Praeger, 2004), 30. See also Dolan, *Immigrant Church*, 1–10; Dolan, *The American Catholic Experience: A History from Colonial Times to the Present* (Notre Dame, Ind.: University of Notre Dame Press, 1992), 127–31, 136–47; Hennesey, *American Catholics*, 101–27; Susannah Ural Bruce, *The Harp and the Eagle: Irish-American Volunteers and the Union Army, 1861–1865* (New York: New York University Press, 2006), 7–17.

11. Although the exact number can never be known, the estimate of two hundred thousand Catholics in the army is based on James McPherson's statement that between 11 and 12 percent of Union soldiers were German or Irish Catholic. It is also the figure used by Randall Miller in his important study of Irish Catholic Union soldiers during the war. James M. McPherson, *What They Fought For, 1861–1865* (New York: Anchor Books, 1995), 37; Randall M. Miller, "Catholic Religion, Irish Ethnicity, and the Civil War," in Randall M. Miller, Harry S. Stout, and Charles Reagan Wilson, eds., *Religion and the American Civil War* (New York: Oxford University Press, 1998), 265. Although fifty-three chaplains was a small number compared to how many ministers other denominations

sent to the front in the Civil War, it was many more than the two or three Catholic chaplains who served in the Mexican War. Blied also gave a figure of six hundred nuns serving in the armies, which is corroborated by Sister Denis Maher, who believed that at least 617 nuns from twenty-different communities served as nurses. The real number may be even higher as many of the archives run by female religious communities I visited, such as the Daughters of Charity in Emmitsburg, Maryland, claimed to have uncovered even more nurses who have served since Maher's study was published. Benjamin J. Blied, *Catholics and the Civil War* (Milwaukee: St. Francis Seminary Press, 1945), 12, 118, 122–23; Sr. Mary Denis Maher, *To Bind Up the Wounds: Catholic Sister Nurses in the U.S. Civil War* (New York: Greenwood Press, 1989), 69. For a list of all known Catholic priests who served in the Union Army or hospital service during the war, and a list of female religious communities that served in Union hospitals, please see Appendices B and C.

12. Bruce, *Harp and the Eagle*, 134; Robert M. Sandow, *Deserter Country: Civil War Opposition in the Pennsylvania Appalachians* (New York: Fordham University Press, 2009), 70–71; George C. Rable, *God's Almost Chosen Peoples: A Religious History of the American Civil War* (Chapel Hill: University of North Carolina Press, 2010), 195–98, 354–55.

13. For an excellent recent study of southern Irishmen, which devotes substantial analysis to their Catholic faith as well as their ethnicity and class, see David T. Gleeson, *The Green and the Gray: The Irish in the Confederate States of America* (Chapel Hill: University of North Carolina Press, 2013), 1–9.

14. See, for example, James Moorhead, *American Apocalypse: Yankee Protestants and the Civil War, 1860–1869* (New Haven, Conn.: Yale University Press, 1978); Gardiner H. Shattuck, Jr., *A Shield and Hiding Place: The Religious Life of the Civil War Armies* (Macon, Ga.: Mercer University Press, 1987); Steven E. Woodworth, *While God Is Marching On: The Religious World of Civil War Soldiers* (Lawrence: University Press of Kansas, 2001), Harry S. Stout, *Upon the Altar of the Nation: A Moral History of the Civil War* (New York: Penguin, 2006). David Goldfield's *America Aflame: How the Civil War Created a Nation* (New York: Bloomsbury, 2011), mentions Catholics only in the context of the anti-Catholicism of Protestant reformers, a group to which he assigns much blame for the war (see pp. 1–16); see also Sean A. Scott, *A Visitation of God: Northern Civilians Interpret the Civil War* (Oxford, U.K.: Oxford University Press, 2011), 7.

15. Recent studies that have made good efforts to discuss Catholics include Miller, Stout, and Wilson, eds., *Religion and the American Civil War*; Noll, *Civil War as a Theological Crisis*; Rable, *God's Almost Chosen Peoples*; and Timothy L. Wesley, *The Politics of Faith during the Civil War* (Baton Rouge: Louisiana State University Press, 2013).

16. Unfortunately, the only other study that approaches Blied's in terms of length and thoroughness is an unpublished dissertation on northern and southern Catholic views of the war that is over thirty years old. While its author did argue that through the war Catholics "were drawn into the mainstream of American life," in fact the study only briefly examined the post-war period and was primarily interested in demonstrating that "earlier church historians" had overlooked Catholic viewpoints on the war: "But Catholic Americans had in fact responded to the war, politically and theologically. These responses to the war provide insights into how Catholics perceived their place in mid-

nineteenth century America." Judith Conrad Wimmer, "American Catholic Interpretations of the Civil War" (Ph.D. diss., Drew University, 1980), 309–11, 345–46.

17. Ella Lonn, *Foreigners in the Union Army and Navy* (Baton Rouge: Louisiana State University Press, 1951); William L. Burton, *Melting Pot Soldiers: The Union's Ethnic Regiments*, 2nd ed. (New York: Fordham University Press, 1998); Bruce, *Harp and the Eagle*; Susannah J. Ural, ed., *Civil War Citizens: Race, Ethnicity, and Identity in America's Bloodiest Conflict* (New York: New York University Press, 2010); Christian G. Samito, *Becoming American under Fire: Irish Americans, African Americans, and the Politics of Citizenship during the Civil War Era* (Ithaca, N.Y.: Cornell University Press, 2009); Christian B. Keller, *Chancellorsville and the Germans: Nativism, Ethnicity, and Civil War Memory* (New York: Fordham University Press, 2007); Christian B. Keller, "New Perspectives in Civil War Ethnic History and Their Implications for Twenty-First-Century Scholarship," in Andrew L. Slap and Michael Thomas Smith, eds., *This Distracted and Anarchical People: New Answers for Old Questions about the Civil War–Era North* (New York: Fordham University Press, 2013), 123–41; David L. Valuska and Christian B. Keller, *Damn Dutch: Pennsylvania Germans at Gettysburg* (Mechanicsburg, Pa.: Stackpole Books, 2004); Ryan W. Keating, "'Give Us War in Our Time': America's Irish Communities at War in the Civil War Era" (Ph.D. diss., Fordham University, 2013). Most scholarship on German Catholics during the nineteenth century generally skips over the Civil War. Even Michael Hochgeschwender's study, written in German, does not add much to our understanding of how average German American Catholic soldiers and their families experienced the war and its hardships. In one of her early studies of German American Catholicism, historian Kathleen Conzen called the German Catholic experience of the conflict "terra incognita." Conzen, like Christian Keller in his more general study of German immigrants, argued that the war was an extremely alienating experience for the German Catholic community. See Philip Gleason, *The Conservative Reformers: German-American Catholics and the Social Order* (Notre Dame, Ind.: University of Notre Dame Press, 1968); Emmet H. Rothan, "The German Catholic Immigrant in the United States (1830–1860)" (Ph.D. diss., Catholic University of America, 1946); Michael Hochgeschwender, *Wahrheit, Einheit, Ordnung: Die Sklavenfrage und der amerikanische Katholizismus, 1835–1870* (Paderborn: Ferdinand Schöningen, 2006); Kathleen Conzen, "Immigrant Religion and the Public Sphere: The German Catholic Milieu in America," in Wolfgang Helbich and Walter D. Kamphoefner, eds., *German-American Immigration and Ethnicity in Comparative Perspective* (Madison, Wis.: Max Kade Institute for German-American Studies, 2004), 114; Kathleen Conzen, "German Catholic Communalism and the American Civil War: Exploring the Dilemmas of Transatlantic Political Integration," in Elisabeth Glaser and Hermann Wellenreuther, eds., *Bridging the Atlantic: The Question of American Exceptionalism in Perspective* (New York: Cambridge University Press, 2002), 119–44.

18. Oscar Handlin's *Boston's Immigrants* argued that the war helped integrate Boston's Catholic Irish into the city's society though prejudice continued to linger. Kevin Kenny also believes that "the Irish military contribution to the American Civil War was in some respects a major step forward in their assimilation." Kenny points to the later immigration of southern and eastern Europeans, who were deemed even stranger by Protestant

Americans than the Irish, as helping to assimilate Irish Catholics by the end of the century. Works written about Catholics during the war have reached different conclusions about whether the conflict promoted tolerance of Catholics in post-war America. Patrick Carey argues that the war "represented a major turning point in American Catholicism," and James T. Fisher similarly argues that "the many sacrifices made by Catholics during the Civil War won a measure of respect for the church and its people." By contrast, John T. McGreevy's *Catholicism and American Freedom* is much more negative. He details the continued persecution of the Catholic Church in the immediate post-war period, for example in the anti-Catholic cartoons of Thomas Nast and the proposed Blaine Amendment to the Constitution to forbid public monies being used to support parochial schools. Michael Hochgeschwender's recent study of American Catholic attitudes toward slavery also paints a largely negative picture, largely self-inflicted, due to the church's alliance with the conservative and immigrant-friendly Democratic Party over other antislavery alternatives. Oscar Handlin, *Boston's Immigrants: A Study in Acculturation*, rev. ed. (Cambridge, Mass.: Belknap Press of Harvard University Press, 1979), 208–11; Kevin Kenny, *The American Irish: A History* (New York: Longman, 2000), 122, 260; Carey, *Catholics in America*, 46; James T. Fisher, *Communion of Immigrants: A History of Catholics in America* (New York: Oxford University Press, 2007), 57; John T. McGreevy, *Catholicism and American Freedom: A History* (New York: W. W. Norton, 2003), 91–94; Hochgeschwender, *Wahrheit, Einheit, Ordnung*, 470, 490.

19. Statistics on the circulation figures for the most prominent newspapers cited throughout this book can be found in Appendix A. *BQR*, July 1860; Madeleine Hooke Rice, *American Catholic Opinion in the Slavery Controversy* (New York: Columbia University Press, 1944), 63; W. Jason Wallace, *Catholics, Slaveholders, and the Dilemma of American Evangelicalism, 1835–1860* (Notre Dame, Ind.: University of Notre Dame Press, 2010), 113.

20. Historians of immigrants and working-class Copperheads have also noted this problem, causing them to rely heavily on opinions of elites and newspapers as the best available way to examine their subjects' daily lives, position on the war, and level of support for Republican policies. Sandow, *Deserter Country*, 13; Ural, ed., *Civil War Citizens*, 8–9.

21. James M. McPherson, *For Cause and Comrades: Why Men Fought in the Civil War* (New York: Oxford University Press, 1997), 66–68.

22. This school of thought, known as "whiteness studies," has reduced the question to racism when opposition to abolitionism was actually based on a number of other factors as well including religion, social conservatism, and political allegiance. The two most important whiteness studies touching on the Irish are David R. Roediger, *The Wages of Whiteness: Race and the Making of the American Working Class*, rev. ed. (New York: Verso, 1998); and Noel Ignatiev, *How the Irish Became White* (New York: Routledge, 1995).

1. The Mexican War and Nativism

1. Robert Francis Hueston, *The Catholic Press and Nativism, 1840–1860* (New York: Arno Press, 1976), 37; Eugene P. Willging and Herta Hatzfeld, *Catholic Serials of the*

Nineteenth Century in the United States: A Descriptive Bibliography and Union List, 1st
and 2nd ser. (Washington, D.C.: Catholic University of America Press, 1959–68), 2nd
ser., Part 15: 118–19, 151–52; Sr. Mary Augustine Kwitchen, "James Alphonsus McMaster:
A Study in American Thought" (Ph.D. diss., Catholic University of America, 1949),
75–77.

2. Sr. Blanche Marie McEniry, "American Catholics in the War with Mexico" (Ph.D.
diss., Catholic University of America, 1937), 13–26.

3. Robert W. Johannsen, *To the Halls of Montezuma: The Mexican War in the American Imagination* (New York: Oxford University Press, 1985), vii–viii; Kevin Doughtery, *Civil War Leadership and Mexican War Experience* (Jackson: University Press
of Mississippi, 2007); Alfred Hoyt Bill, *Rehearsal for Conflict: The War with Mexico,
1846–1848* (New York: Alfred A. Knopf, 1947). Important syntheses of the American
Catholic Church's history, like those written by Father James Hennessey, Jay Dolan, and
John McGreevy, hardly mentioned the Mexican War at all. See Hennessey, *American
Catholics*; Dolan, *American Catholic Experience*; McGreevy, *Catholicism and American
Freedom*. The only lengthy study focusing exclusively on Catholics during the war is
Sr. Blanche Marie McEniry's dissertation, "American Catholics in the War with Mexico."
Fortunately, scholars of the Mexican War have begun to look more closely at immigrants
and Catholics in the U.S. Army. For some examples of this recent scholarship, see Tyler V. Johnson, *Devotion to the Adopted Country: U.S. Immigrant Volunteers in the Mexican War* (Columbia: University of Missouri Press, 2012); John Christopher Pinheiro,
"Crusade and Conquest: Anti-Catholicism, Manifest Destiny, and the U.S.–Mexican War
of 1846–1848" (Ph.D. diss., University of Tennessee, 2001); Paul Foos, *A Short, Offhand,
Killing Affair: Soldiers and Social Conflict during the Mexican–American War* (Chapel
Hill: University of North Carolina Press, 2002), 127–32; William B. Kurtz, "Let Us Hear
No More 'Nativism': The Catholic Press in the Mexican and Civil Wars," *Civil War History* 60, no. 1 (2014): 6–31.

4. Gerald Fogarty, S.J., "Public Patriotism and Private Politics: The Tradition of
American Catholicism," *U.S. Catholic Historical* 4 (1984): 5; Robert Ryal Miller, *Shamrock
and Sword: The Saint Patrick's Battalion in the U.S.–Mexican War* (Norman: University
of Oklahoma Press, 1989) 9, 175. There is some disagreement among both contemporary
sources and subsequent historians as to how many Catholics served in the U.S. Army
prior to the war. Historian Robert Miller states that 50 percent of General Zachary
Taylor's army (3,900 men, totaling about half the entire U.S. Army) on the Nueces River
in October 1845 were foreign-born, of whom 24 percent were Irish and 10 percent German. He does not state the religion of the Irish and Germans, though we can be fairly
sure that many of the Irish would have been Catholic as well as some of the Germans.
Sister McEniry cites a source stating that 1,100 Catholics served in the regulars during
the war, stating the number of Catholic volunteers is unknown. Regardless of the exact
number there were a significant number of Catholics in the regular army, and Catholic
newspapers were constant advocates of their religious rights while also praising them for
their patriotic sacrifices on behalf of the nation. Miller, *Shamrock and Sword*, 9; McEniry,
"American Catholics in the War with Mexico," 99; *Catholic Telegraph* (Cincinnati),
April 2, 1846.

5. *The North American* (Philadelphia), May 18, 1846; Isaac McDaniel, "The Impact of the Mexican War on Anti-Catholicism in the United States" (Ph.D. diss., University of Notre Dame, 1991), 198, 203; *Daily Sentinel and Gazette* (Milwaukee) (excerpt originally from *Cleveland Plain Dealer*), May 28, 1846; Pinheiro, "Crusade and Conquest," 59–60.

6. Richard J. Carwardine, *Evangelicals and Politics in Antebellum America* (New Haven, Conn.: Yale University Press, 1993), 144–45; Pinheiro, "Crusade and Conquest," 130, 142–43, 150–51, 162–64, 215–16.

7. Ibid., 160, 173; Tyler V. Johnson, "Punishing the Lies on the Rio Grande: Catholic and Immigrant Volunteers in Zachary Taylor's Army and the Fight against Nativism," *Journal of the Early Republic* 30 (Spring 2010): 63–64.

8. Raphael Semmes, *Service Afloat and Ashore during the Mexican War* (Cincinnati: Wm. H. Moore & Co., Publishers, 1851), 262–63; Pinheiro, "Crusade and Conquest," 155–56, 188–89; McDaniel, "Impact of the Mexican War on Anti-Catholicism in the United States," 28–30.

9. However, Hughes was invited to address Congress during the war in 1847; he delivered a nondenominational speech about Christianity that seems to have been praised widely. McEniry, "American Catholics in the War with Mexico," 33–46; *New York Freeman's Journal* (hereafter *NYFJ*), May 30, 1846; *U.S. Catholic Miscellany* (Charleston), June 13, 1846; *Catholic Telegraph* (Cincinnati), June 11, 1846. In addition to these two Jesuits from Georgetown who were appointed chaplains, the famous Jesuit missionary, Father Pierre-Jean de Smet of Belgium, may also have been appointed to serve as a chaplain for Catholic soldiers in Utah during the war. McEniry, "American Catholics in the War with Mexico," 110.

10. Daniel Walker Howe, *What Hath God Wrought: The Transformation of America, 1815–1848* (New York: Oxford University Press, 2007), 763–64; *NYFJ*, May 16, 30, 1846; *Le Propagateur Catholique* (New Orleans), June 20, 1846.

11. *The Pilot* (Boston), May 23, 30, 1846. A short biography of Donahoe can be found at the online version of the *Catholic Encyclopedia*. Thomas Meehan, "Patrick Donahoe," in *The Catholic Encyclopedia*, vol. 5 (New York: Robert Appleton Company, 1909), http://www.newadvent.org/cathen/05115c.htm; *Catholic Telegraph*, May 21, 1846; *NYFJ*, August 15, 1846; *U.S. Catholic Miscellany* (Charleston), June 13, 1846.

12. *BQR*, October 1, 1846, July 1, 1847.

13. William M. Lamers, *The Edge of Glory: A Biography of General William S. Rosecrans, U.S.A.* (New York: Harcourt, Brace & World, 1961), 16; Louis Garesché, *Biography of Lieut. Col. Julius P. Garesché, Assistant Adjutant-General, U.S. Army* (Philadelphia: J. B. Lippincott, 1887), 69–71; Foos, *A Short, Offhand, Killing Affair*, 28, 129; E. P. Scammon to Rosecrans, December 1, 1846, Thomas J. Curd to Rosecrans, November 29, 1847, Box 1, William S. Rosecrans Papers, UCLA Special Collections, Los Angeles (hereafter UCLA-Rosecrans Papers).

14. McEniry, "American Catholics in the War with Mexico," 105–12.

15. *Sigma* to Editor, *NYFJ*, May 30, 1846; *NYFJ*, August 8, 1846, January 30, 1847. The *Freeman's Journal* even went so far as to suggest that in the future the Mexicans and the Mexican church might be better off within a functioning republic like the United States rather than under the Mexicans' own corrupt and decidedly un-republican government.

16. Helbich and Kamphoefner, *German-American Immigration and Ethnicity*, 69. A good overview of German Catholic immigration in the three decades before the Civil War is Emmet H. Rothan's "German Catholic Immigrant in the United States." A comparative study of Irish and German immigration in the nineteenth century with statistics is Reinhard R. Doerries, *Iren und Deutsche in Der Neuen Welt* (Stuttgart: Franz Steiner Verlag Wiesbaden GMBH, 1986). While clearly recognizing the war as a subject of great interest to the German Catholic community, the *Katholische Kirchen Zeitung*'s editor, Maximilian Oertel, did not comment on the war's causes or greater importance for German American Catholics or Catholic America. Published in Baltimore during the war with Mexico, this paper had moved to New York City by the time of the Civil War. *Katholische Kirchen-Zeitung* (Baltimore and New York), August 14, 1846; Rothan, "German Catholic Immigrant in the United States," 121; *Der Wahrheits Freund* (Cincinnati), May 28, 1846, July 1, 1847; Johnson, "Punishing the Lies on the Rio Grande," 70–72.

17. *The Pilot* (Boston), June 13, December 12, 1846, January 23, 1847; *The Catholic* (Pittsburgh), May 30, 1846, January 23, 1847; *NYFJ*, November 21, 1846. Similar lists were printed by other Catholic newspapers to demonstrate Catholic loyalty. See also *The Catholic* (Pittsburgh), January 23, 1847; *Civis* to Editor, *NYFJ*, October 3, 1846.

18. Howe asserts that "the great majority of [deserters who joined the Mexican Army] were Catholics and/or immigrants" and that "the largest single national group among the *sanpatricios* was of Irish origin." While this is correct, the perception that most of the San Patricios were Irish or Catholic was actually false. Howe, *What Hath God Wrought*, 751; Johnson, "Punishing the Lies on the Rio Grande," 72–73; Foos, *A Short, Offhand, Killing Affair*, 107–8; Miller, *Shamrock and Sword*, 31–33, 173–74; McEniry, "American Catholics in the War with Mexico," 73–98.

19. Hugh M'Cann to Editor, *The Catholic* (Pittsburgh), March 4, 1848; Miller, *Shamrock and Sword*, 33–34, 173–75. For an example of such a reference to the San Patricios in the 1850s, see William S. Balch, *Romanism and Republicanism Incompatible: A Lecture Delivered in the Broadway Tabernacle, Monday Evening, April 5th, 1852, in Review of "The Catholic Chapter of the United States," as Written by the Most. Rev. John Hughes, D.D., Archbishop of New York* (New York: Dewitt & Davenport, 1852), 28; *Pilot*, October 16, November 6, 1847.

20. Jane Storm to Anthony Blanc, May 4, 1847, Archdiocese of New Orleans Collection, University of Notre Dame Archives, Notre Dame, Ind. (hereafter known as ANO); *The Pilot*, January 23, 1847; *Catholic Herald* (Philadelphia), December 21, 1848; Scammon to Rosecrans, January 6, 1848, Box 2, UCLA-Rosecrans Papers.

21. Pinheiro, "Crusade and Conquest," 187–88; John McElroy, "Chaplains for the Mexican War," in *Woodstock Letters*, vol. 16 (Woodstock, Md.: Woodstock College Press, 1887), 227–28; Fr. John McElroy to Bp. Blanc, May 1, 1847, ANO.

22. *Catholic Herald* (Philadelphia), January 28, 1847; McEniry, "American Catholics in the War with Mexico," 13.

23. Hueston, *Catholic Press and Nativism*, 113–15; Foos, *A Short, Offhand, Killing Affair*, 26–27.

24. *Boston Courier*, June 28, 1849; McGreevy, *Catholicism and American Freedom*, 21–25. For more information about the Roman revolution of 1848, its effect on Pius IX,

and his pontificate, see Frank J. Coppa, *Pope Pius IX: Crusader in a Secular Age* (Boston: Twayne, 1979); Roger Aubert, *Le Pontificat de Pie IX (1846–1878)* (Paris: Bloud & Gay, 1952); Nicholas Atkin and Frank Tallett, *Priests, Prelates, and People: A History of European Catholicism since 1750* (New York: Oxford University Press, 2003), 120–23, 130–33.

25. Alexander Campbell quoted in Noll, *America's God*, 243–44; Balch, *Romanism and Republicanism Incompatible*, 7, 30; McGreevy, *Catholicism and American Freedom*, 33–34; Hamburger, *Separation of Church and State*, 205–6. According to historian Ernest Lee Tuveson, the widely held notion that the millennium was near and that America was a "new chosen people reached a peak of enthusiasm in the years immediately preceding 1860." *Redeemer Nation: The Idea of America's Millennial Role* (Chicago: University of Chicago Press, 1980), x, 116–17, 187. For more about how early-nineteenth-century American Protestantism was linked to American republicanism, see Noll, *America's God*, 3–17; and Gjerde, *Catholicism and the Shaping of Nineteenth-Century America*, 33–47.

26. Billington, *Protestant Crusade*, 200–238; David H. Bennett, *The Party of Fear: From Nativist Movements to the New Right in American History* (Chapel Hill: University of North Carolina Press, 1988), 53–60.

27. Hennesey, *American Catholics*, 126; Billington, *Protestant Crusade*, 289–99, 335; Michael F. Holt, *The Political Crisis of the 1850s* (New York: W. W. Norton, 1978), 159–64.

28. Hennesey, *American Catholics*, 124–25; Anbinder, *Nativism and Slavery*, 27–30; Holt, *Political Crisis of the 1850s*, 125–26, 131–32, 163–64; William W. Freehling, *The Road to Disunion*, vol. 2, *Secessionists Triumphant, 1854–1861* (New York: Oxford University Press, 2007), 86–89; William E. Gienapp, *The Origins of the Republican Party, 1852–1856* (New York: Oxford University Press, 1988), 98.

29. Holt, *Political Crisis of the 1850s*, 156, 162–64; Billington, *Protestant Crusade*, 380–84, 388; Bennett, *Party of Fear*, 129–31; Handlin, *Boston's Immigrants*, 191–201; Gienapp, *Origins of the Republican Party*, 92; David M. Potter, *The Impending Crisis, 1848–1861* (New York: Harper & Row, 1976), 249–50.

30. Billington, *Protestant Crusade*, 387, 408–9; Patrick W. Carey, *Orestes A. Brownson: American Religious Weathervane* (Grand Rapids, Mich.: Eerdmans, 2004), 219; Anbinder, *Nativism and Slavery*, 135–42.

31. Stephan Bell to His Family, October 15, 1854, Auswandererbriefesammlung, Gotha Research Library, Gotha, Germany; Fr. John McCaffrey to Abp. John Purcell, April 4, 1854, Abp. Francis Kenrick to Abp. Purcell, August 5, 1854, Archdiocese of Cincinnati Collection, University of Notre Dame Archives, Notre Dame, Ind. (hereafter known as ACI).

32. Hennesey, *American Catholics*, 125–26; Abp. Blanc to Abp Purcell, March 31, 1854, Bp. Martin Spalding to Abp. Purcell, August 2, 1854, April 11, 1856, Bp. Amadeus Rappe to Abp. Purcell, February 29, 1856, ACI; Fr. Peter McLaughlin to Abp. Blanc, December 11, 1857, ANO.

33. Carey, *Catholics in America*, 31; *The Pilot* (Boston), March 18, July 29, 1854. As historian William Gienapp notes, "From the party's founding its major antagonism was against Catholics, and its supporters despised no group so thoroughly as Irish Catholics." *Origins of the Republican Party*, 93.

34. Kwitchen, "James Alphonsus McMaster," 1, 96–97; *NYFJ*, April 29, 1854; *Catholic Mirror* (Baltimore), September 9, 1854. A number of Catholic bishops and newspapers alike predicted that the church would emerge strengthened from the conflict with the Know-Nothings. Their confidence that God would ultimately preserve Catholicism from its enemies did not mean they did not take the American Party seriously. For examples of their confidence in the church's ultimate victory please see *The Pilot* (Boston), July 8, 1854; Fr. McCaffrey to Abp. Purcell, April 4, 1854, Bp. Spalding to Abp. Purcell, August 2, 1854, ACI.

35. *BQR*, July 1854; James Mulligan to Brownson, August 20, 1856, W. J. Belton to Brownson, July 25, 1854, M. R. Keegan to Brownson, July 29, 1854, J. Mudd to Brownson, August 21, 1854, Orestes Brownson Papers, University of Notre Dame Archives, Notre Dame, Ind. (hereafter BRO).

36. *Catholic Mirror* (Baltimore), July 22, 1854; *The Catholic* (Pittsburgh), July 29, 1854; McGreevy, *Catholicism and American Freedom*, 68; *NYFJ*, July 22, 1854; M. Cody to Brownson, July 22, 1854, BRO; Bp. Spalding to Abp. Purcell, August 2, 1854, ACI.

37. Kenny, *American Irish*, 118; Hennesey, *American Catholics*, 129; Gjerde, *Catholicism and the Shaping of Nineteenth-Century America*, 14–15, 67–90; Jean H. Baker, *Affairs of Party: The Political Culture of Northern Democrats in the Mid-Nineteenth Century* (New York: Fordham University Press, 1998), 325–26.

38. Carey, *Orestes A. Brownson: American Religious Weathervane*, 242–44; Conzen, "Immigrant Religion and the Public Sphere," 73–74; Gjerde, *Catholicism and the Shaping of Nineteenth-Century America*, 14–15; Dolan, *Immigrant Church*, 7–10.

39. Billington, *Protestant Crusade*, 417–30; Eric Foner, *Free Soil, Free Labor, Free Men: The Ideology of the Republican Party before the Civil War* (New York: Oxford University Press, 1995), 240; McGreevy, *Catholicism and American Freedom*, 57–58, 62–64; Potter, *Impending Crisis*, 253–56; Freehling, *Road to Disunion*, 2:93–95; Gienapp, *Origins of Republican Party*, 199.

40. Potter, *Impending Crisis*, 252–53, 258–59; Gienapp, *Origins of the Republican Party*, 420–21; Bp. John Timon to Abp. Purcell, September 17, 1855, ACI; Anbinder, *Nativism and Slavery*, 250–52, 274; McGreevy, *Catholicism and American Freedom*, 62–64.

2. Catholics Rally to the Flag

1. For a good discussion of the united and patriotic way in which leading Catholic thinkers responded to the outbreak of the Civil War, see Walter. G. Sharrow, "Northern Catholic Intellectuals and the Coming of the Civil War," *New York Historical Society Quarterly* 58 (January 1974): 35–56.

2. Shaughnessy, *Has the Immigrant Kept the Faith?* 262; Kenny, *American Irish*, 113–114; Dolan, *American Catholic Experience*, 136–47; Willging and Hatzfeld, *Catholic Serials of the Nineteenth Century*, 2nd. ser., Part 15, p. 152.

3. Rable, *God's Almost Chosen Peoples*, 37, 46, 60–61; Gienapp, *Origins of Republican Party*, 95; Gerald Fogarty, S.J, *Commonwealth Catholicism* (Notre Dame, Ind.: University of Notre Dame Press, 2001), 139; *BQR*, July 1860; Carey, *Orestes A. Brownson: American*

Religious Weathervane, 267–68; *Catholic Herald* (Philadelphia), January 28, February 11, 1860. Perhaps like many native and foreign-born Americans more concerned with personal and family matters, immigrant Catholics in their letters home during this period often conveyed a lack of concern about the political crisis, especially if the writer lived far from the Border States. Katherina Löwen, a resident of Detroit, wrote to her relatives back in Germany in late March without once mentioning the larger political turmoil going on in the United States. Robert Rossi, a Lutheran, likewise wrote to his sister about drinking punch and playing dominoes rather than about political events. Of course no one knew a giant war was about to break out only weeks later. Katharina Löwen to Her Parents and Sister, March 21, 1861, Löwen Papers, and Robert Rossi to Elise Rossi, March 14, 1861, Rossi Papers, Auswandererbriefesammlung, Gotha Research Library, Gotha, Germany.

    4. *NYFJ*, April 7, June 16, 30, July 14, August 4, November 3, 1860; *The Pilot* (Boston), January 28, February 18, May 5, 26, October 20, November 3, 1860; Hennesey, *American Catholics*, 147–48; McGreevy, *Catholicism and American Freedom*, 60–64; Kenny, *American Irish*, 82–86, 118; Walter D. Kamphoefner and Wolfgang Helbich, eds., *Germans in the Civil War: The Letters They Wrote Home* (Chapel Hill: University of North Carolina Press, 2006), 298–302.

    5. *The Pilot* (Boston), November 17, 1860; *New York Tablet*, November 17, 1860, January 19, 1861; *The Catholic* (Pittsburgh), November 24, December 8, 29, 1860, January 5, 1861; *Katholische Kirchen-Zeitung* (Baltimore and New York), November 11, 1860; *Catholic Herald*, November 17, 1860.

    6. This argument that evangelical Protestantism was to blame for much of the nation's troubles in 1860–61 carried on into the war. For an in-depth discussion, see Judith Conrad Wimmer, "American Catholic Interpretations of the Civil War" (Ph.D. diss., Drew University, 1980), 280–91. For a modern historical criticism of evangelical reformers' roles in bringing about sectional discord and social strife which echoes arguments that some mid-nineteenth century Catholics made themselves, see Goldfield, *America Aflame*, 1–16, 17–26, 89–94, 124–25, 170; *NYFJ*, November 17, 1860; *Louisville Guardian*, November 24, 1860, January 12, February 16, 23, 1861; *Catholic Telegraph* (Cincinnati), December 1, 1860, April 13, 1861; *BQR*, April 1861; Rable, *God's Almost Chosen Peoples*, 37, 46, 60–61.

    7. *The Pilot* (Boston), December 1, 15, 1860; *Catholic Mirror* (Baltimore), December 1, 15, 1860; M. Courtney Jenkins is listed as a slaveholder in the 1840 and 1850 censuses; in 1860 he no longer claims any slaves. See M. Courtney Jenkins's Federal Census records of 1840, 1850, and 1860.

    8. *Catholic Telegraph* (Cincinnati), January 5, 1861; *The Catholic* (Pittsburgh), December 29, 1860; *The Pilot* (Boston), January 19, 1861; *NYFJ*, January 12, 1861; *Louisville Guardian*, January 12, 1861.

    9. *Catholic Telegraph* (Cincinnati), March 30, 1861; Bp. Spalding to Abp. Purcell, April 11, 1861, ACI.

    10. *Louisville Guardian*, April 27, 1861; Martin J. Spalding, April 1861, May 5, 1861, in *Bishop M. J. Spalding Journal, 1860–1864* (hereafter *Spalding Journal*), Catholic University of America Archives, Washington, D.C. (hereafter CUA).

11. Thomas W. Spalding, *Martin John Spalding: American Churchman* (Washington, D.C.: Catholic University Press, 1973), 1–2, 129; *Spalding Journal*, August 8, December 1861, January 15, 1862.

12. *Louisville Guardian*, April 27, 1861, May 4, 18, June 22, 1861; *Catholic Mirror* (Baltimore), April 20, 1861; Fogarty, *Commonwealth Catholicism*, 145–47. Not long after the war began, the *Louisville Guardian* ceased publication because wartime disruptions prevented reliable delivery to its subscribers farther south. Willging and Hatzfeld, "Kentucky," in *Catholic Serials of the Nineteenth Century*, 2nd ser., Part 12, pp. 36–37.

13. Fogarty, *Commonwealth Catholicism*, 143–47; James M. McPherson, *The Battle Cry of Freedom* (New York: Oxford University Press, 1988), 285; *Catholic Mirror* (Baltimore), April 27, June 8, August 3, 1861; James J. McGovern, D.D., ed., *The Life and Letters of Eliza Allen Starr* (Chicago: Lakeside Press, 1905), 148, 162–63; Abp. Kenrick to Bp. Spalding, December 2, 1862, Archdiocese of Baltimore Collection, University of Notre Dame Archives, Notre Dame, Ind. (hereafter known as ABA). The two men apparently did not discuss the war with each other, for the *Mirror's* editor admitted he did not know what Kenrick thought of the conflict and reminded readers of his editorials that he was simply expressing his own opinions, not the archbishop's.

14. *New York Times*, May 29, 1861; James F. Simon, *Lincoln and Chief Justice Taney: Slavery, Secession, and the President's War Powers* (New York: Simon & Schuster, 2006), 186–98, 206–32; Mark E. Neely, Jr., *Lincoln and the Triumph of the Nation: Constitutional Conflict in the American Civil War* (Chapel Hill: University of North Carolina Press, 2011), 64–71, 90–95, 201–4.

15. Bruce, *Harp and the Eagle*, 50–52.

16. *Katholische Kirchen-Zeitung* (New York), November 11, 1860, April 18, 1861; *Der Wahrheits Freund* (Cincinnati), April 25, May 9, 1861. James T. Fisher claims that 175,000 German Catholics volunteered but provides no citation for this figure; it is unlikely they served in such numbers, considering that at most 216,000 German-born men served in the army, most German Catholics were Democrats and thus less enthusiastic about the war, and German Catholics are commonly estimated as constituting only one-third of German immigrants to the United States in the 1850s. Fisher, *Communion of Immigrants*, 57; Stephen D. Engle, "Yankee Dutchmen: Germans, the Union, and the Construction of Wartime Identity," in Ural, ed., *Civil War Citizens*, 19; Conzen, "Immigrant Religion and the Public Sphere," 77–78.

17. *Catholic Telegraph* (Cincinnati), March 30, April 20, May 4, 11, 18, 30, 1861; Bp. Spalding to Abp. Purcell, April 21, 1861, ACI; Abp. Purcell to Abraham Lincoln, April 18, 1861, Abraham Lincoln Papers, Library of Congress, Washington, D.C. Scammon got the appointment and served under his old friend Rosecrans in West Virginia. It should be noted that Spalding composed the bishops' pro-peace letter. *Spalding Journal*, May 5, 1861.

18. *NYFJ*, April 20, 1861.

19. *Katholische Kirchen-Zeitung* (New York), May 16, 1861; *Metropolitan Record* (New York), April 27, May 11, 18, 1861.

20. *The Pilot* (Boston), April 27, 1861.

21. *New York Tablet*, April 20, 27, May 4, 1861; *Catholic Telegraph* (Cincinnati) (reprinted from *Catholic Herald* [Philadelphia]), May 11, 1861.

22. *Catholic Telegraph* (Cincinnati), September 14, 1861; Hennesey, *American Catholics*, 149.

23. Abp. Hughes to Card. Barnabo, February 13, 1862, John Hughes Papers, CUA; Hennesey, *American Catholics*, 149.

24. *The Catholic* (Pittsburgh), April 20, 27, 1861; Hennesey, *American Catholics*, 151.

25. Bp. Michael Domenec to Abp. Francis Kenrick, April (?) and May 16, 1861, ABA.

26. *Catholic Herald*, February 2, April 20, August 3, 1861; Bishop James Wood of Philadelphia eventually found a pro-Union editor to replace the pro-southern editor John Duffey. Joseph George, Jr., "Philadelphia's Catholic Herald: The Civil War Years," *Pennsylvania Magazine of History and Biography* 103 (1979): 196–206; Bp. Domenec to Abp. Francis Kenrick, May 16, 1861, ABA.

27. *BQR*, July 1861; Patrick W. Carey, "Orestes Brownson and the Civil War," *U.S. Catholic Historian* 31 (Winter 2013): 6–7; Holt, *Political Crisis of the 1850s*, 189–90; Foner, *Free Soil, Free Labor, Free Men*, 90–102; Leonard L. Richards, *The Slave Power: The Free North and Southern Domination, 1780–1860* (Baton Rouge: Louisiana State University Press, 2000), 1–16.

28. *BQR*, October 1861; Henry S. Hewit to Orestes Brownson, October 6, 1861, M. L. Linton to Brownson, October 16, 1861, Eli Nichols to Brownson, October 22, 1861, R. J. Howard et al. to Brownson, November 10, 1861, BRO; Stout, *Upon the Altar of the Nation*, 39.

29. Abp. Peter Kenrick to Abp. Purcell, November 9, 1853, CACI; Rev. Charles A. Costello, "Episcopate of Rt. Rev. J. M. Young, Bishop of Erie, Pennsylvania, 1854–1866" (M.A. diss., University of Notre Dame, 1951), 59, 159–60; Ellen Sherman to Charles Ewing, July 17, 1861, Charles Ewing Papers, Library of Congress, Washington, D.C. (hereafter LOC: Charles Ewing Papers).

30. Bruce, *Harp and the Eagle*, 64–66; Keating, "Give Us War in Our Time," 26; McGreevy, *Catholicism and American Freedom*, 72; *Chicago Tribune*, May 30, June 4, 1861; Amos A. Lawrence quoted in Thomas H. O'Connor, *Fitzpatrick's Boston, 1846–1866* (Boston: Northeastern University Press, 1984), 197.

31. *New York Times*, April 23, October 11, 1861; John Murray, "John Baptist Purcell," in *The Catholic Encyclopedia*, vol. 12 (New York: Robert Appleton Company, 1911), http://www.newadvent.org/cathen/12570a.htm.

32. *New York Times*, September 27, 1861; Abraham Lincoln to Archbishop Hughes, October 21, 1861, Abraham Lincoln Papers, Library of Congress, Washington, D.C.; Michael J. Bennett, "Saving Jack: Religion, Benevolent Organizations, and Union Sailors during the Civil War," in Paul A. Cimbala and Randall M. Miller, eds., *Union Soldiers and the Northern Home Front: Wartime Experiences, Postwar Adjustments* (New York: Fordham University Press, 2002), 235–36, 245–47.

33. *New York Tablet*, April 27, 1861; *Catholic Telegraph* (Cincinnati), April 20, 1861; *Der Wahrheits Freund*, April 25, 1861; Bruce, *Harp and the Eagle*, 51–52; *New York Times*, April 23, 1861; *BQR*, October 1861.

34. Julie Mujic, "Between Campus and War: Students, Patriotism, and Education at Midwestern Universities during the American Civil War" (Ph.D. diss., Kent State University, 2012), 126–29; *Catholic Mirror* (Baltimore), July 20, 27, 1861; James S. Ruby, ed., *Blue and Gray: Georgetown University and the Civil War* (Baltimore: Garamond Press, 1961), 1–6.

35. Fr. John McCaffrey to Abp. Purcell, September 26, 1861, ACI; Gilbert J. Garraghan, S.J., *The Jesuits of the Middle United States*, 3 vols. (Chicago: Loyola University Press, 1984), 2:147–49, 156–58; Phillip Thomas Tucker, *The Confederacy's Fighting Chaplain Father John B. Bannon* (Tuscaloosa: University of Alabama Press, 1992), 15–17.

36. Edward Sorin, *The Chronicles of Notre Dame Du Lac*, ed. James T. Connelly (Notre Dame, Ind.: University of Notre Dame Press, 1992), 290; James M. Schmidt, *Notre Dame and the Civil War: Marching Onward to Victory* (Charleston: History Press, 2010), 22–24; Mujic, "Between Campus and War," 149.

37. McGreevy, *Catholicism and American Freedom*, 68–69; *NYFJ*, May 4, July 27, 1861, February 7, 1863; *Catholic Mirror* (Baltimore), July 27, 1861; William Nolan (Pennsylvania) to McMaster, June 7, 1861, W. F. McGill (Kentucky) to McMaster, June 15, 1861, Bp. Thomas L. Grace (Minnesota) to McMaster, August 3, 1861, Edward Donnely (New York) to McMaster, August 31, 1861, James A. McMaster Papers, University of Notre Dame Archives, Notre Dame, Ind. (hereafter MMA); *Metropolitan Record* (New York), August 3, 17, 24, 1861; *Catholic Mirror* (Baltimore), August 10, 1861.

38. *Catholic Telegraph* (Cincinnati), August 10, 1861; Abp. Hughes to William H. Seward, July 22, 1861, Seward Papers, University of Rochester Archives, Rochester, N.Y.; Maria Ewing to Charles Ewing, August 1, 1861, LOC: Charles Ewing Papers.

39. *The Pilot* (Boston), August 3, 10, 1861; Christian G. Samito, ed., *Commanding Boston's Irish Ninth: The Civil War Letters of Colonel Patrick R. Guiney, Ninth Massachusetts Volunteer Infantry* (New York: Fordham University Press, 1998), 24; *New York Tablet*, August 3, 1861; *Catholic Telegraph* (Cincinnati), August 3, 10, 1861; *Metropolitan Record* (New York), August 3, 17, 1861.

40. Joseph Dünnebacke blamed the nation's troubles on the abolitionists, "which include a lot of European 48ers." Dünnebacke's linking of antislavery radicalism in the United States to political radicalism in Germany reflected a common Catholic belief that viewed both movements as similarly hostile to social order and the Catholic Church. Nikolaus Pack, a coal miner near Pittsburgh, also called the war "a nice present from Europe that the dear 48ers, those heroes of freedom who have broken with God and their respective monarchs, have brought into this beautiful country." Kamphoefner and Helbich, eds., *Germans in the Civil War*, 117–19, 222–23, 339–41.

41. *New York Times*, April 23, September 24, 1861; Bruce, *Harp and the Eagle*, 3–6, 59–60, 63, 83–84, 145–47; McPherson, *For Cause and Comrades*, 113–14; William Marvel, *Mr. Lincoln Goes to War* (New York: Houghton Mifflin, 2006), 50–62; Bp. Young to Society for the Propagation of the Faith, July 1, 1861, June 30, 1862, Abp. Purcell to Society for the Propagation of the Faith, November 21, 1861, Society for the Propagation of the Faith Collection, University of Notre Dame Archives, Notre Dame, Ind. (hereafter PFP).

42. Peter to Margaret Welsh, February 8, 22, 1863, quoted in Peter Welsh, *Irish Green and Union Blue: The Civil War Letters of Peter Welsh, Color Sergeant, 28th Regiment, Mas-*

sachusetts Volunteers, ed. Lawrence F. Kohl (New York: Fordham University Press, 1986), 6, 69–70, 73–75; Jane McMahon to Fr. Corby, August 26, 1863, William Corby Papers, Indiana Province Archives: Congregation of Holy Cross, Notre Dame, Ind. (hereafter IPAC); Rosana Moleny to Fr. Corby, August 23, 1862, William Corby Papers, University of Notre Dame Archives, Notre Dame, Ind. (hereafter COR); Nina Silber, *Daughters of the Union: Northern Women Fight the Civil War* (Cambridge, Mass.: Harvard University Press, 2005), 1–2. For more on working-class women's dissatisfaction with the war, see Judith Giesberg, *Army at Home: Women and the Civil War on the Northern Home Front* (Chapel Hill: University of North Carolina Press, 2009), 119–42. For a short treatment of lay and religious Catholic women during the war, see James J. Kenneally, *The History of American Catholic Women* (New York: Crossroad Publishing Company, 1990), 80–86.

43. *New York Times*, June 21, 1861; Captain John A. Duff to Judge Daly, September 3, 1862, Charles P. Daly Papers, New York Public Library Archives and Manuscripts.

44. Mary Elizabeth Noyes to William S. Rosecrans, January 20, 1863, Box 8, UCLA-Rosecrans Papers; Garesché, *Biography of Lieut. Col. Julius P. Garesché*, 442–43; Schmidt, *Notre Dame and the Civil War*, 87–88.

45. Ellen Sherman to Charles Ewing, July 24, 1861, LOC: Charles Ewing Papers; Ellen Sherman to William T. Sherman, February 6, 1861, William T. Sherman Family Papers, University of Notre Dame Archives, Notre Dame, Ind. (hereafter SHR). For more on Ellen Sherman and the rest of the Ewing and Sherman families during the war, see Kenneth J. Heineman, *Civil War Dynasty: The Ewing Family of Ohio* (New York: New York University Press, 2013); and William M. Ferraro, "More Than a General's Wife: Ellen Ewing Sherman," *Timeline* 17, no. 1 (2000): 18–33. Ellen Sherman and other lay Catholic women have largely been ignored in gender studies of the war. Ellen, whose papers are readily available at the University of Notre Dame Archives, is only mentioned once in Mary E. Massey's *Women and the Civil War*. The story of Catholic laywomen is a promising avenue for future research into the Catholic experience of the war. As Chapter 4 will argue, Catholic female religious have been much more thoroughly studied, although they, too, are often left out of the most important gender histories of the war. Mary E. Massey, *Women in the Civil War* (1966; repr., Lincoln, Neb.: Bison Books, 1994), 239–40.

46. U.S. Sanitary Commission Fair Flier (1865), Mulligan Papers, Box 3, Folder 5, Chicago History Museum, Research Center; Silber, *Daughters of the Union*, 173–74, 188–89.

47. Henry Major to Abp. Francis Kenrick, December 20, 1861, ABA.

48. Ellen Sherman to William T. Sherman, June 14, 1862, SHR.

3. Catholic Soldiers in the Union Army

1. Although previous historians have attempted to explore Christianity's impact on Union soldiers, scholars such as Steven Woodworth often ignore Catholics due to their status as a religious minority. This is only slowly changing as studies by Randall Miller and George Rable have started to focus on them specifically or in comparison with soldiers of other faiths. Woodworth, *While God Is Marching On*, ix; Miller, "Catholic Religion, Irish Ethnicity, and the Civil War," in Miller, Stout, and Wilson, eds., *Religion and the American Civil War*; Rable, *God's Almost Chosen Peoples*, 6.

2. The earliest study of the brigade was written just two years after the war ended by a former staff member, David Power Conyngham. See Conyngham, *The Irish Brigade and Its Campaigns*, ed. Lawrence Frederick Kohl (1867; repr., New York: Fordham University Press, 1994). Since then a large number of books, and periodical articles, not to mention popular paintings, reenactment groups, and websites, have covered the brigade and the exploits of its commander, Thomas Meagher. Some of the most recent books are Thomas J. Craughwell, *The Greatest Brigade: How the Irish Brigade Cleared the Way to Victory in the American Civil War* (Minneapolis: Fair Winds Press, 2011); Paul R. Wylie, *The Irish General: Thomas Francis Meagher* (Norman: University of Oklahoma Press, 2007); and Phillip Thomas Tucker, *"God Help the Irish!": The History of the Irish Brigade* (Abilene, Tex.: McWhiney Foundation Press, 2007).

3. Lawrence Frederick Kohl, "Introduction," in Conyngham, *The Irish Brigade and Its Campaigns*, ix–x; Bruce, *Harp and the Eagle*, 119–20; Lonn, *Foreigners in the Union Army and Navy*, 578; Miller, "Catholic Religion, Irish Ethnicity, and the Civil War," in Miller, Stout, and Wilson, eds., *Religion and the American Civil War*, 265.

4. Kamphoefner and Helbich, eds., *Germans in the Civil War*, 7, 10–12.

5. Bruce, *Harp and the Eagle*, 58–63; Burton, *Melting Pot Soldiers*, 47–71; *BQR*, October 1861; *Der Wahrheits Freund* (Cincinnati), April 25, 1861.

6. Lonn, *Foreigners in the Union Army and Navy*, 659–62; Burton, *Melting Pot Soldiers*, 213–33; Conyngham, *Irish Brigade and Its Campaigns*, xii.

7. J. C. Fitzgibbon to James Mulligan, February 10, 1862, Mulligan Papers, Chicago History Museum Research Center. The 23rd Illinois Regiment was known, at least in the Midwest, as the "Irish Brigade" during the war, even though it was only a regiment-sized unit. The nickname was simply meant to invoke the exploits of previous "Irish Brigades" from European wars, including a unit known by the same name serving in the papal army in Italy just before the outbreak of war in the United States. The Irish Brigade of the Army of the Potomac, which was actually a brigade-sized unit with several regiments, likewise consciously used the name to promote Irish enlistment. *The Pilot* (Boston), July 7, 1860; Bruce, *Harp and the Eagle*, 63.

8. David P. Conyngham, "Chap. 14: Paul Gillen," in "Soldiers of the Cross: Heroism of the Cross; or, Nuns and Priests of the Battlefield" (unpublished MS, ca. 1883), David P. Conyngham Papers, University of Notre Dame Archives, Notre Dame, Ind. (hereafter "Soldiers of the Cross"); Ron Gancas, *Dear Teres: The Civil War Letters of Andrew Joseph Duff and Dennis Dugan of Company F, the Pennsylvania Seventy-Eighth Infantry*, ed. Dan Coyle, Sr. (Chicora, Pa.: Mechling Bookbindery, 1999), 71.

9. Dom Aidan Henry Germain, S.T.L, M.A., J.C.B., "Catholic Military and Naval Chaplains, 1776–1917" (Ph.D. diss., Catholic University of America, 1929), 84–85; Betty Ann McNeil, D.C., ed. *Dear Masters: Daughters of Charity of Saint Vincent de Paul, Civil War Nurses* (Hanover, Pa.: Sheridan Press, 2011), 36; Fr. A. M. Paresce, S.J., to Fr. Francis McAtee, January 9, 1862, Jesuit Maryland Province Collection, Georgetown University Archives and Special Collections, Washington, D.C.; Lonn, *Foreigners in the Union Army and Navy*, 311–17; Adam Muenzenberger to Mrs. Muenzenberger, May 23, 1863, "Civil War Letters of Corporal Adam Muenzenberger, 1862," http://www.russscott .com/~rscott/26thwis/26pgam62.htm. Given the relative lack of German Catholic priests

in the Union Army, perhaps it should not be surprising then that letters from German Catholic soldiers in the Auswandererbriefesammlung, a collection of letters in Gotha, Germany, that are the best single source of manuscripts on German Americans from the nineteenth century, contain no references to chaplains, going to mass, or practicing Catholic devotions.

10. *Louisville Guardian*, May 25, 1861; *The Pilot* (Boston), April 27, July 6, 1861.

11. *BQR*, October 1861.

12. Peter Cozzens, *No Better Place to Die: The Battle of Stones River* (Urbana: University of Illinois Press, 1990), 204–7; Lamers, *Edge of Glory*, 245–47; George L. Hartstuff to Rosecrans, January 8, 1863, Box 8, UCLA-Rosecrans Papers; James Garfield to Lucretia Garfield, January 26, 27, 1863, Garfield to Austin Garfield, February 18, 1863, quoted in Frederick D. Williams, ed., *The Wild Life of the Army: Civil War Letters of James A. Garfield* (East Lansing: Michigan State University Press, 1964), 225–28, 236–37; *Harper's Weekly*, January 17, 1863; *New York Times*, January 7, 1863; *Catholic Telegraph* (Cincinnati), January 7, 1863; *Catholic Herald*, January 31, 1863 (Philadelphia). Fr. Cooney to Owen Cooney, July 17, 1863, quoted in Thomas McAvoy, C.S.C., "The War Letters of Father Peter Paul Cooney of the Congregation of the Holy Cross," *Records of the American Catholic Historical Society of Philadelphia* 44 (1933): 161–68.

13. Garesché, *Biography of Lieut. Col. Julius P. Garesché*, 439, 446; *The Catholic* (Pittsburgh), January 24, 1863; *Catholic Mirror* (Baltimore), May 23, 1863; *Harper's Weekly*, October 19, 1861; *Chicago Tribune*, November 9, 1861, February 28, 1864; *The Pilot* (Boston), August 13, 20, 27, 1864.

14. *The Pilot* (Boston), August 30, September 6, 1862, September 3, 1864; *Catholic Telegraph* (Cincinnati), January 8, 1862; *Harper's Weekly*, August 30, September 6, 1862; *New York Herald*, March 18, 1863; *New York Times*, October 15, 1861; *Boston Daily Transcript*, November 18, 1864; Bruce, *Harp and the Eagle*, 62, 78–84, 110–11.

15. Bruce, *Harp and the Eagle*, 73; *Harper's Weekly*, August 3, 1861; James Shields to Judge Daly, October 14, 1861, James Shields to Mrs. Daly, August 8, 1862, Charles P. Daly Papers, New York Public Library Archives and Manuscripts; *Chicago Tribune*, June 27, 1862; *Weekly Patriot and Union*, July 3, 1862; William Henry Condon, *Life of Major-General James Shields: Hero of Three Wars and Senator from Three States* (Chicago: Blakely Printing, 1900), 260–61.

16. Burton, *Melting Pot Soldiers*, 118–19, 122–25; Bruce, *Harp and the Eagle*, 89, 272, 276–77; Charles Stone to Abp. Odin, October 25, 1864, ANO; McPherson, *Battle Cry of Freedom*, 362–63; Bruce Tap, *Over Lincoln's Shoulder: The Committee on the Conduct of the War* (Lawrence: University Press of Kansas, 1998), 55–80; *New York Times*, October 24, 1863; Committee of 738 Men to Abraham Lincoln, November 4, 1864, Box 49, UCLA-Rosecrans Papers; William B. Kurtz, "'The Perfect Model of a Christian Hero': The Faith, Anti-Slaveryism, and Post-war Legacy of William S. Rosecrans," *U.S. Catholic Historian* 21, no. 1 (2013): 90–92.

17. W. Springer Menge and J. August Shimrak, eds., *The Civil War Notebook of Daniel Chisholm: A Chronicle of Daily Life in the Union Army, 1864–1865* (New York: Orion Books, 1989), ix–xxii, 196; St. Clair A. Mulholland, *The Story of the 116th Regiment Pennsylvania Volunteers in the War of the Rebellion*, ed. Lawrence Frederick Kohl (1903;

repr., New York: Fordham University Press, 1996), x–xi; Kevin E. O'Brien, ed., *My Life in the Irish Brigade: The Civil War Memoirs of Private William McCarter, 116th Pennsylvania Infantry* (Campbell, Calif.: Savas Publishing, 1996), 49–50, 241.

18. Peter to Margaret Welsh, February 3, 1863, quoted in Welsh, *Irish Green and Union Blue*, xiv–xv, xxi, 64–68; Samito, ed., *Commanding Boston's Irish Ninth*, 11, 47, 161, 246

19. Peter to Margaret Welsh, February 3, 1863, quoted in Welsh, *Irish Green and Union Blue*, 2–3, 64–68; Walter to Richard, July 29, 1863, Walter Elliott Papers, Paulist Archives, Washington, D.C. For more on conservative European Catholics' opinions and their general dislike of the North and the Lincoln government, see Noll, *Civil War as a Theological Crisis*, 138–55.

20. Peter to Margaret Welsh, January 27, April 26, October 7, 1863, April 14, 1864, quoted in ibid., 21, 60–61, 88, 128–29, 150–51.

21. *Der Wahrheits Freund* (Cincinnati), August 6, 1862; *Catholic Telegraph* (Cincinnati), August 13, 1862; Bp. Rosecrans to Abp. Purcell, August 10, 1862, ACI; *History of Saint John's Classis* (Cleveland: Central Publishing House, 1921), 87; Whitelaw Reid, *Ohio in the War: Her Statesmen, Her Generals, and Soldiers: The History of Her Regiments, and Other Military Organizations*, 2 vols. (Cincinnati: Moore, Wilstach & Baldwin, 1868), 1:73, 2:579. To be fair, Reid noted that a similar attempt to raise a second Irish Catholic regiment from the city, the 109th Ohio, failed completely, drawing anger and accusations of draft-dodging from the state adjutant's office.

22. *Daniel Finn Diary*, May 28, 1862, U.S. Military History Institute, Carlisle, Pa.; Edward Brownson to Sarah N. Brownson, January 20, July 25, 1864, BRO; William White to His Family, May 1, [1862?], William White Papers, Philadelphia Archdiocese Historical Research Center (hereafter PAHRC); Robert O'Reilly to His Mother, March 13, 15, April 20, 1864, Robert O'Reilly Papers, PAHRC.

23. Samito, ed., *Commanding Boston's Irish Ninth*, 225–26; Edward Brownson to Sarah N. Brownson, January 28, March 6, August 20, 1864, BRO.

24. Kamphoefner and Helbich, eds., *Germans in the Civil War*, 366–68, 372–74.

25. Peter to Margaret Welsh, undated fragment ca. February 1863, February 3, 8, 1863, quoted in Welsh, *Irish Green and Union Blue*, 62–70; Gary W. Gallagher, *The Union War* (Cambridge, Mass.: Harvard University Press, 2011), 103; Gancas, *Dear Teres*, 243–44. Because so few of the Catholic soldiers' letters examined here discuss how they voted in 1864, determining how many Catholic soldiers voted for Lincoln is extremely difficult. Even though a number of Irishmen, like other northern soldiers, came to see attacking slavery in order to win the war as justified and increasingly supported the Republican Party, the majority probably voted for McClellan as did the majority of Irish Catholic civilians. For example, Colonel Guiney admitted that he was unique in being an Irish Catholic Republican and in supporting Lincoln's presidential campaign in 1864, for "the great bulk of my countrymen differ with me in politics." McPherson, *Battle Cry of Freedom*, 804–805; Samito, ed., *Commanding Boston's Irish Ninth*, xxvii.

26. Peter to Margaret Welsh, October 23, 1862, quoted in Welsh, *Irish Green and Union Blue*, 27–29; Samito, ed., *Commanding Boston's Irish Ninth*, 161.

27. Samito, ed., *Commanding Boston's Irish Ninth*, 243–47.

28. Keating, "Give Us War in Our Time," 277–78; Kamphoefner and Helbich, eds., *Germans in the Civil War*, 133–35.

29. Richard Elliott to Walter Elliott, July 21, 1863, Walter to Richard, July 29, 1863, Pass for Walter Elliott signed by General Martin T. McMahon, December 2, 186[4], Walter Elliott Papers, Paulist Archives, Washington, D.C.; Condon, *Life of Major-General James Shields*, 235.

30. Edward Brownson to Brownson, May 4, 1863, Stanton to Brownson, May 28, 1863, Edward to Sarah Brownson, May 10, 1864, untitled newspaper clippings from August 26, 27, 31, 1864, *New York Tablet*, September 3, 1864, Fr. George McCloskey to Brownson, August 30, 1864, BRO; Carey, *Orestes A. Brownson: American Religious Weathervane*, 280–81.

31. Peter to Margaret Welsh, December 25, 1862, quoted in Welsh, *Irish Green and Union Blue*, 41–43, 156–58.

4. Priests and Nuns in the Army

1. David Endres, "'With a Father's Affection': Chaplain William T. O'Higgins and the Tenth Ohio Volunteer Infantry," *U.S. Catholic Historian* 31 (Winter 2013): 107; Gancas, *Dear Teres*, 15. Sean Fabun recently argued that "many Catholics, particularly the clergy, saw the American Civil War as an opportunity to demonstrate their legitimacy as Americans." While a number of them took great pride in pointing to conversions or changed opinions about Catholicism, they were not "hugely influential" in dispelling prejudice because there were too few of them and they served for too short of a time. They put most of their efforts toward maintaining the faith of soldiers who were already Catholics rather than in trying to dispel nativism. Sean Fabun, "Catholic Chaplains in the Civil War," *Catholic Historical Review* 99 (October 2013): 675, 701.

2. Maher, *To Bind Up the Wounds*, 69–70, 120.

3. Germain, "Catholic Military and Naval Chaplains," 42–45; John W. Brinsfield, William C. Davis, Benedict Maryniak, and James I. Robertson, Jr., eds., *Faith in the Fight: Civil War Chaplains* (Mechanicsburg, Pa.: Stackpole Books, 2003), 9–17.

4. Hugh Harlin quoted in Bruce, *Harp and the Eagle*, 108; Fr. James Fullerton to Abp. Hughes, John Hughes Papers, CUA; Lincoln to Fullerton, August 28, 1861, "The Papers of Abraham Lincoln: New Documents," http://www.papersofabrahamlincoln.org/New_Documents.htm.

5. Fr. Hecker to Bp. Francis McFarland, July 11, 1861, Fr. Augustine Hewit to Bp. McFarland, July 26, 1861, Diocese of Hartford Collection, University of Notre Dame Archives, Notre Dame, Ind. (hereafter DHT); David O'Brien, *Isaac Hecker: An American Catholic* (New York: Paulist Press, 1992), 191–92; Father Purcell quoted in Endres, "With a Father's Affection," 103–4; Abp. Purcell to William S. Rosecrans, March 13, 1863, Box 8, UCLA-Rosecrans Papers; Abp. Hughes to Abp. Francis Kenrick, April 29, 1861, ABA; Abp. Hughes to Gen. Scott, May 7, 1861, Gen. Scott to Abp. Hughes, May 13, 1861, John Hughes Papers, CUA.

6. Abp. John Ireland, "Civil War Memoirs," 4–5, in Peter Paul Cooney Papers, University of Notre Dame, Notre Dame, Ind. (hereafter COO); Warren B. Armstrong, *For

Courageous Fighting and Confident Dying: Union Chaplains in the Civil War (Lawrence: University Press of Kansas, 1998), 18. For more on John Ireland's ten-month-long stint as a Union chaplain and its importance to him in his old age, see Marvin R. O'Connell, *John Ireland and the American Catholic Church* (St. Paul: Minnesota Historical Society Press, 1988), 61–87.

7. This number is derived from dividing the estimated two hundred thousand Catholic soldiers in the Union Army—which had about 2.2 million men in it altogether—by the estimated fifty-three official Catholic Union chaplains. By contrast, in 1861 the church numbered 3.1 million believers with 2,317 priests, yielding a ratio of 1,337 laypeople to each Catholic priest in the United States. This gives an idea of how much harder it would have been for a Catholic soldier to practice his faith in the army than as a civilian. Miller, "Catholic Religion, Irish Ethnicity, and the Civil War," in Miller, Stout, and Wilson, eds., *Religion and the American Civil War*, 265; Blied, *Catholics and the Civil War*, 108; Shaughnessy, *Has the Immigrant Kept the Faith?* 262; *Metropolitan Catholic Almanac and Laity's Directory*, 231.

8. Ireland, "Civil War Memoirs," 1, COO; Oliver Morton to Abraham Lincoln, February 3, 1862, COO; Abp. Purcell to Propaganda Fide, November 29, 1861, Congregatio de Propaganda Fide Collection, University of Notre Dame Archives, Notre Dame, Ind. (hereafter PRF); Abp. Hughes to Abp. Francis Kenrick, April 29, May 9, October 21, 1861, ABA; Abraham Lincoln to Archbishop Hughes, October 21, 1861, Abp. Francis Kenrick to Lincoln, October 24, 1861, Abraham Lincoln Papers, Library of Congress, Washington, D.C.; Abp. Hughes to Gen. Scott, May 7, 1861, Gen. Scott to Abp. Hughes, May 13, 1861, Lincoln to Abp. Hughes, October 21, 1861, John Hughes Papers, CUA; Paresce to Fr. McAtee, December 7, 1862, Jesuit Maryland Province Collection, Colonel Julius Garesché to Fr. Early, July 22, 1861, General Amiel Whipple to Fr. Early, March 31, 1863, Early Papers, Georgetown University Archives and Special Collections, Washington, D.C.

9. Raymond A. Schroth, S.J., *Fordham: A History and Memoir* (Chicago: Loyola University Press, 2002), 169–78; Ruby, ed., *Blue and Gray*, 42–43; Robert Emmett Curran, *A History of Georgetown University: From Academy to University, 1789–1889* (Washington, D.C.: Georgetown University Press, 2010), 246; Julius Garesché to Father Early, July 22, 1861 (and note attached to display case), Early Papers, Georgetown University Archives and Special Collections, Washington, D.C.; William Corby, *Memoirs of Chaplain Life: Three Years with the Irish Brigade in the Army of the Potomac*, ed. Lawrence F. Kohl (New York: Fordham University Press, 1992), 272; Fr. Sorin to Abp. Purcell, January 14, 1862, ACI.

10. Sorin, *Chronicles of Notre Dame Du Lac*, 277–81. Archbishop Ireland, a former Civil War chaplain himself, praised Sorin at the latter's golden jubilee celebration of his fiftieth year as a priest in 1888: "Fathers Corby and Cooney are with us this morning to tell the need there was of priests among our soldiers, and of the great things done for religion by themselves and their fellow-chaplains. There were other priests and other sisters in the war; [but] those of the Holy Cross made up the greater part of the roster. None excelled them in daring and religious fervor. No other order, no diocese, made . . . sacrifices as did that of the Holy Cross. Father Sorin, you saved the honor of the

Church." Marvin O'Connell, *Edward Sorin* (Notre Dame, Ind.: University of Notre Dame Press, 2001), 706.

11. *Catholic Telegraph* (Cincinnati), January 15, 1862; Bp. Lefevere to Abp. Purcell, March 16, April 5, 1861, Bp. Spalding to Abp. Purcell, December 18, 1861, April 25, 1862, ACI; Fr. James Dillon to an unknown CSC priest, July 20, 1863, Box 3, Folder 64, Miscellaneous Manuscript Collection, University of Notre Dame Archives, Notre Dame, Ind. (hereafter known as CMM); Fr. J. A. Naltes to Corby, March 2, 1864, Sorin to Corby, March 10, 1864, COR; Germain, "Catholic Military and Naval Chaplains," 69.

12. Fr. William T. O'Higgins to Abp. Purcell, April 17, May 24, 1861, ACI; Endres, "With a Father's Affection," 99–102; Peter Koch to Bp. Lefevere, December 29, 1860, June 20, September 17, 1861, Diocese of Detroit Collection, University of Notre Dame Archives, Notre Dame, Ind. (hereafter DET); Bp. John McCloskey to Abp. Purcell, August 9, 1863, ACI.

13. *Catholic Mirror* (Baltimore), June 29, 1861; Abp. Hughes to Abp. Francis Kenrick, July 3, 1861, ABA.

14. Fr. Paresce to Fr. McAtee, January 27, 1862, Fr. McAtee to Fr. Paresce, August 8, 1862, Fr. McAtee to Fr. Clarke, November 14, 1862, Fr. McAtee to Fr. Lancaster, January 15, 1863, Jesuit Maryland Province Collection, Georgetown University Archives and Special Collections, Washington, D.C.; *Woodstock Letters*, vol. 17 (1888), 141; Corby, *Memoirs of Chaplain Life*, 37–38; Conyngham, "Chapter 14: Paul E. Gillen," in "Soldiers of the Cross."

15. Conyngham, "Chapters 1–3: Jeremiah F. Trecy," in "Soldiers of the Cross"; W. D. Bickham, *Rosecrans' Campaign with the Fourteenth Army Corps; or, The Army of the Cumberland: A Narrative of Personal Observations with an Appendix, Consisting of Official Reports of the Battle of Stone River* (Cincinnati: Moore, Wilstach, Keys & Co., 1863), 206; Fr. McAtee to Fr. Lancaster, October 26, 1862, February 18, 20, 1863, Jesuit Maryland Province Collection, Georgetown University Archives and Special Collections, Washington, D.C.; Fr. O'Higgins to Abp. Purcell, November 13, 1863, ACI; Fr. Cooney to Owen Cooney, April 26, 1864, quoted in McAvoy, "War Letters of Father Cooney," 223–24.

16. *Woodstock Letters* (1888), 17:271–72.

17. Conyngham, "Chapter 14: Paul E. Gillen" and "Chapter 5: Joseph Carrier," in "Soldiers of the Cross"; Father Cooney to Owen Cooney, October 2, 1862, quoted in McAvoy, "War Letters of Father Cooney," 67–69.

18. "Obituary: Father Joseph B. O'Hagan," in *Woodstock Letters* (1879), 8:179–80; Conyngham, "Chapter 2: J. F. Trecy," in "Soldiers of the Cross"; Father Cooney to Owen Cooney, January 12, 1863, quoted in McAvoy, "War Letters of Father Cooney," 152.

19. Corby, *Memoirs of Chaplain Life*, 181–86; James Quinlan to Father Corby, August 13, 1893, William Corby Papers, IPAC; According to a pamphlet put out in 1911 commemorating the dedication of the Corby monument in Gettysburg, Corby's insistence that his absolution was meant for all soldiers regardless of faith was not theologically unsound. Both baptized and unbaptized non-Catholics could have received the benefits of general absolution if they sincerely desired to confess their sins before God. "Memorials of the Monument Erected on the Battlefield of Gettysburg to Very Rev. William

Corby, C.S.C.," issued by the Catholic Alumni Sodality of Philadelphia (December 1911), 7–8, in Thomas F. McGrath Papers, Notre Dame Special Collections.

20. Father Emmeran Bliemmel of the 10th Tennessee Infantry was killed by a cannonball at the Battle of Jonesboro while assisting a wounded man. Boniface Wimmer, O.S.B., *Letters of an American Abbot*, ed. Jerome Oetgen (Latrobe, Pa.: Saint Vincent Archabbey Publications, 2008), 264–65, 282; *Woodstock Letters* (1889), 18:4–13, 157–58; Conyngham, "Chapter 10: Fr. Thomas Scully," in "Soldiers of the Cross"; Corby, *Memoirs of Chaplain Life*, 72–76; James Quinlan to Father Corby, August 13, 1893, William Corby Papers, IPAC.

21. Father Cooney to Owen Cooney, January 12, 1863, quoted in McAvoy, "War Letters of Father Cooney," 152; B. F. Mullen, *Stones River Report*, January 5, 1863, in U.S. War Department, *War of the Rebellion: A Compilation of the Official Records of the Union and Confederate Armies* (Washington, D.C., 1887), 1st ser., vol. 20, Part 1, p. 612; Nathan Kimball, January 6, 1865, August G. Tassin, December 19, 1864, U.S. War Department, *War of the Rebellion* (1894), 1st ser., vol. 45, Part 1, pp. 183, 203; Conyngham, "Chapter 3: J. F. Trecy," in "Soldiers of the Cross"; Sorin, *Chronicles of Notre Dame Du Lac*, 280; Arthur J. Hope, C.S.C., *Notre Dame One Hundred Years* (Notre Dame, Ind.: University of Notre Dame Press, 1943), 125–26, 132.

22. Blied, *Catholics and the Civil War*, 108–9; Abp. Francis Kenrick to Lincoln, October 24, 1861, Abraham Lincoln Papers, Library of Congress, Washington, D.C.; Fr. Edward McGlynn to Propaganda Fide, December 30, 1864, Sisters of Charity of New York Archives, Bronx, N.Y.; Ireland, "Civil War Memoirs," 3, Cooney, *Diary*, July 5, 1864, COO.

23. Conyngham, *Soldiers of the Cross*, Chapter 14: Paul E. Gillen; "Letters from a Chaplain in the War of 1861," in *Woodstock Letters*, vol. 16 (1887), 23–24, 248; vol. 17 (1888), 15; vol. 19 (1890), 154; Miller, "Catholic Religion, Irish Ethnicity, and the Civil War," in Miller, Stout, and Wilson, eds., *Religion and the American Civil War*, 270–71; *New York Tablet*, January 28, 1865.

24. Fr. Cooney to Owen Cooney, April 26, 1864, quoted in McAvoy, "War Letters of Father Cooney," 223; *Woodstock Letters*, vol. 18 (1889), 323–24.

25. Fr. Cooney to R. O'Connor, July 16, 1863, COO; Fr. Cooney to Owen Cooney, June 17, 1863, quoted in McAvoy, "War Letters of Father Cooney," 158–59; Corby, *Memoirs of Chaplain Life*, 122–27; Cooney, *Diary*, July 5, 1864, COO; Rable, *God's Almost Chosen Peoples*, 136, 169–70.

26. *Woodstock Letters*, vol. 18 (1889), 10–11; vol. 19 (1890), 22–23; "Obituary: Father Joseph B. O'Hagan," vol. 8 (1879), 179–81; Brinsfield et al., eds., *Faith in the Fight*, 124–25.

27. General Walter C. Whitaker quoted in McAvoy, "War Letters of Father Cooney," 232; Corby, *Memoirs of Chaplain Life*, 184–86.

28. Ireland, "Civil War Memoirs," 1–16, COO.

29. James McPherson's still important synthesis, *Battle Cry of Freedom*, does not mention sister nurses even once. Major gender studies of the Civil War, such as Catherine Clinton and Nina Silber's *Divided Houses*, Drew Gilpin Faust's *Mothers of Invention*, Nina Silber's *Gender and the Sectional Conflict*, and Judith Giesberg's *Army at Home*, do not mention the nuns at all, while Mary E. Massey's *Women in the Civil War* and Silber's

Daughters of the Union refers to them only in passing as a thorn in Protestant nurses' side. While Silber and Clinton's *Battle Scars* includes an essay on Catholic nuns along the Gulf Coast and also discusses the Marylander Mary Surratt, gender historians of the North have largely focused on Protestant women to the exclusion of Catholic laywomen and nuns alike. See Massey, *Women in the Civil War*; Drew G. Faust, *Mothers of Invention: Women of the Slaveholding South in the American Civil War* (Chapel Hill: University of North Carolina Press, 1996); Catherine Clinton and Nina Silber, *Battle Scars: Gender and Sexuality in the American Civil War* (New York: Oxford University Press, 2006), 41–60, 110–16; Catherine Clinton and Nina Silber, *Divided Houses: Gender and the Civil War* (New York: Oxford University Press, 1992); Silber, *Daughters of the Union*, and *Gender and the Sectional Conflict* (Chapel Hill: University of North Carolina Press, 2008); Giesberg, *Army at Home*.

30. Mary D. Lee to Fr. Thomas Sim Lee, October 26 [before 1865], Thomas Sim Lee Papers, CUA. Given the relative paucity of preserved letters and diaries written by laywomen during the conflict, the Catholic sisters are in history and historiography the most visible Catholic women who took an active role in the Civil War. Catholic scholars, some verging close to the realm of hagiography, have universally celebrated nuns' apolitical devotion to soldiers' spiritual and bodily health as a remarkable example of Catholic Christian charity in American history. Sister Mary Denis Maher's *To Bind Up the Wounds* (1989) is more than forty years newer than the last general study of Catholics during the war, Rev. Benjamin Blied's 1945 *Catholics in the Civil War*. Only the Irish Brigade outpaces the nuns when it comes to writing about aspects of the Catholic war experience. For more on the most important studies of nuns during the war, see Betty Ann McNeil, D.C., "Daughters of Charity: Courageous and Compassionate Civil War Nurses," *U.S. Catholic Historian* 31 (Winter 2013): 51–52.

31. Maher, *To Bind Up the Wounds*, 1–3, 120, 155–60. For example, Jean V. Berlin writes in a new introduction to Massey's classic book on women in the war, "Scholars generally agree that the Civil War was as important a watershed in the history of American women as it was in the history of the nation." Massey, *Women in the Civil War*, vii.

32. Barbara J. Howe and Margaret A. Brennan, "The Sisters of St. Joseph in Wheeling, West Virginia, during the Civil War," *U.S. Catholic Historian* 31 (Winter 2013): 29–45; Maher, *To Bind Up the Wounds*, 69–70.

33. Abp. Hughes to Abp. Francis Kenrick, May 9, 1861, ABA; clippings from "CHR" on chaplains in the Civil War, Peter Guilday Papers, CUA.

34. Abp. Purcell to William S. Rosecrans, March 13, 1863, Box 8, UCLA-Rosecrans Papers; Maher, *To Bind Up the Wounds*, 81; Sorin, *Chronicles of Notre Dame Du Lac*, 276–77, 279–81.

35. Maher, *To Bind Up the Wounds*, 13–14, 58; Carol K. Coburn and Martha Smith, *Spirited Lives: How Nuns Shaped Catholic Culture and American Life, 1836–1920* (Chapel Hill: University of North Carolina Press, 1999), 42–43; Helen Sweeney, *The Golden Milestone, 1846–1896* (New York: Benziger Brothers, 1896), 70.

36. Mother Angela to Anna Harman, December 4, 1861, Mother Liguori to Gen. Laz. Noble, November 8, 1861, Gen. Sherman to Dr. Murray, August 2, 1862, Box 3.1, Civil

War Records, Sisters of the Holy Cross Archives (hereafter SHCA); Mother Angela to
Fr. Lambert, September 29, 1885, Louis Aloysius Lambert Papers, CUA; Sister Marie de
Lourdes Walsh, *The Sisters of Charity of New York, 1809–1959*, vol. 3 (New York: Fordham
University Press, 1960), 166–67; McNeil, *Dear Masters*, 32–33.

37. Sr. August to Fr. Sorin, March 30, 1863, Box 3.1, *Chronicles of St. Mary's, Notre
Dame, Indiana 1834–1878*, transcribed by Sr. Julie McGuire, C.S.C., Part 1, pp. 88, 90–91,
SHCA; Sweeney, *Golden Milestone*, 123.

38. Maher, *To Bind Up the Wounds*, 99; Walsh, *Sisters of Charity of New York*, 171;
Sister Mary of the Holy Cross Narrative, Box 3.1, Civil War Records, SHCA; McNeil,
Dear Masters, 61.

39. *Spalding Journal*, October 1, 1862, CUA; McNeil, *Dear Masters*, 127–28; *Chronicles
of St. Mary's*, Part 1, p. 94, Part 2, p. 4, SHCA.

40. Judith Metz, S.C., *The Sisters of Charity of Cincinnati in the Civil War* (Cincinnati: Sisters of Charity of Cincinnati, 2012), 9; Maher, *To Bind Up the Wounds*, 140–46;
McNeil, *Dear Masters*, 9–10.

41. Sweeney, *Golden Milestone*, 79; McNeil, *Dear Masters*, 99–100; Maher, *To Bind Up
the Wounds*, 142–43; Fr. Neil Gillespie to His Mother, December 13, 1861, Box 3.1, Civil
War Records, SHCA.

42. William A. Hammond to Abraham Lincoln, July 16, 1862, Abraham Lincoln
Papers, Library of Congress, Washington, D.C.; Maher, *To Bind up the Wounds*, 125–35;
Ellen Ryan Jolly, *The Nuns of the Battlefield* (Providence: Providence Visitor, 1927),
236, 245. While Lincoln certainly appreciated the nuns' efforts on behalf of the Union,
post-war claims that Lincoln had a painting commissioned to honor the nuns are
probably apocryphal, and a quote in which he praised the "charity and benevolence"
of "Catholic Sisters" was actually said by a Treasury official. Maher, *To Bind Up the
Wounds*, 143.

43. Although there is no Sister Beatrice listed among the records of the Sisters of the
Holy Cross, Mrs. Wallace might be thinking of Sister Bartholomew, who served in a
St. Louis Hospital at this time. "Sisters Who Served (as Sisters) in the Army/Navy during
the Civil War," Mother Angela, "Civil War Narrative," Susan E. Wallace to Her Mother,
December 18, 1861, Box 3.1, Civil War Records, SHCA; McNeil, *Dear Masters*, 81–82;
Maher, *To Bind Up the Wounds*, 130; Conyngham, "Introduction," in "Soldiers of the
Cross."

44. *Harper's Weekly*, May 9, 1863, Box 3.4, Fr. Neil Gillespie to His Mother, December 13, 1861, Governor Morton to Mother Angela, May 6, 1862, Captain J. Lewis
to Captain Woolfolk, November 20, 1863, Box 3.1, Civil War Records, SHCA; A. W.
Pennock to Sister M. Angela, October 14, 1862, C. H. Davis to First Master A. M. Grant,
September 19, 1862, in U.S. War Department, *War of the Rebellion: A Compilation of the
Official Records of the Union and Confederate Navies* (Washington, D.C., 1910), 1st ser.,
vol. 23, pp. 364–65; L. J. Harwood, Chairman of Salvage Committee of St. Joseph County
to Mother M. Vincentia, C.S.C., September 18, 1942, Box 3.4, Civil War Records, SHCA.

45. Sister Josephine Meagher to Joseph, June 5, 1911, Sister Josephine Meagher Collection, Chicago History Museum Research Center; "Abraham Lincoln: The Unveiling of
the Monument to Him," *New York Times*, October 16, 1874.

46. Bp. John Henry Luers to the Society for the Propagation of the Faith, February 25, 1864, PFP.

5. Slavery Divides the Church

1. Eric Foner, *The Fiery Trial: Abraham Lincoln and American Slavery* (New York: W. W. Norton, 2010), 217–47; Rev. Boniface Wimmer to Ludwig I, December 12, 1860, quoted in Wimmer, *Letters of an American Abbot*, 236–37.

2. McGreevy, *Catholicism and American Freedom*, 49–66, 75–78.

3. Hochgeschwender, *Wahrheit, Einheit, Ordnung*, 8–9; McGreevy, *Catholicism and American Freedom*, 51–52; Ignatiev, *How the Irish Became White*, 69, 76, 106–20.

4. Freesoilism was a political position that opposed the extension of slavery into the western territories of the United States. *NYFJ*, July 15, September 9, 1843; *The Pilot* (Boston), July 8, 22, 1854; Angela F. Murphy, *American Slavery, Irish Freedom: Abolition, Immigrant Citizenship, and the Transatlantic Movement for Irish Repeal* (Baton Rouge: Louisiana State University Press, 2010), 9–15, 22–23.

5. *NYFJ*, June 5, 1854; *BQR*, January 1857.

6. McPherson, *Battle Cry of Freedom*, 170–78; Don E. Fehrenbacher, *The Dred Scott Case: Its Significance in American Law and Politics* (New York: Oxford University Press, 1978), 1–3, 226–28, 557–61.

7. Hennesey, *American Catholics*, 147; *NYFJ*, September 12, 1857; *BQR*, April 1857; *The Liberator* (Boston), April 24, 1857; *The Pilot* (Boston), April 11, 1857; "A Maryland Catholic Democrat," *Daily Ohio Statesmen* (Columbus), April 23, 1857.

8. *The Pilot* (Boston), November 5, 1859; *Catholic Mirror* (Boston), October 29, 1859; *Louisville Guardian*, November 12, 1859; *BQR*, July 1860; *NYFJ*, October 29, 1859.

9. McPherson, *Battle Cry of Freedom*, 311–12, 352–53; Gary W. Gallagher, *The Union War* (Cambridge, Mass.: Harvard University Press, 2011), 2, 45–50; *NYFJ*, July 20, 1861; James Oakes, *Freedom National: The Destruction of Slavery in the United States, 1861–1865* (New York: W. W. Norton, 2013), xi–xxiv.

10. Maria Lydig Daly, *Diary of a Union Lady, 1861–1865*, ed. Harold Earl Hammond (New York: Funk & Wagnalls, 1962), 152; McGreevy, *Catholicism and American Freedom*, 49–56; Blied, *Catholics and the Civil War*, 19–22; Rice, *American Catholic Opinion in the Slavery Controversy*, 11–85; John Francis Maxwell, *Slavery and the Catholic Church: The History of Catholic Teaching concerning the Moral Legitimacy of the Institution of Slavery* (London: Barry Rose, 1975), 10, 28–79.

11. *BQR*, October 1861.

12. Ibid.

13. Henry S. Hewit to Brownson, October 6, 1861, M. L. Linton to Brownson, October 16, 1861, Eli Nichols to Brownson, October 22, 1861, R. J. Howard et al. to Brownson, November 10, 1861, BRO; *The Catholic* (Pittsburgh), October 5, 1861; *Catholic Mirror* (Baltimore), October 5, 1861.

14. *Metropolitan Record* (New York), October 12, 1861. Archbishop Hughes's authorship of this letter was an open secret. *The Pilot* identified him as the author when it reprinted the letter, approvingly, on October 19, 1861.

15. *BQR*, January 1862; Abp. Hughes to Seward, October 10, 1861, Seward Papers, University of Rochester Archives, Rochester, N.Y.; McGreevy, *Catholicism and American Freedom*, 79–80.

16. *Metropolitan Record* (New York), April 26, 1862; *NYFJ*, April 26, July 19, 1862; *Catholic Mirror* (Baltimore), January 11, 1862.

17. *New York Tablet*, January 18, 1862; *The Pilot* (Boston), April 19, 1862; *The Catholic* (Pittsburgh), January 18, 1862; *Catholic Telegraph* (Cincinnati), January 22, 1862.

18. Brownson to Charles Sumner, September 1862, Sumner to Brownson, October 12, 1862, Brownson to Fr. Sorin, November 5, 1862, Brownson to Bp. James R. Bayley (Draft), 1861–62, BRO; *New York Times*, November 2, 1862; *BQR*, July 1863; *The Catholic* (Pittsburgh), July 18, 1863; *BQR*, January 1864; Carey, *Orestes A. Brownson: American Religious Weathervane*, 280.

19. *Catholic Telegraph*, October 1, 1862; Alison Clark Efford, "The Appeal of Racial Neutrality in the Civil War–Era North: German Americans and the Democratic New Departure," *Journal of the Civil War Era* 5 (March 2015): 78; Bp. Young to Henry Meline," April 2, 1861, BRO; Bp. Spalding to Propaganda Fide, December 1, 1864, PRF. Ironically, given the *Catholic Telegraph*'s firm support of emancipation, Young once reviled Bishop Rosecrans as traitorous and proslavery. Bp. Rosecrans to Abp. Purcell, August 10, 1862, ACI.

20. Henry F. Brownson, *Orestes A. Brownson's Middle Life: From 1845 to 1855* (Detroit: H. F. Brownson, 1899), 501–9; Anthony H. Deye, "Archbishop John Baptist Purcell and the Civil War" (Ph.D. diss., University of Cincinnati, 1944), 65–67; *Catholic Telegraph* (Pittsburgh), June 29, 1861, January 15, July 23, 1862.

21. McGreevy, *Catholicism and American Freedom*, 84; *Catholic Telegraph* (Pittsburgh), August 27, September 3, October 1, 1862.

22. *BQR*, October 1862; General Rosecrans to Ann Rosecrans, September 8, November 5, 14, 1862, Box 59, UCLA-Rosecrans Papers; Garesché, *Biography of Lieut. Col. Julius P. Garesché*, 419.

23. *The Catholic* (Pittsburgh), October 4, 1862; *Metropolitan Record* (New York), October 4, 1862; *NYFJ*, October 4, 1862; *The Pilot* (Boston), October 4, 1862; *Catholic Telegraph* (Cincinnati), October 1, 1862.

24. *Spalding Journal*, September 29, November 1, 1862, January 1, March 1, 1863; McGreevy, *Catholicism and American Freedom*, 86; Garesché, *Biography of Lieut. Col. Julius P. Garesché*, 351–52.

25. McGreevy, *Catholicism and American Freedom*, 82–85; *Catholic Telegraph* (Cincinnati), March 25, 1863; *NYFJ*, April 4, 1863.

26. *Catholic Telegraph* (Cincinnati), April 8, 22, June 24, 1863; Deye, "Archbishop John Baptist Purcell and the Civil War," 69–73. The *Telegraph*'s appeal can be compared to Daniel O'Connell's efforts to enlist Irish Catholics to support abolition during the repeal debates in the early 1840s. Both O'Connell and the *Catholic Telegraph* were largely unsuccessful.

27. Peter to Margaret Welsh, February 3, 1863, quoted in Welsh, *Irish Green and Union Blue*, 64–68; *BQR*, July 1863; *Catholic Telegraph* (Cincinnati), May 6, 1863; Fr. O'Higgins to Abp. Purcell, May 28, 1863, ACI; McGreevy, *Catholicism and American Freedom*, 85.

28. *Spalding Journal*, April 12, June–July 1863; McGreevy, *Catholicism and American Freedom*, 86–87.

29. David Spalding, C.F.X., "Martin John Spalding's 'Dissertation on the American Civil War,'" *Catholic Historical Review* 52, no. 1 (1966): 66–69, 76–81, 83–85.

30. *NYFJ*, July 11, 1863; *The Pilot* (Boston), July 25, 1863; *Metropolitan Record* (New York), July 11, 1863; David Endres, "Rectifying the Fatal Contrast: Archbishop John Purcell and the Slavery Controversy among Catholics in Civil War Cincinnati," *Ohio Valley History* 2 (Fall 2002): 30; *Catholic Telegraph* (Cincinnati), December 16, 1863.

31. *Der Wahrheits Freund*, October 1, 1862, September 30, 1863; Deye, "Archbishop John Purcell and the Civil War," 87–88.

32. *Der Wahrheits Freund*, August 5, October 14, 1863, July 6, November 2, 1864; *Katholische Volkszeitung* (Baltimore), August 15, 1863.

33. *Katholische Kirchen-Zeitung* (New York), October 17, 1861, January 8, May 7, 1863; *Katholische Volkszeitung* (Baltimore), June 23, October 24, 1863.

34. Bp. Elder to Abp. Purcell, September 14, 1863, Bp. Spalding to Abp. Purcell, October 5, 1863, ACI; Kenneth J. Zanca, ed., *American Catholics and Slavery, 1789–1866: An Anthology of Primary Documents* (New York: University Press of America, 1994), 249–50; entries for July, August, and September in Bishop William H. Elder, *Civil War Diary (1862–1865) of Bishop William Henry Elder, Bishop of Natchez*, ed. Rev. R. O. Gerow (Natchez, 1960), 53–66.

35. Bp. Spalding to Abp. Purcell, October 21, 1863, Bp. James Wood to Abp. Purcell, October 23, 1863, Bp. Elder to Abp. Purcell, December 30, 1863, February 18, 1864, ACI.

36. *Catholic Telegraph* (Cincinnati), November 16, 1864; *NYFJ*, February 11, 1865, November 24, 1866; *Catholic Telegraph* (Cincinnati), February 8, 1865; Brownson to Charles Sumner, January 2, 1866, BRO; Carey, *Orestes A. Brownson: American Religious Weathervane*, 347–51. Unlike McMaster, the editor of *Catholic Mirror*, usually an outspoken critic of the war, declined to comment on the amendment when it was passed by Congress in late January or when it was finally ratified later in early December. The editor's constant opposition to abolition and his support for President Andrew Johnson against his radical critics meant that he was certainly critical of the thirteenth amendment in private. *Catholic Mirror*, November 25, 1865.

37. Fr. Pacciarini to Fr. Lancaster, October 14, 1864, Box 15, Jesuit Maryland Province Collection, Georgetown University Archives and Special Collections, Washington, D.C. Father Lancaster's response, unfortunately, has not been found. Ruby, ed., *Blue and Gray*, 43; *New York Tribune*, December 20, 1864. While Greeley's paper was probably overstating its case somewhat and completely ignored the Purcell brothers' support of emancipation, it was undoubtedly correct that most Catholic Democrats had no sympathy for abolition. The *Tribune*'s accusations, rightly or wrongly, probably reinforced the common pre-war conviction that slavery and Catholicism went hand in hand, much to the detriment of Catholics after the war. McGreevy, *Catholicism and American Freedom*, 62–63.

38. *Catholic Mirror* (Baltimore), December 2, 1865.

39. Hennesey, *American Catholics*, 161–63; Zanca, ed., *American Catholics and Slavery*, 256.

40. Francis X. Weninger, *Memoirs*, trans. Susan X. Blakely, 201, Francis Weninger Collection, Jesuit Archives of the Central United States, St. Louis.

6. Catholics' Opposition to the War

1. Frank Klement, "Catholics as Copperheads during the Civil War," *Catholic Historical Review* 80 (January 1994): 36. For more on Copperheads and anti-war dissent, see Jennifer L. Weber, *Copperheads: The Rise and Fall of Lincoln's Opponents in the North* (New York: Oxford University Press, 2006); and Sandow, *Deserter Country*.

2. Although McMaster and others cited religious reasons for their dissent, they did not oppose all wars out of principle, as did the perfectionist pacifist Protestant leaders of the radical peace movement during the war. Thomas F. Curran, *Soldiers of the Peace: Civil War Pacifism and the Postwar Radical Peace Movement* (New York: Fordham University Press, 2003), xii.

3. Maria Lydig Daly quoted in Weber, *Copperheads*, 50. Of recent studies of wartime dissent, Robert Sandow has persuasively shown that "Democrats considered themselves champions of laws and of the Constitution." Melinda Lawson has similarly noted that Democrats "framed their own ideas of loyalty to the nation—ideas rooted in republican traditions of liberty, vigilance, and civic virtue." Anti-war Catholic leaders, who were all Democrats, repeated such partisan claims verbatim while often expressing additional Catholic reasons for opposing the war as well. Sandow, *Deserter Country*, 71; Melinda Lawson, *Patriot Fires: Forging a New American Nationalism in the Civil War North* (Lawrence: University Press of Kansas, 2002), 92.

4. McPherson, *Battle Cry of Freedom*, 600–609; Hennesey, *American Catholics*, 150.

5. McGreevy, *Catholicism and American Freedom*, 73; Rable, *God's Almost Chosen Peoples*, 266; Iver Bernstein, *The New York City Draft Riots: Their Significance for American Society and Politics in the Age of the Civil War* (New York: Oxford University Press, 1990), 263–64. Historian Randall Miller argues that the riots overshadowed the heroism and sacrifice of the Irish Brigade, requiring a considerable amount of damage control by Irish Catholics after the war. Miller, "Catholic Religion, Irish Ethnicity," in Miller, Stout, and Wilson, eds., *Religion and the American Civil War*, 283.

6. Keating, "Give Us War in Our Time," 238–39.

7. *Catholic Telegraph* (Cincinnati), August 10, 1861; Bp. Young to Society for Propagation of the Faith, July 1, 1861, June 30, 1862, Abp. Purcell to Society for Propagation of the Faith, November 21, 1861, PFP; Sandow, *Deserter Country*, 59; Wimmer to Gregory Scherr, February 26, 1863, quoted in Wimmer, *Letters of an American Abbot*, 266. For more on the war as an alienating experience for German Catholics, see Kathleen Conzen, "German Catholic Communalism and the American Civil War: Exploring the Dilemmas of Transatlantic Political Integration," in Elisabeth Glaser and Hermann Wellenreuther, eds., *Bridging the Atlantic: The Question of American Exceptionalism in Perspective* (New York: Cambridge University Press, 2002), 119–44.

8. *Catholic Telegraph* (Cincinnati), July 23, 1862; *NYFJ*, August 16, 1862.

9. Bernstein, *New York City Draft Riots*, 18–42, 78, 112–13; Hennesey, *American Catholics*, 150–51; Giesberg, *Army at Home*, 127–36; *New York Times*, July 16, 1863; *Abendzeitung* quoted in *New York Tribune*, July 23, 1863.

10. O'Brien, *Isaac Hecker*, 193–94; *New York Tablet*, July 25, 1863; Sister Mary Ulrica O'Reilly file, Sisters of Charity New York Archives; *Harper's Weekly*, August 1, 1863.

11. *New York Times*, July 16, 18, 1863; *New York Tablet*, July 25, 1863; *The Liberator* (Boston), July 31, 1863; *BQR*, August 1863. Hughes began his speech by saying, "They call you rioters. I cannot see a riotous face among you." Hennesey, *American Catholics*, 150–51.

12. *The Catholic* (Pittsburgh), July 18, August 1, 1863; Edward Brownson to Sally Brownson, July 15, 1863, BRO; *Catholic Mirror* (Baltimore), July 25, 1863; *Metropolitan Record* (New York), July 25, 1863; *Der Wahrheits Freund* (Cincinnati), July 22, 1863.

13. Samito, ed., *Commanding Boston's Irish Ninth*, 203; Peter to Margaret Welsh, July 17, July 22, August 2, 1863, quoted in Welsh, *Irish Green and Union Blue*, 108–16; Gancas, ed., *Dear Teres*, 242.

14. *NYFJ*, July 18, August 1, 1863; *Metropolitan Record* (New York), July 25, 1863; *Katholische Kirchen-Zeitung* (Baltimore and New York), July 23, 1863; *BQR*, October 1863; *Catholic Telegraph* (Cincinnati), July 22, 1863.

15. *The Catholic* (Pittsburgh), August 8, 1863; *New York Tablet*, July 25, 1863; *BQR*, October 1863.

16. *Catholic Telegraph* (Cincinnati), August 26, 1863; *NYFJ*, July 18, 25, 1863; *Metropolitan Record* (New York), July 18, 1863; *Catholic Herald* (Philadelphia), July 29, 1863.

17. *The Pilot* (Boston), August 1, 8, 15, 22, 1863; *Metropolitan Record* (New York), July 25, 1863; *NYFJ*, August 1, 1863.

18. Weber, *Copperheads*, 18, 154; Wimmer to Lincoln, June 10, 1863, quoted in Wimmer, *Letters of an American Abbot*, 267–69; *The Pilot* (Boston), August 8, 1863; Archbishop Spalding to Archbishop Purcell, January 4, 1864, CACI.

19. Kwitchen, "James Alphonsus McMaster," 138–43; Clint Johnson, *A Vast and Fiendish Plot: The Confederate Attack on New York City* (New York: Citadel Press, 2010), 165, 182, 226.

20. *NYFJ*, July 20, 1861, August 16, 23, 1862, March 19, 1864.

21. Hennesey, *American Catholics*, 156; McGreevy, *Catholicism and American Freedom*, 87–88; *New York Tablet*, August 1, 1863; *American Quarterly Church Review*, October 1863. The *Washington Chronicle*, a secular pro-war paper, similarly drew connections between the riots and the peace letters, which it dismissed as full of "impertinence and the presumption." Quoted in *Catholic Mirror* (Baltimore), August 22, 1863.

22. Hennesey, *American Catholics*, 156–57; McGreevy, *Catholicism and American Freedom*, 87–88; Spalding, *Martin John Spalding*, 146; *New York Times*, August 3, 1863; *The Independent* (New York), August 20, 1863, January 28, 1864; Pius IX to Abp. Purcell, November 15, 1864, ACI; Pius IX to Jefferson Davis, December 3, 1863, quoted in U.S. War Department, *War of the Rebellion*, 4th ser., vol. 3, 401; *NYFJ*, January 23, 1864.

23. *Catholic Telegraph* (Cincinnati), January 20, March 16, 1864. The *New York Times* also reprinted Father Purcell's article on January 24, 1864. See also *Spalding Journal*, January 1864; *The Catholic* (Pittsburgh), August 15, 1863.

24. *BQR*, October 1863.

25. *Catholic Mirror* (Baltimore), August 22, 29, 1863; *Metropolitan Record* (New York), August 15, 1863; *NYFJ*, March 19, 1864.

26. Hennesey, *American Catholics*, 156; Leo Francis Stock, "The United States at the Court of Pius IX," *Catholic Historical Review* 9 (1923–24): 116–20; Fr. Bernard Smith to Abp. Hughes, September 12, 27, 1862, John Hughes Papers, CUA.

27. Bp. Lynch to Isaac Hecker, December 21, 1879, Isaac Hecker Papers, Paulist Archives, Washington, D.C.; *New York Tablet*, June 25, 1864.

28. McPherson, *Battle Cry of Freedom*, 718; *BQR*, April 1864; Samito, ed., *Commanding Boston's Irish Ninth*, 242, 246–47; *The Pilot* (Boston), May 7, 1864; *Catholic Herald* (Philadelphia), January 9, 1864; Gancas, ed., *Dear Teres*, 277, 287–88.

29. *The Catholic* (Pittsburgh), May 14, July 9, 1864; *Catholic Herald* (Philadelphia), July 30, 1864; *The Pilot* (Boston), May 7, July 9, 23, 1864.

30. *Catholic Telegraph* (Cincinnati), August 3, September 21, 28, 1864; *New York Tablet*, June 18, 1864.

31. *Der Wahrheits Freund* (Cincinnati), July 6, November 2, 1864; Deye, "Archbishop John Baptist Purcell and the Civil War," 88; *The Pilot* (Boston), September 17, October 22, 29, 1864; *NYFJ*, August 20, 1864; *Metropolitan Record* (New York), November 5, 1864; *New York Times*, July 2, October 28, 1864; *BQR*, July and October 1864.

32. *Catholic Herald* (Philadelphia), August 27 1864; *The Catholic* (Pittsburgh), November 26, 1864; *The Pilot* (Boston), November 12, 1864; *NYFJ*, November 19, 1864.

33. *Catholic Herald* (Philadelphia), December 24, 1864 (the *Catholic Herald* was now named *The Universe* after Louis Veuillot's famous, conservative Catholic newspaper published in France); *Catholic Telegraph* (Cincinnati), February 1, 1865; *New York Tablet*, February 11, 18, April 8, 1865; *BQR*, October 1864; Carey, *Orestes A. Brownson: American Religious Weathervane*, 280–81. Later, Brownson admitted to his Radical Republican friend Charles Sumner a secular cause for his paper's demise: his unwise support for Frémont in 1864. Brownson to Sumner, January 17, 1865, BRO.

34. *Katholische Kirchen-Zeitung* (Baltimore and New York), January 12, April 13, 1865; *Catholic Mirror* (Baltimore), March 25, 1865; *Metropolitan Record* (New York), January 14, February 11, April 8, 1865; *NYFJ*, February 4, 11, 18, 25, March 4, 11, 25, 1865.

35. *The Pilot* (Boston), March 4, April 8, 1865; *New York Tablet*, April 1, 8, 1865; *Der Wahrheits Freund* (Cincinnati), April 12, 1865; *The Catholic* (Pittsburgh), March 25, April 8, 1865, 52; *Catholic Telegraph* (Cincinnati), April 5, 1865.

36. *The Pilot* (Boston), April 22, 1865; *Der Wahrheits Freund* (Cincinnati), April 19, 1865; *Katholische Kirchen-Zeitung* (Baltimore and New York), April 20, 1865.

37. *Catholic Telegraph* (Cincinnati), April 19, 1865; *Catholic Mirror* (Baltimore), April 22, 1865; *NYFJ*, April 22, 1865; *Metropolitan Record* (New York), April 22, 1865; *New York Tablet*, April 22, 1865; *The Catholic* (Pittsburgh), April 22, 1865.

38. *San Francisco Bulletin*, April 17, 1865. Regardless of what some see as its other shortcomings, Robert Redford's recent film *The Conspirator* (2010) accurately portrays

Mary Surratt's devout Catholicism, Father John Walter's role as her confessor, and how priests aided John Surratt after he arrived in Canada. The best published treatment of Mary Surratt's trial and the public reaction to it from a Catholic point of view is Kenneth J. Zanca, *The Catholics and Mrs. Mary Surratt: How They Responded to the Trial and Execution of the Lincoln Conspirator* (New York: University of America Press, 2008). Some recent general examinations of Mrs. Surratt include Elizabeth Steger Trindal, *Mary Surratt: An American Tragedy* (Gretna, La.: Pelican Publishing, 1996); and Kate Clifford Larson, *The Assassin's Accomplice: Mary Surratt and the Plot to Kill Abraham Lincoln* (New York: Basic Books, 2008).

39. *Catholic Telegraph* (Cincinnati), July 12, 1865; *The Pilot* (Boston), July 22, 1865; *The Catholic* (Pittsburgh), July 1, 1865; *New York Tablet*, July 15, 22, 1865; *NYFJ*, July 15, 22, 1865; *New York Tribune*, July 17, 21, 1865; Hennesey, *American Catholics*, 159; *NYFJ*, August 10, 17, 1867. Father Purcell's defense of General Hardie against Father Jacob Walter, Surratt's confessor, showed that not all Catholics saw the incident as one of religious prejudice. *Catholic Telegraph* (Cincinnati), July 26, 1865.

40. *New York Tribune*, December 20, 1864.

41. *The Pilot* (Boston), February 25, April 22, 1865; *New York Tablet*, January 7, 1865; *NYFJ*, December 31, 1864.

42. *The Catholic* (Pittsburgh), January 28, 1865; *Catholic Telegraph* (Cincinnati), January 4, 18, 1865; *Katholische Kirchen-Zeitung* (Baltimore and New York), November 30, 1865; *The Pilot* (Boston), June 3, 1865.

43. *The Pilot* (Boston), June 3, 1865; Pierre-Jean de Smet, S.J., *Life, Letters and Travels of Father Pierre-Jean de Smet, S.J., 1801–1873*, 4 vols. (New York: Francis P. Harper, 1905), 4:1443–46; Stock, "United States at the Court of Pius IX," 121–22.

7. Post-war Anti-Catholicism

1. Gleeson, *Green and the Gray*, 1–9; McGreevy, *Catholicism and American Freedom*, 111–12; Bruce, *Harp and the Eagle*, 249–51; Wimmer to Michael Reger, November 12, 1876, quoted in Wimmer, *Letters of an American Abbot*, 404–5.

2. McGreevy, *Catholicism and American Freedom*, 93–98; Carey, *Orestes A. Brownson: American Religious Weathervane*, 289–94; *Catholic Telegraph* (Cincinnati), January 25, 1865; *New York Tablet*, February 11, 18, 1865.

3. Carey, *Orestes A. Brownson: American Religious Weathervane*, 296–320; Michael B. Gross, *The War against Catholicism: Liberalism and the Anti-Catholic Imagination in Nineteenth-Century Germany* (Ann Arbor: University of Michigan Press, 2004), 242–43.

4. Bruce, *Harp and the Eagle*, 236–44; Mitchell Snay, *Fenians, Freedmen and Southern Whites: Race and Nationalities in the Era of Reconstruction* (Baton Rouge: Louisiana State Press, 2007), 43–48; William Sherman to O. O. Howard, April 21, 1866, William T. Sherman Papers, Missouri Historical Society, Columbia, Mo.; Samito, *Becoming American under Fire*, 172–215.

5. *Chicago Tribune*, February 2, 1864; Bp. James Wood, Circular to the Clergy and People of the Diocese of Philadelphia, January 17, 1864, ACI.

6. *Chicago Tribune*, February 2, 1864; J. K. Barrett to James Mulligan, February 9, 1864, Mulligan Papers, Chicago History Museum Research Center; John P. Brophy to Abp. Martin J. Spalding, April 28, 1869, ABA; Snay, *Fenians, Freedmen, and Southern Whites*, 130–31.

7. David Montgomery, *Beyond Equality: Labor and the Radical Republicans, 1862–1872* (Urbana: University of Illinois Press, 1981), 120–34; McGreevy, *Catholicism and American Freedom*, 127–31; *Chicago Tribune*, February 28, 1864. Historian William Burton contended that Mulligan wrote this letter only as a smokescreen to hide his true sympathies, which were fully with the Irish nationalists. Mulligan's wartime diaries, with their abundant and devout references to religion and God, however, show that his faith was in fact just as important to him as his love for Ireland. Burton, *Melting Pot Soldiers*, 11–12; Mulligan, *Diary*, October 18, December 20, 1862, January 1, 1863, Mulligan Papers, Chicago History Museum Research Center.

8. Maurice Wolfe to his uncle, May 12, 1867, undated [1867–68?], Maurice Wolfe Letters, National Library of Ireland, Dublin; Bruce, *Harp and Eagle*, 242–43; In the several Fenian raids into Canada in 1866, at most only a few thousand men took part. By the time the Fenians launched another invasion in 1870, they could only muster a few hundred men. They were easily repulsed in both cases. Snay, *Fenians, Freedmen, and White Southerners*, 1–3, 171; W. S. Neidhart, *Fenianism in North America* (University Park: Pennsylvania State University Press, 1975), 45–50, 58–75, 77–81, 120–28.

9. Bp. Wood to Abp. Spalding, August 14, 1865, Bishop Wood Collection, PAHRC; *Catholic Mirror* (Baltimore), June 9, 1866; Snay, *Fenians, Freedmen, and White Southerners*, 171–72.

10. Joseph G. Bilby, *The Irish Brigade in the Civil War: The 69th New York and Other Irish Regiments of the Army of the Potomac* (Boston: Da Capo Press, 1998), 28; Peter D'Agostino, *Rome in America: Transnational Catholic Identity from the Risorgimento to Fascism* (Chapel Hill: University of North Carolina Press, 2004), 19–51; Charles A. Coulombe, *The Pope's Legion: The Multinational Fighting Force That Defended the Vatican* (New York: Palgrave Macmillan, 2008), 143–45.

11. *NYFJ*, November 9, 1867, January 25, July 11, 1868; *The Pilot* (Boston), January 11, 1868; *New York Times*, February 23, 1868.

12. *Proceedings of the Fourth National Congress of the Fenian Brotherhood, at Pittsburgh, Pa., February 1866, with the Constitution of the F.B., and Addenda Thereto* (New York: J. Craft, 1866), 11; *NYFJ*, February 15, March 28, April 18, May 2, 16, 23, 1868; *The Pilot* (Boston), June 13, 20, 1868.

13. *Catholic Mirror* (Baltimore), March 7, 1868; *The Pilot* (Boston), May 9, 1868; Card. Barnabo to Bp. Lefevere, May 16, 1868, DET; Abp. Purcell to Abp. Spalding, June 12, 1868, Gen. Hardie to Abp. Spalding, May 30, 1868, ABA; Abp. Spalding to Propaganda Fide, May 21, 1868, PRF; Gen. Hardie to Abp. Spalding, June 5, 20, 21, 1868, ABA; Abp. Spalding to Abp. Purcell, June 9, 1868, Abp. McCloskey to Abp. Purcell, June 10, 1868, ACI. Archbishop John McCloskey of New York complained with that the *New York Herald* had gotten a copy of the papal letter concerning the raising of the American battalion before even he did.

14. Abp. Spalding to Abp. Purcell, June 9, 1868, ACI; Abp. McCloskey to Abp. Spalding, June 15, 16, 19, 29, 30 1868, ABA; *Catholic Mirror* (Baltimore), July 4, 1863. Upon seeing the archbishops' refusal in print, Archbishop Odin expressed his approval, saying that local collections for the pope's defense had been rather underwhelming anyway. Abp. Odin to Abp. Spalding, July 8, 1868, ABA.

15. In his address to the Canadian Papal Zouaves at a Mass held in their honor in February 1868, McCloskey had lavishly praised the Canadians for volunteering to serve the pope. As even McMaster himself acknowledged, however, McCloskey had at that time given good reasons for why no American Catholics had joined them (or were likely to). *NYFJ*, July 11, 1868; *New York Times*, February 23, 1868; Propaganda Fide to Abp. Spalding, July 11, 22, 1868, Propaganda Fide to Abp. McCloskey, July 11, 1868, PRF; *The Pilot* (Boston), July 11, August 1, 1868; *Catholic Mirror* (Baltimore), July 18, 1868; *NYFJ*, August 8, 22, 1868; Tevis to McMaster, November 16, 1868, MMA; D'Agostino, *Rome in America*, 47–48; Coulombe, *Pope's Legion*, 107–8, 120–21, 205–6; Carey, *Orestes A. Brownson: American Religious Weathervane*, 316–17.

16. Atkin and Tallett, *Priests, Prelates, and People*, 141–59; McGreevy, *Catholicism and American Freedom*, 96–105; Ward M. McAfee, *Religion, Race, Reconstruction: The Public School in the Politics of the 1870s* (Albany: State University of New York Press, 1998), 47–58.

17. Billington, *Protestant Crusade*, 142–58; Gjerde, *Catholicism and the Shaping of Nineteenth-Century America*, 67–69, 93, 141, 144–75; McGreevy, *Catholicism and American Freedom*, 19–42, 112–22.

18. McAfee, *Religion, Race, and Reconstruction*, 27–29.

19. McAfee, *Religion, Race, and Reconstruction*, 29, 54; *Harper's Weekly*, March 19, 1870.

20. McAfee, *Religion, Race, and Reconstruction*, 29, 55–60, 74; Bruce, *Harp and the Eagle*, 251; *New York Tablet*, October 30, 1875.

21. Conzen, "German Catholic Communalism and the American Civil War," 141; *Catholic Telegraph* (Cincinnati), April 10, 1873; McAfee, *Race, Religion, and Reconstruction*, 24, 53–54; McGreevy, *Catholicism and American Freedom*, 98–114.

22. McAfee, *Religion, Race, and Reconstruction*, 40, 192–94; McGreevy, *Catholicism and American Freedom*, 91–93.

23. *Western Watchman* (St. Louis), October 30, November 6, December 11, 1875; *New York Tablet*, October 30, 1875; *Catholic Mirror* (Baltimore) [reprint from *New York Tablet*], November 6, 1875; *The Catholic* (Pittsburgh), December 4, 1875.

24. *NYFJ*, November 27, December 18, 1875; *Catholic Mirror* (Baltimore), December 4, 1875, January 8, 1876; *The Pilot* (Boston), December 11, 1875; John Y. Simon, ed., *The Papers of Ulysses S. Grant*, 32 vols. (Carbondale: Southern Illinois University Press, 2003), 26:532; *Catholic World* (New York), January 1876; Louis Adrian Rosecrans to Rosecrans, January 18, 28, 1876, Box 63, UCLA-Rosecrans Papers; *Chicago Tribune*, December 21, 1875.

25. The Blaine amendment read, "No State shall make any law respecting an establishment of religion, or prohibiting the free exercise thereof; and no money raised by

taxation in any state for the support of public schools, or derived from any public fund therefor, nor any public lands devoted thereto, shall ever be under the control of any religious sect, nor shall any money so raised or lands so devoted be divided between religious sects or denominations." McAfee, *Race, Religion, and Reconstruction*, 186–88, 194–95, 197, 200–2.

26. McAfee, *Race, Religion, and Reconstruction*, 198, 203–20; *Harper's Weekly*, September 30, 1876; Wimmer to Michael Reger, November 12, 1876, quoted in Wimmer, *Letters of an American Abbot*, 404–5.

27. Samito, *Becoming American under Fire*, 172–215; Sr. Josephine Meagher, May 6, 1911, Sister Josephine Meagher Collection, Chicago History Museum Research Center; *The Independent* (New York), July 19, 1883; Kenny, *American Irish*, 122; Handlin, *Boston's Immigrants*, 210–15; Fogarty, *Commonwealth Catholicism*, 176, 188–89.

28. Abp. John Ireland to Fr. Aloysius Lambert, February 3, 1895, Louis Aloysius Lambert Papers, CUA; Abp. Ireland to Fr. Cooney, October 15, 1884, John Hyde to Fr. Cooney, October 13, 1884, Box 1, Cooney, Notes from a Total Abstinence Meeting, March 12, 1887, Box 3, COO; *Chicago Tribune*, August 3, 1894; O'Connell, *John Ireland and the American Catholic Church*, 74, 85–134, 322–47, 394–401.

29. George M. Fredrickson, *The Inner Civil War: Northern Intellectuals and the Crisis of Union* (Champaign: University of Illinois Press, 1993), 199–216; McGreevy, *Catholicism and American Freedom*, 91–114; McAfee, *Religion, Race, and Reconstruction*, 3–7, 47–48, 53–54.

30. Hennesey, *American Catholics*, 172–83; Dolan, *American Catholic Experience*, 257–61; Christopher J. Kauffman, *Faith and Fraternalism: The History of the Knights of Columbus*, rev. ed. (New York: Simon & Schuster, 1992), xiii–xvi, xxv–xxvi; Carol K. Coburn and Martha Smith, *Spirited Lives: How Nuns Shaped Catholic Culture and American Life, 1836–1920* (Chapel Hill: University of North Carolina Press, 1999), 222; John Higham, *Strangers in the Land: Patterns of American Nativism, 1860–1925*, 2nd ed. (New Brunswick, NJ: Rutgers University Press, 1988), 60–63; Bruce, *Harp and the Eagle*, 234–35.

31. Dolan, *American Catholic Experience*, 306–20.

8. Catholics Remember the Civil War

1. Hennesey, *American Catholics*, 182–83; Higham, *Strangers in the Land*, 52–63; Stephen Railton, "Yankee Anti-Catholicism" and "Fifty Years in the Church of Rome," *Mark Twain, His Times, Catholic Church*, http://twain.lib.virginia.edu/yankee/cycathhp.html. For more on anti-Catholicism in nineteenth-century literature, see Elizabeth A. Fenton, *Religious Liberties : Anti-Catholicism and Liberal Democracy in Nineteenth-Century* (Oxford, U.K.: Oxford University Press, 2011).

2. June Granatir Alexander, *Daily Life in Immigrant America, 1870–1920* (Westport, Conn.: Greenwood Press, 2007), 18–23, 25–26; Dolan, *American Catholic Experience*, 127–57.

3. Gleeson, *Green and the Gray*, 208–10.

4. Orestes Brownson, "The American Republic," in Henry F. Brownson, ed., *The Works of Orestes A. Brownson*, 20 vols. (New York: AMS Press, 1966), 18:5–8, 192, 194; Garesché, *Biography of Lieut. Col. Julius P. Garesché*, 433; George Barton, *Angels of the Battlefield: A History of the Labors of the Catholic Sisterhood in the Late Civil War* (Philadelphia: Catholic Art Publishing, 1897), iii–iv, 297; Hochgeschwender, *Wahrheit, Einheit, Ordnung*, 458, 470.

5. Bruce, *Harp and the Eagle*, 234–36; Miller, "Catholic Religion, Irish Ethnicity, and the Civil War," in Miller, Stout, and Wilson, eds., *Religion and the American Civil War*, 284; Caroline E. Janney, *Remembering the Civil War: Reunion and the Limits of Reconciliation* (Chapel Hill: University of North Carolina Press, 2013), 108–10; Hennesey, *American Catholics*, 188.

6. Bruce, *Harp and the Eagle*, 257–62; Conyngham, *Irish Brigade and Its Campaigns*; Mulholland, *Story of the 116th Regiment*, xvii–xxiii.

7. Corby, *Memoirs of Chaplain Life*; Conyngham, *Irish Brigade and Its Campaigns*; Barton, *Angels of the Battlefield*; Joseph Taggart, *Biographical Sketches of the Eminent American Patriots, Charles Carroll, of Carrollton; Roger Brooke Taney; William Starke Rosecrans; John Barry; Philip Henry Sheridan, and a Sketch of the Early History of Maryland* (Kansas City, Mo.: Burton Company, 1907); L. W. Mulhane, *Major-General William Stark Rosecrans: Hero of Iuka, Corinth and Stone River, and Father of the Army of the Cumberland* (Columbus, Ohio: Columbian Print Company, 1898); John H. Lamott, S.T.D., *History of the Archdiocese of Cincinnati, 1821–1891* (Cincinnati: Frederick Pustet Company, 1921), 70–85, 87–88; William B. Sprague to Abp. John Purcell, November 21, 1864, quoted in Endres, "Rectifying the Fatal Contrast," 31; David W. Blight, *Race and Reunion: The Civil War in American Memory* (Cambridge, Mass.: Harvard University Press, 2001). There are no entries for slavery or emancipation in Lawrence Kohl's modern edited editions of Corby's *Memoirs* and Conyngham's *The Irish Brigade*.

8. The two most important challenges to David Blight's thesis of white reconciliation at the expense of African Americans are Janney, *Remembering the Civil War*; and Barbara A. Gannon, *The Won Cause: Black and White Comradeship in the Grand Army of the Republic* (Chapel Hill: University of North Carolina Press, 2011). William S. Rosecrans, Circulars, July 26, August 4, 1880, Box 48, UCLA-Rosecrans Papers; Barton, *Angels of the Battlefield*, iv; "Memorial of the Monument Erected on the Battlefield of Gettysburg to Very Rev. William Corby, C.S.C.," *Catholic Alumni Sodality of Philadelphia* (December 1911), 7, 9.

9. Blied, *Catholics and the Civil War*, 7–8, 19–35.

10. Sorin, *Chronicles of Notre Dame Du Lac*, 291; Hochgeschwender, *Wahrheit, Einheit, Ordnung*, 460–63.

11. *Notre Dame Scholastic* (South Bend, Ind.), May 13, 1905; Abp. John Ireland to Fr. Aloysius Lambert, February 3, 1895, Louis Aloysius Lambert Papers, CUA; Abp. John Ireland to Fr. Cooney, October 15, 1884, John Hyde to Fr. Cooney, October 13, 1884, Cooney, Notes from a Total Abstinence Meeting, March 12, 1887, COO; *Chicago Tribune*, August 3, 1894; Corby, *Memoirs of Chaplain Life*, xvii–xx; Corby to John B. Bachelder, January 4, 1879, COR.

12. "Rev. P. P. Cooney," *New Record* (n.p.), December 1, 1887, and "Fr. Cooney's Lecture," *Catholic Record* (Indianapolis), March 20, 1890, Rosecrans to Father Cooney, April 14, 1890, COO.

13. Kohl, "Introduction," in Corby, *Memoirs of Chaplain Life*, xx–xxiii, 66–70, 191–95, 271–391; W. L. D. O'Grady to Corby, May 24, 1888, Abp. John Gibbons to Corby, December 14, 1891, Fr. Ouellet, S.J., to Corby, August 26, 1891, Ouellet to Corby, July 4, 1893, Charles F. McKenna to Corby, July 26, 1893, Fr. P. J. Boland to Corby, June 26, 1893, Carrie Stevens Walter to Corby, May 21, 1894, Circular Promotion of "Memoirs of Chaplain Life," Box 1, William Corby Papers, IPAC.

14. W. L. D. O'Grady to Corby, October 26, 1892, Mulholland to Corby, November 10, 1892, Record and Pension Office of War Department to Mulholland, August 12, 1893, William Corby Papers, IPAC; Corby, *Memoirs* of Chaplain Life, xx–xxiv, 393–96; Peter J. Lysy, *Blue for the Union and Green for Ireland: The Civil War Flags of the 63rd Regiment New York Volunteers, Irish Brigade* (South Bend, Ind.: Mossberg and Company, 2001), 16–17, 53; Schmidt, *Notre Dame and the Civil War*, 104.

15. Fr. Cooney to Fr. Peter A. Baart, February 11, 1899, Box 1, Folder 11, COO; *Notre Dame Scholastic* (South Bend, Ind.), August 1899. Even the Republican *Chicago Tribune* reported the story favorably, pronouncing on July 3, 1899, the music for the occasion to be "especially fine." Unfortunately Cooney's Civil War chalice seems to be missing according to Holy Cross and Notre Dame archivists.

16. Corby, *Memoirs of Chaplain Life*, xxiv; John Finn to Corby, February 14, 1896, Z. A. Smith to William Olmstead, April 3, 1896, Smith to Corby, September 28, 1896, Charles Grainger to Corby, January 9, 1895, J. D. Hamilton to Corby, January 21, 1894, William A. Olmsted to Corby, November 18, 1895, Orville T. Chamberlain to Corby, April 1, 1896, William Corby Papers, IPAC; Bruce, *Harp and the Eagle*, 234–35; *The Pilot* (Boston), March 7, 1868; *New York Times*, October 10, 1895; Schmidt, *Notre Dame and Civil War*, 113.

17. Schmidt, *Notre Dame and the Civil War*, 113; *New York Times*, July 28, 31, 1897; *Notre Dame Scholastic* (South Bend, Ind.), October 9, 1897; *Atlanta Constitution*, November 7, 1897; *Chicago Tribune*, November 7, 1897; *Washington Post*, November 7, 1897; Corby to Thomas Kennedy, October 27, November 12, 14, 1897, COR.

18. Corby, *Memoirs of Chaplain Life*, xxv; *Notre Dame Scholastic* (South Bend, Ind.), January 15, 1898, May 13, 1905.

19. Corby, *Memoirs of Chaplain Life*, 397–400; "Memorial of the Rev. Corby Monument," 3, 8–16; *Notre Dame Scholastic* (South Bend, Ind.), October 8, 1910. President Father John Cavanaugh called on alumni asking them not to "miss the opportunity" of contributing to "a gratifying proof of the patriotism of Notre Dame." Fr. John Cavanaugh to Notre Dame Alumni, November 15, 1909, Box 1, Folder 48, COR.

20. "Memorial of the Rev. Corby Monument," 18–36; *Notre Dame Scholastic* (South Bend, Ind.), November 5, 1910; *The Times* (South Bend, Ind.), May 30, 1911, Folder 48, "Notre Dame at Gettysburg, 1863–1963," COR; Rev. Thomas J. O'Donnell to James Meyers, August 30, 1962, 17–27, "Father William Corby Statue" folder, Gettysburg National Military Park Library and Research Center, Gettysburg, Pa.; Rev. John Jenkins, C.S.C., "Battle of Gettysburg 150th Anniversary Address," Gettysburg National Military Park,

Gettysburg, Pa., June 22, 2013, http://president.nd.edu/writings-addresses/2013
-addresses/battle-of-gettysburg-150th-anniversary-address/.

21. *NYFJ*, November 19, 1864, May 18, 1867; *The Pilot* (Boston), November 26, 1864,
August 10, 1867; *The Congregationalist* (Boston), January 12, 1881; Fogarty, *Commonwealth Catholicism*, 160–62.

22. Paul Andrew Hutton, *Phil Sheridan and His Army* (Lincoln: University of Nebraska Press, 1985), 369, 372. Sheridan's surviving correspondence at the Library of Congress seems to make no reference at all to his religious faith. According to one Catholic
observer, Sheridan was "annoyed" by the "persecutive snubbing" he received at the
hands of Protestants in the War Department, including the secretary of war, George W.
McCray, "who believes . . . that to have a Roman Catholic Commander-in-chief to the
army is really and truly dangerous to Republican liberties and principles." Ella L. Dorsey
to Fr. Daniel L. Hudson, July 1, 1887, Daniel E. Hudson Papers, Notre Dame Archives,
University of Notre Dame Archives, Notre Dame, Ind. See also *New York Tribune*,
August 6, 1888; *Christian Advocate* (New York), August 9, 1888; *NYFJ*, August 11, 18, 1888;
Zion's Herald (Boston), August 29, 1888; *New York Evangelist*, August 16, 1888.

23. For more on how the battle shaped perceptions of Rosecrans, see Bradley S.
Keefer, *Conflicting Memories of the "River of Death": The Chickamauga Battlefield and the
Spanish–American War, 1863–1933* (Kent, Ohio: Kent State University Press, 2013), 66–68,
100; Fr. Joseph Havens Richards, S.J., to Rosecrans, January 31, 1889, Box 43, UCLA-
Rosecrans Papers.

24. *Notre Dame Scholastic* (South Bend, Ind.), March 15, April 5, 1896; Laetare Medal
Certificate: William Rosecrans, Box 124, UCLA-Rosecrans Papers; *Western Watchman*
(St. Louis), March 26, 1896; *NYFJ*, March 21, 1896; *San Francisco Monitor*, March 21,
1896. Even the *Freeman's Journal*, which had previously been one of Rosecrans's big-
gest critics, approvingly put the news on its front cover. Notre Dame had previously
awarded it ten years earlier to General John Newton, Rosecrans's old friend, thus making
Rosecrans the second Civil War general to receive the award. Newton, however, won the
award primarily for his engineering accomplishments in New York State after the war. In
fact, of the five Union veterans to win the award (the other three were Henry Brownson,
Timothy Edward Howard, and Richard C. Kerens), only Rosecrans won it explicitly for
his service. Coming just a few years after Father Corby published his successful memoirs
celebrating his chaplaincy during the war, the decision to honor Rosecrans was a part
of the university's larger goal of celebrating the roles of the church and the Order of the
Holy Cross in the conflict. In 1914 Edward Douglas White became the only Confederate
veteran to receive the award. *Notre Dame Scholastic* (South Bend, Ind.), April 3, 1886,
March 26, 1892, March 12, 1898, March 12, 1904, March 21, 1914.

25. *The Pilot* (Boston), March 26, 1898; *Los Angeles Times*, March 17, 1898; *San
Francisco Chronicle*, Mar 17, 1898; *New York Tribune*, Mar 12, 19, 1898; "In Memoriam [of
General Rosecrans]," memorial adopted by Board of Directors of Los Angeles Cham-
ber of Commerce, March 17, 1898, "Resolution," signed by R. G. Denforth, S. S. Yoder,
E. S. Gilman, Union Veterans' Union, Hancock Command, No. 1, 1898, "Resolutions of
Sympathy on the Death of William S. Rosecrans," signed by S. A. Thorpe, Commander,
Wm. Cole Harrison, Vice Commander and Surgeon, and A. M. Fulkerson, Adjutant,

March 4, 1898, Los Angeles Confederate Veterans Association of California, Camp 770, United Confederate Veterans, UCLA-Rosecrans Papers; *New York Times,* March 12, 1898; *Chicago Tribune,* March 12, 1898; *Washington Post,* April 5, May 18, 1902; *San Francisco Chronicle,* April 29, 1902.

26. *Western Watchman* (St. Louis), March 17, 1898; *Irish World and American Industrial Liberator* (New York), June 11, 1898; *The Pilot* (Boston), March 19, 1898; *Notre Dame Scholastic* (South Bend, Ind.), March 12, 1898.

27. Mulhane, *Major-General William Stark Rosecrans,* preface; Taggart, *Biographical Sketches of the Eminent American Patriots,* 299.

28. Lamers, *Edge of Glory;* David Moore, *William S. Rosecrans and the Union Victory: A Civil War Biography* (Jefferson, NC: McFarland Press, 2014); Frank P. Varney, *General Grant and the Rewriting of History: How the Destruction of General William S. Rosecrans Influenced Our Understanding of the Civil War* (El Dorado Hills, Calif.: Savas Beatie, 2013). In writing to a Georgetown priest about his book, Lamers said, "Please pray for the success of our Rosecrans. . . . Catholics should be proud to point to him as one of their own. America never had a better citizen, the U.S. Army [a] better general, or the Church a more devoted & worthy son." William Lamers to Fr. Repetti, "Rosecrans, William S. 3–16," Varia Collection, Georgetown University Archives and Special Collections, Washington, D.C.

29. "General Rosecrans Elementary School," http://www.bigwalnut.k12.oh.us/school_home.aspx?schoolID=7; *Sunbury News* (Ohio), April 23, 2009; http://rosecransheadquarters.org/News/SN4-23-09.htm; "Statue," http://rosecransheadquarters.org/Statue/Campaign.htm; "Support the Statue" (printed by Rosecrans Headquarters, n.d.), https://centralohiocwrt.files.wordpress.com/2011/03/general-rosecrans1.pdf. Biographical material on the site does talk about Rosecrans's faith in some detail, but the issue is not mentioned on the main "Statue" page or in a promotional flyer dedicated to raising funds for the monument.

30. Conzen, "German Catholic Communalism and the American Civil War," 119–44; Keller, *Chancellorsville and the Germans,* 147–67.

31. Minutes of the National Convention of the Central Verein, 1855–65, Central Verein of America Records, University of Notre Dame Archives, Notre Dame, Ind.; Central Verein National Convention Pamphlet Collection, Central Verein Library, St. Louis; Keller, *Chancellorsville and the Germans,* 2–4; *Katholische Kirchen-Zeitung* (Baltimore and New York), May 14, 1863.

32. Scheuermann Papers, Auswandererbriefesammlung, Gotha Research Library (Gotha, Germany); Hennesey, *American Catholics,* 194–96. Out of the twenty-five men listed as constituting the "Corby Monument Committee," no more than five of them had German last names. While Irish and American names were prominent among those among the clergy and laity who supported building the monument to Father Corby at Gettysburg, only one German Catholic bishop, no German Catholic newspapers, and no German Catholic societies appeared in the Monument Committee's memorial publication of 1911. "Memorial of the Rev. Corby Monument," 3–19.

33. Knights of Columbus of Gettysburg, Pa., *28th Annual Convention and Memorial Dedication, May 10–13, 1925* (n.p., 1925), Ellen Ryan Jolly to Mother Margaret O'Keefe,

July 15, 1920, Civil War Collection, Daughters of Charity Archives, Emmitsburg, Md.; Abp. J. Cardinal Gibbons to Ellen Ryan Jolly, September 26, 1914, Box 3.3, Civil War Records, SHCA; Ellen Ryan Jolly, *The Nuns of the Battlefield* (Providence: Providence Visitor, 1927); Corby, *Memoirs*, 400; Kathleen Szpila, "Lest We Forget: Ellen Ryan Jolly and the Nuns of the Battlefield Monument," *American Catholic Studies* 123, no. 4 (2012): 23–43; Keating, "Give Us War in Our Time," 332.

34. Peter Guilday, "Contributions of Catholics to Nation during the Civil War," *NCWC News Service*, February 2, 1934, Peter Guilday Papers, CUA; "Notre Dame at Gettysburg, 1863–1963," COR; Higham, *Strangers in the Land*, 311–30; Hennesey, *American Catholics*, 237, 246–48.

Conclusion

1. Hennesey, *American Catholics*, 226–28.

2. Ibid., 246–48, 276–80; Thomas Bruscino, *A Nation Forged in War: How World War II Taught Americans to Get Along* (Knoxville: University of Tennessee Press, 2010), 1–16; McGreevy, *Catholicism and American Freedom*, 212–15.

3. Jenkins, "Battle of Gettysburg 150th Anniversary Address."

Bibliography

Archival Sources

Catholic University of America Archives (CUA) (Washington, D.C.)
  Charles Ewing Papers (LOC: Charles Ewing Papers)
  Peter Guilday Papers
  John Hughes Papers
  Louis Aloysius Lambert Papers
  Thomas Sim Lee Papers
  Bernard Smith Papers
  Bishop M. J. Spalding Journal, 1860–1864 (*Spalding Journal*)
Central Verein Library (St. Louis)
  National Conventions Pamphlet Collection
Chicago History Museum Research Center
  Sister Josephine Meagher Collection
  Mulligan Papers
Daughters of Charity Archives (Emmitsburg, Md.)
  Civil War Collection
Georgetown University Archives and Special Collections (Washington, D.C.)
  Early Papers
  Jesuit Maryland Province Collection
  Julius Garesché Papers
  Varia Collection
Gettysburg National Military Park Library and Research Center (Gettysburg, Pa.)
  "Father William Corby Statue" Folder
Gotha Research Library (Gotha, Germany)
  Auswandererbriefesammlung
Indiana Historical Society (Indianapolis, Ind.)
  Hugh D. Gallagher Diary and Papers
Indiana Province Archives: Congregation of Holy Cross (IPAC) (Notre Dame, Ind.)
  William Corby Papers
  Holy Cross Personnel Files
  Edward Sorin Papers
Jesuit Archives of the Central United States (St. Louis)
  Francis Weninger Papers
Library of Congress (Washington, D.C.)
  Charles Ewing Papers
  Abraham Lincoln Papers

William S. Rosecrans Collection
Philip H. Sheridan Papers
Missouri Historical Society (Columbia, Mo.)
William T. Sherman Papers
National Library of Ireland (Dublin)
Maurice Wolfe Letters
New-York Historical Society
Regimental Collection, McIvor Papers
New York Public Library Archives and Manuscripts
Charles P. Daly Papers
Paulist Archives (Washington, D.C.)
Walter Elliot Papers
Isaac Hecker Papers
Philadelphia Archdiocese Historical Research Center (PAHRC)
Robert O'Reilly Papers
William White Papers
Bishop Wood Collection
James Wood Papers
Sisters of Charity of New York Archives (Bronx, N.Y.)
Sisters of the Holy Cross Archives (SHCA) (Notre Dame, Ind.)
Chronicles of St. Mary's, Notre Dame, Ind., 1834–1878 (transcription)
Civil War Records
University of California–Los Angeles Archives
William S. Rosecrans Papers (UCLA-Rosecrans Papers)
University of Notre Dame Archives (UNDA) (Notre Dame, Ind.)
Archdiocese of Baltimore Collection (ABA)
Archdiocese of Cincinnati Collection (ACI)
Archdiocese of New Orleans Collection (ANO)
Henry Brownson Papers
Orestes Brownson Papers (BRO)
Central Verein of America Records
Congregatio de Propaganda Fide Collection (PRF)
Congregation of Holy Cross Priests Collection (SCP)
David P. Conyngham Papers
David P. Conyngham, "Soldiers of the Cross: Heroism of the Cross; or,
Nuns and Priests of the Battlefield" (unpublished MS, ca. 1883).
Peter P. Cooney Papers (COO)
William Corby Papers (COR)
Diocese of Detroit Collection (DET)
Diocese of Hartford Collection (DHT)
Daniel E. Hudson Papers
James A. McMaster Papers (MMA)
Miscellaneous Manuscript Collection (CMM)
Notre Dame Printed and Reference Material Dropfiles

William S. Rosecrans Papers
William T. Sherman Family Papers (SHR)
Society for the Propagation of the Faith Collection (PFP)
University of Notre Dame Special Collections (Notre Dame, Ind.)
Thomas F. McGrath Papers
University of Rochester Archives (Rochester, N.Y.)
Seward Papers
U.S. Military History Institute (Carlisle, Pa.)
Daniel Finn Diary
U.S. National Archives I (Washington, D.C.)
Compiled Military Service Records
Court Martial Records

Periodicals

American Protestant Magazine (New York)
Atlanta Constitution
Boston Courier
Boston Daily Transcript
Brownson's Quarterly Review (BQR) (Boston and New York)
The Catholic (Pittsburgh)
Catholic Herald (Philadelphia)
Catholic Mirror (Baltimore)
Catholic Record (Indianapolis)
Catholic Telegraph (Cincinnati)
Catholic World (New York)
Chicago Tribune
Christian Advocate (New York)
The Congregationalist (Boston)
Daily Ohio Statesmen (Columbus)
Daily Sentinel and Gazette (Milwaukee)
Der Wahrheits Freund (Cincinnati)
The Independent (New York)
Irish World and American Industrial Liberator (New York)
Katholische Kirchen-Zeitung (Baltimore and New York)
Katholische Volkszeitung (Baltimore)
The Liberator (Boston)
Louisville Guardian
Los Angeles Times
Metropolitan Record (New York)
New Record (n.p.)
New York Evangelist
New York Freeman's Journal (NYFJ)
New York Herald

New York Tablet
New York Times
New York Tribune
The North American (Philadelphia)
Notre Dame Scholastic (South Bend, Ind.)
The Pilot (Boston)
Le Propagateur Catholique (New Orleans)
San Francisco Bulletin
San Francisco Monitor
Sunbury News (Ohio)
The Times (South Bend, Ind.)
U.S. Catholic Miscellany (Charleston)
Washington Post
Western Watchman (St. Louis)
Zion's Herald (Boston)

Published Primary Sources

Balch, William S. *Romanism and Republicanism Incompatible: A Lecture Delivered in the Broadway Tabernacle, Monday Evening, April 5th, 1852, in Review of "The Catholic Chapter of the United States," as Written by the Most. Rev. John Hughes, D.D., Archbishop of New York.* New York: Dewitt & Davenport, 1852.

Brownson, Henry, ed. *The Works of Orestes Brownson.* 20 vols. 1882–87. Reprint, New York: AMS Press, 1966.

Corby, William. *Memoirs of Chaplain Life: Three Years with the Irish Brigade in the Army of the Potomac.* Edited by Lawrence F. Kohl. New York: Fordham University Press, 1992.

Crackel, Theodore J., ed. *The Papers of George Washington Digital Edition.* Charlottesville: University of Virginia Press, Rotunda, 2007.

Daly, Maria Lydig. *Diary of a Union Lady, 1861–1865.* Edited by Harold Earl Hammond. New York: Funk & Wagnalls, 1962.

Elder, William H. *Civil War Diary (1862–1865) of Bishop William Henry Elder, Bishop of Natchez.* Edited by Rev. R. O. Gerow. Natchez, 1960.

Gancas, Ron, ed. *Dear Teres: The Civil War Letters of Andrew Joseph Duff and Dennis Dugan of Company F, the Pennsylvania Seventy-Eighth Infantry.* Edited by Dan Coyle, Sr. Chicora, Pa.: Mechling Bookbindery, 1999.

Grant, Ulysses S. *Personal Memoirs of U.S. Grant, Selected Letters, 1839–1865.* New York: Library of America, 1990.

"The Hierarchy of the Catholic Church." http://www.catholic-hierarchy.org/.

Jenkins, Rev. John, C.S.C. "Battle of Gettysburg 150th Anniversary Address." Gettysburg National Military Park (June 22, 2013). http://president.nd.edu/communications/address-to-the-nd-club-of-gettysburg.

Kamphoefner, Walter D., and Wolfgang Helbich, eds. *Germans in the Civil War: The Letters They Wrote Home*. Chapel Hill: University of North Carolina Press, 2006.

Kehoe, Lawrence, ed. *The Complete Works of the Most. Rev. John Hughes*. New York: Lawrence Kehoe, 1866.

Kenneally, Finbar. *United States Documents in the Propaganda Fide Archives: 13 vols*. Washington, D.C.: Academy of American Franciscan History, 1966–2006.

McAvoy, Thomas, C.S.C. "The War Letters of Father Peter Paul Cooney of the Congregation of the Holy Cross." *Records of the American Catholic Historical Society of Philadelphia* 44 (1933): 47–69, 151–69, 220–37.

McGovern, James J., D.D., ed. *The Life and Letters of Eliza Allen Starr*. Chicago: Lakeside Press, 1905.

McNeil, Betty Ann, D.C., ed. *Dear Masters: Daughters of Charity of Saint Vincent de Paul, Civil War Nurses*. Hanover, Pa.: Sheridan Press, 2011.

"Memorial of the Monument Erected on the Battlefield of Gettysburg to Very Rev. William Corby, C.S.C." *Catholic Alumni Sodality of Philadelphia* (December 1911).

Menge, W. Springer, and J. August Shimrak, eds. *The Civil War Notebook of Daniel Chisholm: A Chronicle of Daily Life in the Union Army, 1864–1865*. New York: Orion Books, 1989.

The Metropolitan Catholic Almanac and Laity's Directory. Baltimore: John Murphy & Co., 1861.

Mulholland, St. Clair. *The Story of the 116th Regiment Pennsylvania Volunteers in the War of the Rebellion*. Edited by Lawrence Frederick Kohl. 1903. Reprint, New York: Fordham University Press, 1996.

O'Brien, Kevin E., ed. *My Life in the Irish Brigade: The Civil War Memoirs of Private William McCarter, 116th Pennsylvania Infantry*. Campbell, Calif.: Savas Publishing, 1996.

Proceedings of the Fourth National Congress of the Fenian Brotherhood, at Pittsburgh, Pa., February 1866, with the Constitution of the F.B., and Addenda Thereto. New York: J. Craft, 1866.

Samito, Christian, ed. *Commanding Boston's Irish Ninth: The Civil War Letters of Colonel Patrick R. Guiney, Ninth Massachusetts Volunteer Infantry*. New York: Fordham University Press, 1998.

Simon, John Y., ed. *The Papers of Ulysses S. Grant*. 32 vols. Carbondale: Southern Illinois University Press, 1967–2012.

Smet, Pierre-Jean de, S.J. *Life, Letters and Travels of Father Pierre-Jean de Smet, S.J., 1801–1873*. 4 vols. New York: Francis P. Harper, 1905.

University of Notre Dame Archives. "Calendar." http://archives.nd.edu/calendar.htm.

U.S. War Department. *War of the Rebellion: A Compilation of the Official Records of the Union and Confederate Armies*. 128 vols. Washington, D.C., 1880–1901.

———. *War of the Rebellion: A Compilation of the Official Records of the Union and Confederate Navies*. 30 vols. Washington, D.C., 1894–1922.

Welsh, Peter. *Irish Green and Union Blue: The Civil War Letters of Peter Welsh, Color Sergeant, 28th Regiment, Massachusetts Volunteers*. Edited by Lawrence F. Kohl. New York: Fordham University Press, 1986.

Williams, Frederick D., ed. *The Wild Life of the Army: Civil War Letters of James A. Garfield*. East Lansing: Michigan State University Press, 1964.

Wimmer, Boniface, O.S.B. *Letters of an American Abbot*. Edited by Jerome Oetgen. Latrobe, Pa.: Saint Vincent Archabbey Publications, 2008.

Woodstock Letters. 98 vols. Woodstock, Md.: Woodstock College Press, 1872–1969.

Zanca, Kenneth J., ed. *American Catholics and Slavery, 1789–1866: An Anthology of Primary Documents*. New York: University Press of America, 1994.

Secondary Sources

Ahlstrom, Sydney. *A Religious History of the American People*. 2nd ed. New Haven, Conn.: Yale University Press, 2004.

Alexander, June Granatir. *Daily Life in Immigrant America, 1870–1920*. Westport, Conn.: Greenwood Press, 2007.

Anbinder, Tyler. *Nativism and Slavery: The Northern Know Nothings and the Politics of the 1850s*. New York: Oxford University Press, 1992.

Appleby, Joyce. *Liberalism and Republicanism in the Historical Imagination*. Cambridge, Mass.: Harvard University Press, 1992.

Armstrong, Warren B. *For Courageous Fighting and Confident Dying: Union Chaplains in the Civil War*. Lawrence: University Press of Kansas, 1998.

Atkin, Nicholas, and Frank Tallett. *Priests, Prelates, and People: A History of European Catholicism since 1750*. New York: Oxford University Press, 2003.

Aubert, Roger. *Le Pontificat de Pie IX (1846–1878)*. Paris: Bloud & Gay, 1952.

Baker, Jean H. *Affairs of Party: The Political Culture of Northern Democrats in the Mid-Nineteenth Century*. New York: Fordham University Press, 1998.

Barton, George. *Angels of the Battlefield: A History of the Labors of the Catholic Sisterhood in the Late Civil War*. Philadelphia: Catholic Art Publishing, 1897.

Bennett, David H. *The Party of Fear: From Nativist Movements to the New Right in American History*. Chapel Hill: University of North Carolina Press, 1988.

Bennett, Michael J. "Saving Jack: Religion, Benevolent Organizations, and Union Sailors during the Civil War." In Paul A. Cimbala and Randall M. Miller, eds., *Union Soldiers and the Northern Home Front: Wartime Experiences, Postwar Adjustments*, 219–62. New York: Fordham University Press, 2002.

Bernstein, Iver. *The New York City Draft Riots: Their Significance for American Society and Politics in the Age of the Civil War*. New York: Oxford University Press, 1990.

Bickham, W. D. *Rosecrans' Campaign with the Fourteenth Army Corps; or, The Army of the Cumberland: A Narrative of Personal Observations with an Appendix, Consisting of Official Reports of the Battle of Stone River*. Cincinnati: Moore, Wilstach, Keys & Co., 1863.

Bilby, Joseph G. *The Irish Brigade in the Civil War: The 69th New York and Other Irish Regiments of the Army of the Potomac*. Boston: Da Capo Press, 1998.

Bill, Alfred Hoyt. *Rehearsal for Conflict: The War with Mexico, 1846–1848*. New York: Alfred A. Knopf, 1947.

Billington, Ray Allen. *The Protestant Crusade, 1800–1860*. New York: Macmillan, 1938.

Blied, Benjamin J. *Catholics and the Civil War*. Milwaukee: St. Francis Seminary Press, 1945.

Blight, David W. *Race and Reunion: The Civil War in American Memory*. Cambridge, Mass.: Harvard University Press, 2001.

Brinsfield, John W., William C. Davis, Benedict Maryniak, and James I. Robertson, Jr., eds. *Faith in the Fight: Civil War Chaplains*. Mechanicsburg, Pa.: Stackpole Books, 2003.

Brownson, Henry F. *Orestes A. Brownson's Middle Life: From 1845 to 1855*. Detroit: H. F. Brownson, 1899.

———. *Orestes A. Brownson's Latter Life: From 1856 to 1876*. Detroit: H. F. Brownson, 1900.

Bruce, Susannah Ural. *The Harp and the Eagle: Irish-American Volunteers and the Union Army, 1861–1865*. New York: New York University Press, 2006.

Bruscino, Thomas. *A Nation Forged in War: How World War II Taught Americans to Get Along*. Knoxville: University of Tennessee Press, 2010.

Burton, William L. *Melting Pot Soldiers: The Union's Ethnic Regiments*. 2nd ed. New York: Fordham University Press, 1998.

Carey, Patrick W. *Catholics in America: A History*. Westport, Conn.: Praeger, 2004.

———. *Orestes A. Brownson: A Bibliography, 1826–1876*. Milwaukee: Marquette University Press, 1997.

———. *Orestes A. Brownson: American Religious Weathervane*. Grand Rapids, Mich.: Eerdmans, 2004.

———. "Orestes Brownson and the Civil War." *U.S. Catholic Historian* 31 (Winter 2013): 1–20.

———. *People, Priests, and Prelates: Ecclesiastical Democracy and the Tensions of Trusteeism*. Notre Dame, Ind.: University of Notre Dame, 1987.

Carwardine, Richard J. *Evangelicals and Politics in Antebellum America*. New Haven, Conn.: Yale University Press, 1993.

The Catholic Encyclopedia. 15 vols. New York: Robert Appleton Company, 1907–14. http://www.newadvent.org/cathen/.

Clinton, Catherine, and Nina Silber. *Battle Scars: Gender and Sexuality in the American Civil War*. New York: Oxford University Press, 2006.

———. *Divided Houses: Gender and the Civil War*. New York: Oxford University Press, 1992.

Coburn, Carol K., and Martha Smith. *Spirited Lives: How Nuns Shaped Catholic Culture and American Life, 1836–1920*. Chapel Hill: University of North Carolina Press, 1999.

Condon, William Henry. *Life of Major-General James Shields: Hero of Three Wars and Senator from Three States*. Chicago: Blakely Printing, 1900.

Conyngham, David Power. *The Irish Brigade and Its Campaigns*. Edited by Lawrence Frederick Kohl. 1867. Reprint, New York: Fordham University Press, 1994.

Conzen, Kathleen. "German Catholic Communalism and the American Civil War: Exploring the Dilemmas of Transatlantic Political Integration." In *Bridging the Atlantic: The Question of American Exceptionalism in Perspective*, edited by Elisabeth Glaser and Hermann Wellenreuther, 119–44. New York: Cambridge University Press, 2002.

———. "Immigrant Religion and the Public Sphere: The German Catholic Milieu in America." In Wolfgang Helbich and Walter D. Kamphoefner, eds., *German-American Immigration and Ethnicity in Comparative Perspective*, 69–114. Madison, Wis.: Max Kade Institute for German-American Studies, 2004.

———. "Immigrant Religion and the Republic: German Catholics in Nineteenth-Century America." *German Historical Institute Bulletin* 35 (Fall 2004): 43–56.

Coppa, Frank J. *Pope Pius IX: Crusader in a Secular Age*. Boston: Twayne, 1979.

Costello, Rev. Charles A. "Episcopate of Rt. Rev. J. M. Young, Bishop of Erie, Pennsylvania, 1854–1866." M.A. diss., University of Notre Dame, 1951.

Coulombe, Charles A. *The Pope's Legion: The Multinational Fighting Force That Defended the Vatican*. New York: Palgrave Macmillan, 2008.

Cozzens, Peter. *No Better Place to Die: The Battle of Stones River*. Urbana: University of Illinois Press, 1990.

Craughwell, Thomas J. *The Greatest Brigade: How the Irish Brigade Cleared the Way to Victory in the American Civil War*. Minneapolis: Fair Winds Press, 2011.

Curran, Robert Emmett. *A History of Georgetown University: From Academy to University, 1789–1889*. 3 vols. Washington, D.C.: Georgetown University Press, 2010.

Curran, Thomas F. *Soldiers of the Peace: Civil War Pacifism and the Postwar Radical Peace Movement*. New York: Fordham University Press, 2003.

D'Agostino, Peter. *Rome in America: Transnational Catholic Identity from the Risorgimento to Fascism*. Chapel Hill: University of North Carolina Press, 2004.

Daniel, Larry J. *Days of Glory: The Army of the Cumberland, 1861–1865*. Baton Rouge: Louisiana State Press, 2004.

Deye, Anthony H. "Archbishop John Baptist Purcell and the Civil War." Ph.D. diss., University of Cincinnati, 1944.

Doerries, Reinhard R. *Iren und Deutsche in Der Neuen Welt*. Stuttgart: Franz Steiner Verlag Wiesbaden GMBH, 1986.

Dolan, Jay P. *The American Catholic Experience: A History from Colonial Times to the Present*. Notre Dame, Ind.: University of Notre Dame Press, 1992.

———. *The Immigrant Church: New York's Irish and German Catholics, 1815–1865*. Baltimore: Johns Hopkins University Press, 1975).

Doughtery, Kevin. *Civil War Leadership and Mexican War Experience*. Jackson: University Press of Mississippi, 2007.

Efford, Alison Clark. "The Appeal of Racial Neutrality in the Civil War–Era North: German Americans and the Democratic New Departure." *Journal of the Civil War Era* 5 (March 2015): 68–96.

———. *German Immigrants, Race, and Citizenship in the Civil War Era*. New York: Cambridge University Press, 2013.

Endres, David. "Rectifying the Fatal Contrast: Archbishop John Purcell and the Slavery Controversy among Catholics in Civil War Cincinnati." *Ohio Valley History* 2 (Fall 2002): 23–32.

——. "'With a Father's Affection': Chaplain William T. O'Higgins and the Tenth Ohio Volunteer Infantry." *U.S. Catholic Historian* 31 (Winter 2013): 97–127.

Fabun, Sean. "Catholic Chaplains in the Civil War." *Catholic Historical Review* 99 (October 2013): 675–702.

Faherty, William Barnaby, S.J. *Exile in Erin: A Confederate Chaplain's Story: The Life of John B. Bannon.* St. Louis: Missouri Historical Society Press, 2002.

Faust, Drew G. *Mothers of Invention: Women of the Slaveholding South in the American Civil War.* Chapel Hill: University of North Carolina Press, 1996.

Fehrenbacher, Don E. *The Dred Scott Case: Its Significance in American Law and Politics.* New York: Oxford University Press, 1978.

Fenton, Elizabeth A. *Religious Liberties: Anti-Catholicism and Liberal Democracy in Nineteenth-Century.* Oxford, U.K.: Oxford University Press, 2011.

Ferraro, William M. "More Than a General's Wife: Ellen Ewing Sherman." *Timeline* 17, no. 1 (2000): 18–33.

Fisher, James T. *Communion of Immigrants: A History of Catholics in America.* New York: Oxford University Press, 2007.

Fogarty, Gerald, S.J. *Commonwealth Catholicism.* Notre Dame, Ind.: University of Notre Dame Press, 2001.

——. "Public Patriotism and Private Politics: The Tradition of American Catholicism." *U.S. Catholic Historical* 4 (1984): 1–48.

Foner, Eric. *The Fiery Trial: Abraham Lincoln and American Slavery.* New York: W. W. Norton, 2010.

——. *Free Soil, Free Labor, Free Men: The Ideology of the Republican Party before the Civil War.* New York: Oxford University Press, 1995.

Foos, Paul. *A Short, Offhand, Killing Affair: Soldiers and Social Conflict during the Mexican–American War.* Chapel Hill: University of North Carolina Press, 2002.

Fredrickson, George M. *The Inner Civil War: Northern Intellectuals and the Crisis of Union.* Champaign: University of Illinois Press, 1993.

Freehling, William W. *The Road to Disunion.* Vol. 2, *Secessionists Triumphant, 1854–1861.* New York: Oxford University Press, 2007.

Gallagher, Gary W. *The Union War.* Cambridge, Mass.: Harvard University Press, 2011.

Gannon, Barbara A. *The Won Cause: Black and White Comradeship in the Grand Army of the Republic.* Chapel Hill: University of North Carolina Press, 2011.

Garesché, Louis. *Biography of Lieut. Col. Julius P. Garesché, Assistant Adjutant- General, U.S. Army.* Philadelphia: J. B. Lippincott, 1887.

Garraghan, Gilbert J., S.J. *The Jesuits of the Middle United States.* 3 vols. Chicago: Loyola University Press, 1984.

George, Joseph, Jr.. "Philadelphia's Catholic Herald: The Civil War Years." *Pennsylvania Magazine of History and Biography* 103 (1979): 196–221.

Germain, Dom Aidan Henry, S.T.L., M.A., J.C.B. "Catholic Military and Naval Chaplains, 1776–1917." Ph.D. diss., Catholic University of America, 1929.

Gienapp, William E. *The Origins of the Republican Party, 1852–1856*. New York: Oxford University Press, 1988.

Giesberg, Judith. *Army at Home: Women and the Civil War on the Northern Home Front*. Chapel Hill: University of North Carolina Press, 2009.

Gjerde, Jon. *Catholicism and the Shaping of Nineteenth-Century America*. Edited by S. Deborah King. Cambridge, U.K.: Cambridge University, 2012.

Gleason, Philip. *The Conservative Reformers: German-American Catholics and the Social Order*. Notre Dame, Ind.: University of Notre Dame Press, 1968.

Gleeson, David T. *The Green and the Gray: The Irish in the Confederate States of America*. Chapel Hill: University of North Carolina Press, 2013.

Goldfield, David. *America Aflame: How the Civil War Created a Nation*. New York: Bloomsbury, 2011.

Gross, Michael B. *The War against Catholicism: Liberalism and the Anti-Catholic Imagination in Nineteenth-Century Germany*. Ann Arbor: University of Michigan Press, 2004.

Hamburger, Philip. *Separation of Church and State*. Cambridge, Mass.: Harvard University Press, 2002.

Handlin, Oscar. *Boston's Immigrants: A Study in Acculturation*. Rev. ed. Cambridge, Mass.: Belknap Press of Harvard University Press, 1979.

Hassard, John. *Life of the Most Reverend John Hughes, D.D.: First Archbishop of New York, with Extracts from His Private Correspondence*. New York: D. Appleton and Company, 1866.

Heineman, Kenneth J. *Civil War Dynasty: The Ewing Family of Ohio*. New York: New York University Press, 2013.

Hennesey, James, S.J. *American Catholics: A History of the Roman Catholic Community in the United States*. New York: Oxford University Press, 1981.

———. "The Baltimore Council of 1866." *American Catholic Historical Society of Philadelphia* 3 (September 1965): 157–73.

Higham, John. *Strangers in the Land: Patterns of American Nativism, 1860–1925*. 2nd ed. New Brunswick, NJ: Rutgers University Press, 1988.

History of Saint John's Classis. Cleveland: Central Publishing House, 1921.

Hochgeschwender, Michael. *Wahrheit, Einheit, Ordnung: Die Sklavenfrage und der amerikanische Katholizismus, 1835–1870*. Paderborn: Ferdinand Schöningen, 2006.

Holt, Michael F. *The Political Crisis of the 1850s*. New York: W. W. Norton, 1978.

Hope, Arthur J., C.S.C. *Notre Dame One Hundred Years*. Notre Dame, Ind.: University of Notre Dame Press, 1943.

Howe, Barbara J., and Margaret A. Brennan. "The Sisters of St. Joseph in Wheeling, West Virginia, during the Civil War." *U.S. Catholic Historian* 31 (Winter 2013): 21–49.

Howe, Daniel Walker. *What Hath God Wrought: The Transformation of America, 1815–1848*. New York: Oxford University Press, 2007.

Hueston, Robert Francis. *The Catholic Press and Nativism, 1840–1860*. New York: Arno Press, 1976.

Hutton, Paul Andrew. *Phil Sheridan and His Army.* Lincoln: University of Nebraska Press, 1985.

Ignatiev, Noel. *How the Irish Became White.* New York: Routledge, 1995.

Janney, Caroline E. *Remembering the Civil War: Reunion and the Limits of Reconciliation.* Chapel Hill: University of North Carolina Press, 2013.

Johannsen, Robert W. *To the Halls of Montezuma: The Mexican War in the American Imagination.* New York: Oxford University Press, 1985.

Johnson, Clint *A Vast and Fiendish Plot: The Confederate Attack on New York City.* New York: Citadel Press, 2010.

Johnson, Tyler V. *Devotion to the Adopted Country: U.S. Immigrant Volunteers in the Mexican War.* Columbia: University of Missouri Press, 2012.

———. "Punishing the Lies on the Rio Grande: Catholic and Immigrant Volunteers in Zachary Taylor's Army and the Fight against Nativism." *Journal of the Early Republic* 30 (Spring 2010): 63–84.

Jolly, Ellen Ryan. *The Nuns of the Battlefield.* Providence: Providence Visitor, 1927.

Kauffman, Christopher J. *Faith and Fraternalism: The History of the Knights of Columbus.* Rev. ed. New York: Simon & Schuster, 1992.

Keating, Ryan W. "'Give Us War in Our Time': America's Irish Communities at War in the Civil War Era." Ph.D. diss., Fordham University, 2013.

Keefer, Bradley S. *Conflicting Memories of the "River of Death": The Chickamauga Battlefield and the Spanish–American War, 1863–1933.* Kent, Ohio: Kent State University Press, 2013.

Keller, Christian B. *Chancellorsville and the Germans: Nativism, Ethnicity, and Civil War Memory.* New York: Fordham University Press, 2007.

———. "New Perspectives in Civil War Ethnic History and Their Implications for Twenty-First-Century Scholarship." In Andrew L. Slap and Michael Thomas Smith, eds., *This Distracted and Anarchical People: New Answers for Old Questions about the Civil War–Era North,* 123–41. New York: Fordham University Press, 2013.

Kenneally, James J. *The History of American Catholic Women.* New York: Crossroad Publishing Company, 1990.

Kenny, Kevin. *The American Irish: A History.* New York: Longman, 2000.

Klement, Frank. "Catholics as Copperheads during the Civil War." *Catholic Historical Review* 80 (January 1994): 36–57.

Knobel, Dale T. *Paddy and the Republic: Ethnicity and Nationality in Antebellum America.* Middletown, Conn.: Wesleyan University Press, 1986.

Kurtz, William B. "Let Us Hear No More 'Nativism': The Catholic Press in the Mexican and Civil Wars." *Civil War History* 60, no. 1 (2014): 6–31.

———. "'The Perfect Model of a Christian Hero': The Faith, Anti-Slaveryism, and Postwar Legacy of William S. Rosecrans." *U.S. Catholic Historian* 21, no. 1 (2013): 73–96.

Kwitchen, Sister Mary Augustine. "James Alphonsus McMaster: A Study in American Thought." Ph.D. diss., Catholic University of America, 1949.

Lamers, William M. *The Edge of Glory: A Biography of General William S. Rosecrans, U.S.A.* New York: Harcourt, Brace & World, 1961.

Lamott, John H., S.T.D. *History of the Archdiocese of Cincinnati, 1821–1891.* Cincinnati: Frederick Pustet Company, 1921.

Larson, Kate Clifford. *The Assassin's Accomplice: Mary Surratt and the Plot to Kill Abraham Lincoln.* New York: Basic Books, 2008.

Lawson, Melinda. *Patriot Fires: Forging a New American Nationalism in the Civil War North.* Lawrence: University Press of Kansas, 2002.

Lonn, Ella. *Foreigners in the Union Army and Navy.* Baton Rouge: Louisiana State University Press, 1951.

Lysy, Peter J. *Blue for the Union and Green for Ireland: The Civil War Flags of the 63rd Regiment New York Volunteers, Irish Brigade.* South Bend, Ind.: Mossberg and Company, 2001.

Maher, Sr. Mary Denis. *To Bind Up the Wounds: Catholic Sister Nurses in the U.S. Civil War.* New York: Greenwood Press, 1989.

Marty, Martin, O.S.B. *Dr. Johann Martin Henni, erster bischof und erzbischof von Milwaukee: Ein lebensbild aus der pionier-zeit von Ohio und Wisconsin.* New York: Benziger Brothers, 1888.

Marvel, William. *Mr. Lincoln Goes to War.* New York: Houghton Mifflin, 2006.

Massey, Mary E. *Women in the Civil War.* 1966. Reprint, Lincoln, Neb.: Bison Books, 1994.

Maxwell, John Francis. *Slavery and the Catholic Church: The History of Catholic Teaching concerning the Moral Legitimacy of the Institution of Slavery.* London: Barry Rose, 1975.

McAfee, Ward M. *Religion, Race, and Reconstruction: The Public School in the Politics of the 1870s.* Albany: State University of New York Press, 1998.

McDaniel, Isaac. "The Impact of the Mexican War on Anti-Catholicism in the United States." Ph.D. diss., University of Notre Dame, 1991.

McEniry, Sr. Blanche Marie. "American Catholics in the War with Mexico." Ph.D. diss., Catholic University of America, 1937.

McGreevy, John T. *Catholicism and American Freedom: A History.* New York: W. W. Norton, 2003.

McNeil, Betty Ann, D.C. "Daughters of Charity: Courageous and Compassionate Civil War Nurses." *U.S. Catholic Historian* 31 (Winter 2013): 51–72.

McPherson, James M. *The Battle Cry of Freedom.* New York: Oxford University Press, 1988.

———. *For Cause and Comrades: Why Men Fought in the Civil War.* New York: Oxford University Press, 1997.

———. *What They Fought For, 1861–1865.* New York: Anchor Books, 1995.

McSorley, Joseph. *Isaac Hecker and His Friends.* Rev ed. New York: Paulist Press, 1972.

Metz, Judith, S.C. *The Sisters of Charity of Cincinnati in the Civil War.* Cincinnati: Sisters of Charity of Cincinnati, 2012.

Miles, Michael J. "An Irish Philadelphian in the Civil War: The Civil War Letters of William C. White." B.A. diss., St. Joseph University, 2002.

Miller, Kerby A. *Emigrants and Exiles: Ireland and the Irish Exodus to North America.* New York: Oxford University Press, 1985.

Miller, Randall M., Harry S. Stout, and Charles Reagan Wilson, eds. *Religion and the American Civil War.* New York: Oxford University Press, 1998.

Miller, Robert Ryal. *Shamrock and Sword: The Saint Patrick's Battalion in the U.S.-Mexican War.* Norman: University of Oklahoma Press, 1989.

Montgomery, David. *Beyond Equality: Labor and the Radical Republicans, 1862–1872.* Urbana: University of Illinois Press, 1981.

Moore, David. *William S. Rosecrans and the Union Victory: A Civil War Biography.* Jefferson, N.C.: McFarland Press, 2014.

Moorhead, James. *American Apocalypse: Yankee Protestants and the Civil War, 1860–1869.* New Haven, Conn.: Yale University Press, 1978.

Mujic, Julie. "Between Campus and War: Students, Patriotism, and Education at Midwestern Universities during the American Civil War." Ph.D. diss., Kent State University, 2012.

Mulhane, L. W. *Major-General William Stark Rosecrans: Hero of Iuka, Corinth and Stone River, and Father of the Army of the Cumberland.* Columbus, Ohio: Columbian Print Company, 1898.

Murphy, Angela F. *American Slavery, Irish Freedom: Abolition, Immigrant Citizenship, and the Transatlantic Movement for Irish Repeal.* Baton Rouge: Louisiana State University Press, 2010.

Neely, Jr., Mark E. *Lincoln and the Triumph of the Nation: Constitutional Conflict in the American Civil War.* Chapel Hill: University of North Carolina Press, 2011.

Neidhart, W. S. *Fenianism in North America.* University Park: Pennsylvania State University Press, 1975.

Noll, Mark A. *America's God: From Jonathan Edwards to Abraham Lincoln.* New York: Oxford University Press, 2002.

———. *The Civil War as a Theological Crisis.* Chapel Hill: University of North Carolina Press, 2006.

Oakes, James. *Freedom National: The Destruction of Slavery in the United States, 1861–1865.* New York: W. W. Norton, 2013.

O'Brien, David J. *Isaac Hecker: An American Catholic.* New York: Paulist Press, 1992.

O'Connell, Marvin. *Edward Sorin.* Notre Dame, Ind.: University of Notre Dame Press, 2001.

———. *John Ireland and the American Catholic Church.* St. Paul: Minnesota Historical Society Press, 1988.

O'Connor, Thomas H. *Fitzpatrick's Boston, 1846–1866.* Boston: Northeastern University Press, 1984.

Pinheiro, John Christopher. "Crusade and Conquest: Anti-Catholicism, Manifest Destiny, and the U.S.–Mexican War of 1846–1848." Ph.D. diss., University of Tennessee, 2001.

Pocock, J. G. A. "Between Gog and Magog: The Republican Thesis and the Ideologia Americana." *Journal of the History of Ideas* 48 (April–June 1987): 325–46.

Potter, David M. *The Impending Crisis, 1848–1861.* New York: Harper & Row, 1976.

Rable, George C. *God's Almost Chosen Peoples: A Religious History of the American Civil War*. Chapel Hill: University of North Carolina Press, 2010.

Railton, Stephen. "Yankee Anti-Catholicism" and "Fifty Years in the Church of Rome." *Mark Twain, His Times, Catholic Church*. http://twain.lib.virginia.edu/yankee/cycathhp.html.

Reid, Whitelaw. *Ohio in the War: Her Statesmen, Her Generals, and Soldiers: The History of Her Regiments, and Other Military Organizations*. 2 vols. Cincinnati: Moore, Wilstach & Baldwin, 1868.

Rice, Madeleine Hooke. *American Catholic Opinion in the Slavery Controversy*. New York: Columbia University Press, 1944.

Richards, Leonard L. *The Slave Power: The Free North and Southern Domination, 1780–1860*. Baton Rouge: Louisiana State University Press, 2000.

Rodgers, Daniel T. *Contested Truths: Keywords in American Politics since Independence*. New York: Basic Books, 1987.

Roediger, David R. *The Wages of Whiteness: Race and the Making of the American Working Class*. Rev. ed. New York: Verso, 1998.

Rothan, Emmet H. "The German Catholic Immigrant in the United States (1830–1860)." Ph.D. diss., Catholic University of America, 1946.

Ruby, James S., ed. *Blue and Gray: Georgetown University and the Civil War*. Baltimore: Garamond Press, 1961.

Samito, Christian G. *Becoming American under Fire: Irish Americans, African Americans, and the Politics of Citizenship during the Civil War Era*. Ithaca, N.Y.: Cornell University Press, 2009.

Sandow, Robert M. *Deserter Country: Civil War Opposition in the Pennsylvania Appalachians*. New York: Fordham University Press, 2009.

Schmidt, James M. *Notre Dame and the Civil War: Marching Onward to Victory*. Charleston: History Press, 2010.

Schroth, Raymond A., S.J. *Fordham: A History and Memoir*. Chicago: Loyola University Press, 2002.

Scott, Sean A. *A Visitation of God: Northern Civilians Interpret the Civil War*. Oxford, U.K.: Oxford University Press, 2011.

Semmes, Raphael. *Service Afloat and Ashore during the Mexican War*. Cincinnati: Wm. H. Moore & Co., Publishers, 1851.

Sharrow, Walter G. "Northern Catholic Intellectuals and the Coming of the Civil War." *New York Historical Society Quarterly* 58 (January 1974): 35–56.

Shattuck, Gardiner H., Jr. *A Shield and Hiding Place: The Religious Life of the Civil War Armies*. Macon, Ga.: Mercer University Press, 1987.

Shaughnessy, Gerald. *Has the Immigrant Kept the Faith? A Study of Immigration and Catholic Growth in the United States, 1790–1920*. New York: Macmillan, 1925.

Silber, Nina. *Daughters of the Union: Northern Women Fight the Civil War*. Cambridge, Mass.: Harvard University Press, 2005.

———. *Gender and the Sectional Conflict*. Chapel Hill: University of North Carolina Press, 2008.

Simon, James F. *Lincoln and Chief Justice Taney: Slavery, Secession, and the President's War Powers*. New York: Simon & Schuster, 2006.

Snay, Mitchell. *Fenians, Freedmen, and Southern Whites: Race and Nationalities in the Era of Reconstruction*. Baton Rouge: Louisiana State Press, 2007.

Sorin, Edward. *The Chronicles of Notre Dame Du Lac*. Edited by James T. Connelly. Notre Dame, Ind.: University of Notre Dame Press, 1992.

Spalding, David, C.F.X. "Martin John Spalding's 'Dissertation on the American Civil War.'" *Catholic Historical Review* 52, no. 1 (1966): 66–85.

Spalding, Thomas W. *Martin John Spalding: American Churchman*. Washington, D.C.: Catholic University Press, 1973.

Stock, Leo Francis. "The United States at the Court of Pius IX." *Catholic Historical Review* 9 (1923–24): 103–22.

A Story of Fifty Years: From the Annals of the Congregation of the Sisters of the Holy Cross. Notre Dame, Ind.: Ave Maria Press, 1905.

Stout, Harry S. *Upon the Altar of the Nation: A Moral History of the Civil War*. New York: Penguin, 2006.

Sweeney, Helen. *The Golden Milestone, 1846–1896*. New York: Benziger Brothers, 1896.

Szpila, Kathleen. "Lest We Forget: Ellen Ryan Jolly and the Nuns of the Battlefield Monument." *American Catholic Studies* 123, no. 4 (2012): 23–43.

Taggart, Joseph. *Biographical Sketches of the Eminent American Patriots, Charles Carroll, of Carrollton; Roger Brooke Taney; William Starke Rosecrans; John Barry; Philip Henry Sheridan, and a Sketch of the Early History of Maryland*. Kansas City, Mo.: Burton Company, 1907.

Tap, Bruce. *Over Lincoln's Shoulder: The Committee on the Conduct of the War*. Lawrence: University Press of Kansas, 1998.

Trindal, Elizabeth Steger. *Mary Surratt: An American Tragedy*. Gretna, La.: Pelican Publishing, 1996.

Tucker, Phillip Thomas. *The Confederacy's Fighting Chaplain Father John B. Bannon*. Tuscaloosa: University of Alabama Press, 1992.

———. *"God Help the Irish!": The History of the Irish Brigade*. Abilene, Tex.: McWhiney Foundation Press, 2007.

Tuveson, Ernest Lee. *Redeemer Nation: The Idea of America's Millennial Role*. Chicago: University of Chicago Press, 1980.

Ural, Susannah J., ed. *Civil War Citizens: Race, Ethnicity, and Identity in America's Bloodiest Conflict*. New York: New York University Press, 2010.

Valuska, David L., and Christian B. Keller. *Damn Dutch: Pennsylvania Germans at Gettysburg*. Mechanicsburg, Pa.: Stackpole Books, 2004.

Varney, Frank P. *General Grant and the Rewriting of History: How the Destruction of General William S. Rosecrans Influenced Our Understanding of the Civil War*. El Dorado Hills, Calif.: Savas Beatie, 2013.

Wallace, W. Jason. *Catholics, Slaveholders, and the Dilemma of American Evangelicalism, 1835–1860*. Notre Dame, Ind.: University of Notre Dame Press, 2010.

Walsh, Sister Marie de Lourdes. *The Sisters of Charity of New York, 1809–1959*. Vol. 2. New York: Fordham University Press, 1960.

Weber, Jennifer L. *Copperheads: The Rise and Fall of Lincoln's Opponents in the North.*
New York: Oxford University Press, 2006.

Wesley, Timothy L. *The Politics of Faith during the Civil War.* Baton Rouge: Louisiana
State University Press, 2013.

Willging, Eugene P., and Herta Hatzfeld. *Catholic Serials of the Nineteenth Century in
the United States: A Descriptive Bibliography and Union List.* 1st and 2nd ser.
Washington, D.C.: Catholic University of America Press, 1959–68.

Wimmer, Judith Conrad. "American Catholic Interpretations of the Civil War." Ph.D.
diss., Drew University, 1980.

Woodworth, Steven E. *While God Is Marching On: The Religious World of Civil War
Soldiers.* Lawrence: University Press of Kansas, 2001.

Wylie, Paul R. *The Irish General: Thomas Francis Meagher.* Norman: University of Oklahoma Press, 2007.

Index

69th New York Infantry Regiment, 44, 46
108th Ohio Infantry Regiment, 62

abolition: Catholic Church's position on,
  93–94, 100–1, 147; Catholic soldiers'
  views on, 63–64; northern Catholic
  views on, 89–107
absolutions, 75–76, 150
African Americans: Catholic missions to,
  104–5, 106–7; Catholic soldiers' views
  of, 63, 64; labor riots against, 111
American Party. See Know-Nothings
American Protective Association (APA),
  144
American Republican Party, 21–22
Anderson, Robert, 12, 14
Andrew, John A., 43
Angels of the Battlefield (Barton), 145, 146
antebellum period: growth of Catholicism,
  3, 22; growth of Catholic subculture,
  3, 26–27; growth of nativism and anti-
  Catholicism, 2–3, 20–28
anti-Catholicism: in American history
  and thought, 2–3; antebellum growth
  of, 2–3, 20–28; Catholic patriotism to
  counteract, 1, 4, 14–15, 16–18, 42–43,
  46, 50–51, 144–45, 148–49, 160, 161–64;
  at end of Civil War, 126–28; faced by
  Catholic nuns and chaplains, 71–72,
  77–80, 82–83, 85–87; influenced by
  European events, 20, 129–36; instances
  of decline in post-war period, 141–42;
  of Know-Nothings, 3, 10, 22–28; Manifest Destiny influenced by, 10–11; during Mexican War, 11–12, 14–15, 18–19;
  reinforced by public school debates,
  136–41; in Union Army, 55, 77–80

anti-Prostestantism: expressed by Catholic
  chaplains, 78–79; expressed by Catholic
  commentators, 32, 117
anti-war Catholics: complex motivations
  of, 108–9; during Mexican War, 15–16;
  New York City draft riots, 109–16;
  reactions to Lincoln's assassination,
  125–26; reaction to papal peace letters,
  119–20; wartime views of, 4, 36–37, 100,
  116–24
Antonelli, Card. Giacomo, 120
assimilation, 26–27. See also Catholic
  subculture

Balch, Rev. William S., 21
Banks, Nathaniel P., 23, 28, 131
Bannon, John, 44
Bapst, Fr. John, 24
Bardstown College, 44
Barry, John, 2
Barton, George, 145, 146, 147
battlefield absolutions, 75–76, 150
Battle of Gettysburg absolution, 76, 150
Beauregard, Pierre Gustave Toutant, 16,
  29, 45
Becoming American under Fire (Samito), 5
Bedini, Abp. Gaetano, 22
Bell, John, 31
Bell, Stephan, 23
Biographical Sketches of the Eminent
  American Patriots (Taggart), 156
Bismarck, Otto von, 131, 136
Blaine, James G., 140
Blaine amendment, 140, 203–4n25
Blied, Benjamin, 5, 147
Boffinger, Peter, 65, 159
Booth, John Wilkes, 125

Border State Catholics: reactions to Fort Sumter attack, 33–35; reactions to secession, 31–33

Bourget, Fr. Julien-Prosper, 77

Brady, Fr. Thomas, 73

Breckinridge, John, 31

Brophy, John P., 132

Brown, John, 92

Brownson, Edward P., 63–64, 66, 113, 123

Brownson, Henry, 66

Brownson, Orestes A.: on Catholic patriotism, 1, 30, 44, 57, 145; on Mexican War, 15; nativist views of, 25–26; on New York City draft riots, 113, 114, 115; on papal peace letters, 119; pro-war views of, 40–42, 121, 122–24; on role of Catholic press, 6; on secession, 1, 32; sons' deaths, 66, 123; support for Lincoln, 31, 122–23; views on slavery and emancipation, 91–92, 94–97, 99, 106

Brownson, William, 66, 123

Brownson's Quarterly Review, 42, 95, 97

Bucklin, Sophia, 87

Bullenhaar, Anton, 64, 159

Burns, Anthony, 22, 90

Butler, Gen. Benjamin, 86, 120

Callnan, Sr. Elizabeth, 84

Campaign of General Scott, The (Semmes), 16

Campbell, Alexander, 21

Carrier, Fr. Joseph, 75

Carroll, Charles, 2

Catholic, The: on anti-Catholicism, 127; on Orestes Brownson's nativism, 26; on New York City draft riots, 113, 114; pro-war views of, 40; views on slavery and emancipation, 97, 99

Catholic chaplains: anti-Catholicism faced by, 71–72, 77–80; Civil War service of, 43, 68–77; lack of German speakers among, 55–56, 62, 69; post-war commemoration of, 152–53

Catholic Church: antebellum growth of, 3, 22; missions to African Americans, 104–5, 106–7; position on slavery and emancipation, 31–32, 93–94, 100–1, 147; response to Fenians, 131; as solution to sectionalism, 31–32, 117

Catholic clergy: antebellum political neutrality of, 30; on Catholic assimilation, 26–27; Civil War service of, 43, 68–77; drafting of, 116; lack of support for Fenians, 131, 133; reactions to New York City draft riots, 112–13; on requests for chaplains and nuns, 69–70, 82, 87–88; on "Roman Question," 134–35. See also individual clergymen

Catholic colleges: enlistment from, 44–45; as source of Civil War chaplains, 71–72

Catholic Copperheads, 116–17. See also anti-war Catholics

"Catholic Department" at Chicago Fair, 50

Catholic Encyclopedia, The, 43, 158

Catholic Herald, 19, 38, 57, 121, 123

Catholic laity, wartime views of, 46–50

Catholic Mirror: anti-war views of, 34, 46, 73, 124; on Know-Nothings and Orestes Brownson's nativism, 25, 26; on New York City draft riots, 113; on papal peace letters, 119; on public school debates, 140; on "Roman Question," 135; views on slavery and emancipation, 95, 96, 106

Catholic nuns: anti-Catholicism faced by, 82–83, 85–87; Civil War service of, 68, 80–88; post-war commemoration of, 87, 159–60

Catholic patriotism: attacks on, 126–28, 137, 139–41; celebrated by Catholic press, 14–15, 37–38, 46, 56–60; commemoration of (see post-war commemoration); to counteract anti-Catholicism, 1, 4, 14–15, 16–18, 42–43, 46, 50–51, 144–45, 148–49, 160, 161–64; German Catholics, 158–59; Irish Catholics, 1, 37–38, 56, 57, 59; during

Mexican War, 14–15, 16–18; Pittsburgh Catholics, 39–40

Catholic press: antebellum political neutrality of, 30; on anti-Catholicism, 14–15, 126–28; anti-war views, 37, 108–28; celebration of Catholic patriotism, 14–15, 37–38, 46, 56–60; debate over slavery and emancipation, 89–106; German language, 17 (*see also* German Catholic press); on Know-Nothings, 24–26; on Lincoln's assassination, 125–26; on Mexican War, 9–10, 14–15, 16–20; on New York City draft riots, 114–16; overview of, 9–10; on presidential election of 1864, 122–23; pro-war views, 33–40, 121–25; on public school debates, 139–40; on secession, 31–33; tributes to Gen. Rosecrans, 155–56. *See also individual newspapers and editors*

Catholics and the Civil War (Blied), 5, 147

Catholic soldiers: anti-Catholicism faced by, 43, 55, 60; celebrated by Catholic press, 46, 56–60; Civil War service of, 43–45, 52–67; German Catholics, 53–54, 55–56, 62–63; hardships of families of, 64–66; Irish Catholics, 53, 54, 57, 59–61; key aspects of Civil War experience, 52–53; Mexican War service of, 11, 15–19; post-war commemoration of (*see* post-war commemoration); reactions to New York City draft riots, 113–14; religious life of, 43, 55–56, 62, 69; Revolutionary War service of, 2; views of African Americans, 63, 64; views on slavery and emancipation, 63–64

Catholic subculture: antebellum growth of, 3, 26–27; German Catholics and, 27, 159; post-war growth of, 4–5, 142–43

Catholic Telegraph: on anti-Catholicism, 127; on Catholic patriotism, 46, 127; on Cincinnati labor riots, 111; on Mexican War, 15; on papal peace letters, 118–19;

pro-war views of, 36, 123; on secession and sectionalism, 32, 33; views on slavery and emancipation, 97, 98, 100–1, 102, 103

Catholic University of America, 142

Catholic veterans' groups, 146

Catholic women: nuns' Civil War service, 68, 80–88; post-war commemoration by, 159–60; role in New York City draft riots, 112; wartime views of, 47–50

Cavanaugh, John W., 153

Central Verein, 159

Chase, Salmon P., 27

Chicago Tribune, 131

Chiniquy, Charles, 144

Chisholm, Alex, 60–61

Chisholm, Daniel, 60–61

Christian Advocate and Journal, 11

Christy, Fr. Richard, 55

Cincinnati Gazette, 111

Cincinnati (OH): Catholic reaction to Fort Sumter attack, 36; labor riots, 111; public school debates, 137, 138

Cleveland Plain Dealer, 11

Colfax, Schuyler, 28

College of Notre Dame. *See* University of Notre Dame

colonies, anti-Catholicism in, 2

confessions, 75

conscription. *See* draft

conversions, 84–85

Conyngham, David Powers, 146

Conzen, Kathleen, 158

Cook, James, 84

Cooney, Fr. Peter Paul: as Civil War chaplain, 70, 74, 75–76, 77, 78–79; death of, 152; post-war career and commemoration, 141, 148–49, 150, 151, 152; on Gen. Rosecrans, 57

Corby, Fr. William: as Civil War chaplain, 62, 72, 73, 74, 76, 79, 80, 146; death of, 152; post-war career and commemoration, 4, 147, 148, 149–53, 163–64

Corcoran, Col. Michael, 44, 54, 57, 59, 60

Curd, Thomas J., 16
Curtin, Andrew, 86

Daly, Charles, 48
Daly, Maria Lydig, 108
Daughters of Charity, *81*, 82, 83, 85
Davis, Jefferson, 118
Democratic Catholics: party loyalty of, 26, 29, 30–31, 63; views on Civil War, 4, 36–38
Denny, James, 114
desertion, 18–19
Deshon, Fr. George, 155
De Smet, Fr. Pierre-Jean, 128
Dieden, Johann, 31
Dillon, Fr. James, *72*, 72–73, 76, 77
Domenec, Bp. Michael, 39, 40, 125
Donahoe, Patrick: on anti-Catholicism, 127, 128; on drafting of Catholic clergy, 116; on Irish Catholic patriotism, 1, 37–38, 46, 127; on Know-Nothings, 24–25; on Lincoln's assassination, 125; on Mexican War, 15; on New York City draft riots, 115, 116; pro-war views of, 121–22, 124; "Roman Question" involvement of, 134, 135; on secession, 32; views on slavery and emancipation, 90, 96–97, 100, 103
Douglas, Stephen A., 30–31
draft, 109, 111, 116
draft riots, 109–16
Dred Scott decision, 91–92
Duff, Joe, 64, 121
Duggan, Dennis, 55
Duggan, Bp. James, 131
Dunne, Edmund E., 140
Dupanloup, Bp. Felix, 98

Early, Fr. John, 71
Edge of Glory (Lamers), 156
Edwards, Frank, 12
Elder, Bp. William H., 105, 122
Elliott, Fr. Walter, 62, 65–66, 153
Elliott, William, 65

emancipation: Catholic Church's position on, 93–94, 100–1, 147; Catholic soldiers' views on, 63–64; ignored in post-war commemorations, 146–48; northern Catholic views on, 89–107
European nationalist movements, 136
European revolutions of 1848, 20
Ewing, Maria T., 46

Farran, James, 103
fast day (January 4, 1861), 32–33
Fenians, 35, 131–33
Fillmore, Millard, 27
First Battle of Bull Run, 45–46
Fitzpatrick, Bp. John B., 43
For Cause and Comrades (McPherson), 7
Fordham University, 71
Fort Sumter attack, 1, 29, 33–36
Forty-Eighters, 20
Freeman's Journal. See New York Freeman's Journal
Frémont, John, 122
Fullerton, Fr. James, 69

GAR. *See* Grand Army of the Republic
Garesché, Col. Julius, 16, 57, 71, 99, 100
Garesché, Louis, 100, 145
Gavazzi, Alessandro, 20
General Grant and the Rewriting of History (Varney), 156–57
Georgetown College, 44, 71
Georgetown University, 154
German Catholic press: debate over slavery and emancipation, 103–4; on Mexican War, 17. *See also individual newspapers and editors*
German Catholics: civilians' experiences, 47, 110, 158; Civil War service of, 53–54, 55–56, 62–63; lack of German-speaking chaplains, 55–56, 62, 69; lack of post-war commemoration, 157–59; reactions to Fort Sumter attack, 35–36; separatism of, 27, 159
Gillen, Fr. Paul, 55, 72–73, 74, 75, 78

Gillespie, Mother Angela, 83, 86, 87
Grand Army of the Republic (GAR), 146, 150–52
Grant, Gen. Ulysses S., 121, 131, 139–40
"Gray Nuns Act," 138
Greeley, Horace, 112, 126–28
Guilday, Fr. Peter, 160
Guiney, Col. Patrick, 46, 57, 61, 65, 113, 121

Hammond, William A., 86
Hancock, Gen. Winfield Scott, 76
Hardie, Gen. James A., 126, 134
Harlin, Hugh, 69
Harney, Col. William Selby, 16
Harp and the Eagle, The (Ural), 5
Harper's Weekly, 59, 112, 115
Hatala, Fr. Aloysius, 62
Hayes, Rutherford B., 138, 140
Hecker, Fr. Isaac, 112
Henni, Bp. Martin, 97–98
Herberg, Will, 163
Hett, Matthew, 17
Hewit, Augustine, 112
Hewit, Henry S., 42, 104–5
Hochgeschwender, Michael, 145
Hughes, Abp. John, 13; on Catholic separatism, 26–27; on draft, 111; during Mexican War, 14; New York City draft riots and, 112–13; Protestant criticism of, 21; pro-war views of, 37, 38–39, 46; on requests for Catholic chaplains, 70, 73; views on slavery and emancipation, 95–96

immigrant Catholics: in antebellum period, 3; Democratic loyalty of, 26; involvement with Fenians, 35, 131–33; post-war diversity of, 144; reactions to Fort Sumter attack, 35. See also German Catholics; Irish Catholics
Independent, The, 118
infallibility doctrine, 130–31
Ingersoll, Robert G., 141
Ireland, Abp. John, 70, 77, 80, 141–42

Irish Brigade, 53, 60–61, 76
Irish Brigade and Its Campaigns, The (Conyngham), 146
Irish Brigade Association, 146, 150
Irish Catholics: in antebellum period, 3, 30; Orestes Brownson's criticisms of, 25–26; Cincinnati riots, 111; Civil War service of, 43, 44, 47, 53, 54, 57, 59–61; involvement with Fenians, 35, 131–33; Mexican War service of, 11, 15, 18–19; New York City draft riots, 109–16; patriotism of, 1, 37–38, 56, 57, 59; post-war commemoration of, 146, 157; southern, 5; views of African Americans, 63, 64; views on slavery and emancipation, 63, 64, 90–91
Irish independence movement. See Fenians
Irish Repealers, 18
Irish World and American Industrial Liberator, 156

Jenkins, Courtney, 32, 45
Jenkins, Fr. John, 153, 163–64
Johansen, Robert, 10
John Brown's raid, 92
Johnson, Andrew, 131
Johnston, Gen. Joseph E., 45
Jolly, Ellen Ryan, 159–60
Judge Daly Guards, 48
"just war" theology, 119

Katholische Kirchen-Zeitung, 17, 35, 104, 125, 127–28
Katholische Volkszeitung, Die, 104
Keller, Christian, 159
Kennedy, John F., 163
Kenrick, Abp. Francis P., 24, 34–35, 70–71, 73, 77, 102
Kenrick, Abp. Peter R., 105
King, Rufus, 120
Know-Nothing Order, 22
Know-Nothings, 3, 10, 22–28. See also nativism

Koehler, Rev. Robert, 62
Kulturkampf, 136

Laetare Medal, 155
Lambert, Fr. Louis A., 141
Lamers, William, 156
Lane, Maj. Henry, 12, 14
Lawlor, Sr. Fidelis, 82, 84
Lee, Mary D., 80
Lee, Col. William R., 55
Lefevere, Bp. Peter Paul, 72, 73
Leveque, Fr. Joseph, 77
Liberator, The, 92, 113
Lincoln, Abraham, 31, 43, 70, 122–23,
    125–26
Lincoln assassination, 125–26
Louisville Guardian, 31–32, 33, 92
Luers, Bp. John H., 87
Lynch, Bp. Patrick, 38, 120
Lynch, William F., 45
Lyon, Nathaniel, 44

Manifest Destiny, 10–11
Mann, A. Dudley, 120
Mann, Horace, 136
Maria Monk, 83
Maryland Catholics, 34–35, 106
Maryland colony, 2
Massachusetts Know-Nothings, 22–23
McAtee, Fr. Francis, 56, 74
McCaffrey, Fr. John, 23–24, 44
McCarter, William, 61
McClellan, Gen. George B., 121, 122
McCloskey, Bp. John, 73, 134, 135
McDowell, Gen. Irwin, 45
McElroy, Fr. John, 11, 14, 19
McFarland, Bp. Francis P., 70
McGlynn, Fr. Edward, 77
McKinley, William, 155
McMahon, Fr. Laurence, 62
McMaster, James A.: on anti-Catholicism,
    122, 127, 140; anti-war views of, 36–37,
    45, 116–17, 120, 122, 123, 124; editorship
    of, 10; on Know-Nothings and nativ-

ism, 25, 26; on Lincoln's assassination,
    125, 126; on New York City draft riots,
    115; on papal peace letters, 120; on pub-
    lic school debates, 140; "Roman Ques-
    tion" involvement of, 133–34, 135; on
    secession and sectionalism, 31, 32–33,
    92; views on slavery and emancipation,
    93, 99–100, 101, 103, 105–6, 111
McPherson, James, 7
Meagher, Gen. Thomas F., 35, 54, 59, 60, 63
Memoirs of Chaplain Life (Corby), 146, 149
Merriman, John, 35
Metropolitan Record, 37, 46, 95–96, 103, 113
Mexican Catholicism, 12
Mexican War: anti-Catholicism during,
    11–12, 14–15, 18–19; Catholic press on,
    9–10, 14–15, 16–20; Catholic service in,
    11, 15–19; effect on Catholics, 10–11
Miettinger, Fr. Gustavus, 55–56
Military Order of the Loyal Legion, 150
Miller, Robert, 18
Montgomery, Bp. George T., 155
Mooney, Fr. Thomas F., 73
Moore, David, 156
Morrissey, Fr. Andrew, 150
Morton, Oliver P., 70
Mount Saint Mary's College, 44
Moylan, Gen. Stephan, 2
Muenzenberger, Adam, 56
Mulhane, Fr. L. W., 156
Mulholland, Gen. St. Clair A., 76, 146,
    151–52, 153
Mullay, John: on anti-Catholicism, 116;
    anti-war views of, 37, 45, 122, 124; on
    New York City draft riots, 115; on papal
    peace letters, 119–20; views on slavery
    and emancipation, 99, 124
Mulligan, Col. James A., 29, 54, 55, 57, 59,
    132
Murray, Samuel A., 152–53

Nash, Fr. Michael, 71, 74–75, 76, 78, 79
Nast, Thomas, 137
National Catholic War Council, 163

Native American Party, 3, 21–22
nativism: antebellum growth of, 2–3, 10,
    20–28; of Orestes Brownson, 25–26;
    Catholic patriotism to counteract, 1, 4,
    14–15, 16–18, 42–43, 46, 50–51, 144–45,
    148–49, 160, 161–64; of Republican
    Party, 27–28
Newton, Gen. John, 71, 74
New York City draft riots, 109–16
New York Freeman's Journal: editorship
    of, 10; on Know-Nothings, 25; on
    Mexican War, 14, 16–18; on papal peace
    letters, 120; on "Roman Question," 134;
    views on slavery and emancipation,
    91, 96
New York Tablet: on anti-Catholicism,
    127, 138, 139; on draft riots, 112, 114–15;
    pro-war views of, 38, 46, 96, 123; on
    secession, 31, 38
New York Times, 57, 59, 60
northern Catholics: anti-war views of, 4,
    36–37, 100, 116–24 (see also anti-war
    Catholics); New York City draft riots,
    109–16; pro-war views of, 46, 48–51,
    96–97, 121–25 (see also pro-war Catho-
    lics); reactions to end of war, 124–25;
    reactions to First Battle of Bull Run,
    45–46; reactions to Lincoln assassina-
    tion, 125–26; reactions to outbreak of
    Civil War, 1, 29, 35–42; reactions to
    secession, 31–33; studies of Civil War's
    effect on, 5–6; Union Army service of,
    43–44, 45, 52–67; views on slavery and
    emancipation, 89–107; wartime views
    of laity, 46–50
Notre Dame. See University of Notre
    Dame
Notre Dame GAR Post 569, 151–52
Notre Dame Scholastic, 152, 156
Noyes, Mary, 48
"Nuns of the Battlefield" monument, 159

O'Brien, Sr. Elise, 82
O'Connell, Daniel, 90

Oertel, Maximillian, 35, 37, 104, 114, 124
O'Grady, Maj. William, 149–50
O'Hagan, Fr. Joseph, 75, 79
O'Higgins, Fr. William, 73, 74, 99, 102
Ohio Catholics, 36, 98
O'Reilly, Fr. Bernard, 93
O'Reilly, Robert, 63
O'Reilly, Sr. Ulrica, 112
Ouellet, Fr. Thomas, 149
Overland Campaign, 121–22

Pacciarini, Fr. Basil, 106
papal infallibility doctrine, 130–31
papal peace letters, 117–20
Papal States, 20, 133–35
Parker, Theodore, 21
parochial schools, funding of. See public
    school debates
Patterson, Gen. Robert, 59
Paul, Tom, 157
Paulists, 69–70
Pierpont, Edward, 83
Pilot, The: on Irish Catholic patriotism, 1,
    37, 56, 57; on Mexican War, 15, 17, 18–19;
    pro-war views of, 37; on public school
    debates, 140; tribute to Gen. Rosecrans,
    156; views on slavery and emancipa-
    tion, 90, 92
Pittsburgh Catholics, 39–40
Pius IX: controversy over peace letters of,
    117–20; overthrown in revolution of
    1848, 20; perceived reactionary policies
    of, 130–31; "Roman Question" and,
    133–35; views on Civil War, 120–21
Polk, James K., 11
post-war commemoration: of Catholic
    chaplains, 152–53; of Catholic Civil War
    heroes, 153–57; of Catholic nuns' ser-
    vice, 87, 159–60; by Catholic veterans
    and apologists, 144–48; to counteract
    anti-Catholicism, 144–45, 160; German
    Catholics' lack of, 157–59; Notre Dame's
    contributions to, 148–53; slavery ig-
    nored in, 146–48

post-war period: anti-Catholicism influenced by European events, 129–36;
anti-Catholicism reinforced by public
school debates, 136–41; growth of
Catholic subculture, 4–5, 142–43;
instances of religious tolerance, 141–42;
southern Irish Catholics, 5
presidential elections: 1852, 22; 1860, 29;
1864, 122–23; 1876, 140
Propagateur Catholique, Le, 14
Protestants: clergy's anti-Catholic views,
11, 21; Know-Nothings, 3, 10, 22–28; in
public school debates, 136–41; reactions
to papal peace letters, 117–18; soldiers'
interactions with Catholics during
Civil War, 55, 77–80; soldiers' views on
Catholics during Mexican War, 11–12,
14; views of Catholic nuns, 82–83, 85–87
pro-war Catholics: during Mexican War,
14–15, 16–18; reactions to Lincoln's
assassination, 125–26; reactions to
outbreak of Civil War, 35–36, 37–42;
reactions to papal peace letters, 118–19;
wartime views of, 46, 48–51, 96–97,
121–25
public school debates, 136–41
Purcell, Fr. Edward: on Cincinnati labor
riots, 111; on Lincoln's assassination,
125; on New York City draft riots, 114,
115; on papal peace letters, 118–19;
pro-war views of, 36, 46, 69, 122;
public school debates and, 137; views
on slavery and emancipation, 101, 103,
122, 125, 127
Purcell, Abp. John: on labor issues, 110;
pro-war views of, 42–43; public school
debates and, 137; on requests for
Catholic chaplains, 70, 82; on "Roman
Question," 134, 135; views on slavery
and emancipation, 98–99, 102, 105, 147

Quarterly Review. See *Brownson's Quarterly Review*
Quigley, Fr. Hugh, 72

Rappe, Bp. Amadeus, 24
Reconstruction. *See* post-war period
Republican Party: lack of Catholic support
for, 31, 63–64; in public school debates,
136–41; "Slave Power Conspiracy"
paradigm, 40; ties to Know-Nothings,
27–28
Revolutionary War, Catholic service in, 2
Rey, Fr. Anthony, 11, 19
Richards, Fr. Joseph, 154
Riley, John, 18
"Roman Question," 133–35
Roosevelt, Theodore, 155
Rosecrans, Adrian Louis, 140, 154
Rosecrans, Bp. Sylvester, 36, 101
Rosecrans, Gen. William S., 58; anti-
Catholic attacks on, 60; as Catholic
Civil War hero, 57, 154–57; death of, 155;
during Mexican War, 15–16; post-war
career and commemoration, 147, 149;
support for Catholic chaplains, 74, 76;
views on slavery and emancipation,
99, 102
Ruff, Carl, 64

Sadlier, Dennis and James, 38, 115, 122, 124
Saint Louis University, 44
Saint Mary's College, 48
Samito, Christian, 5
San Francisco Monitor, 126
San Patricio Battalion, 16, 18–19
Scammon, Eliakim P., 16, 36
Scheuermann, Joseph, 159
Scott, Gen. Winfield, 12, 22
Scully, Fr. Thomas, 76
secession crisis, 1, 31–33
Second Army Corps Association, 150
Second Plenary Council of Baltimore,
106–7
Semmes, Raphael, 12, 16
Service Afloat and Ashore (Semmes), 16
Seward, William Henry, 45
Sheridan, Gen. Philip, 57, 154
Sherman, Ellen Ewing, 42, 48, 49, 50, 51

Sherman, Minnie, 48
Sherman, Gen. William, 131
Shields, Gen. James, 16, 59–60
Sisters of Charity of New Orleans, 86
Sisters of Charity of New York, 83
Sisters of St. Joseph, 82
Sisters of the Holy Cross, 82, 87
"Slave Power Conspiracy" paradigm, 40
slavery: Catholic Church's position on, 31–32, 93–94, 100–1, 147; Catholic soldiers' views on, 63–64; ignored in post-war commemoration, 146–48; northern Catholic views on, 89–107
Smith, William R., 23
Sorin, Fr. Edward, 45, 71
southern Catholics: criticism of pro-war views, 38; in post-war period, 5
Spalding, Bp. Martin J.: anti-war views of, 33–34, 36; on Lincoln's assassination, 125; reactions to Know-Nothings, 24, 26; on requests for Catholic missions, 105; on "Roman Question," 134, 135; views on slavery and emancipation, 100, 102–3
St. Joseph's College, 44
Stanley, Gen. David, 74
Steele, William G., 97
Stone, Gen. Charles P., 60
Storm, Jane, 19
Story of the 116th Regiment, Pennsylvania Infantry, The (Mulholland), 146
Surratt, Mary, 126
Syllabus of Errors, 130

Taggart, Joseph, 156
Tammany Ring, 138
Taney, Roger B., 35, 91–92
Tevis, Charles Carroll, 134–35
Thirteenth Amendment, 105–6
Timon, Bp. John, 28, 113, 121
Tissot, Fr. Peter, 71
Tooney, Fr. D. B., 151
Trecy, Fr. Jeremiah, 74, 75, 77
Twain, Mark, 144

Tweed, William, 138
Twichell, Rev. Joseph H., 79

Ullman, Daniel, 28
Union Army: anti-Catholicism in, 55, 77–80; Catholic chaplains' service in, 68–80; Catholic nuns' service in, 68, 80–88; Catholic religious life in, 43, 55–56, 62, 69, 77–80; German Catholic service in, 53–54, 55–56, 62–63; Irish Catholic service in, 43, 44, 47, 53, 54, 57, 59–61; key aspects of Catholic experience in, 52–53; lack of German-speaking chaplains in, 55–56, 62, 69; northern Catholic service in, 43–44, 45, 52–67. See also Catholic soldiers
University of Notre Dame: contributions to post-war commemoration, 148–53; recognition of Gen. Rosecrans, 154–55; role in Civil War, 45, 71–72
Upham, John Baxter, 83
Ural, Susannah, 5, 47
U.S. Catholic Miscellany, 15

Vallandigham, Clement, 117
Varney, Frank P., 156–57
Verot, Bp. Augustine, 34
Virginia Catholics, 141

Wahrheits Freund, Der: on Catholic patriotism, 17; on Lincoln's assassination, 125; on New York City draft riots, 113; pro-war views of, 35–36, 124; views on slavery and emancipation, 103–4, 122
Wallace, Mrs. Lew, 86–87
War Democrats, 37–38. See also pro-war Catholics
Washington, George, 2
Washington Daily Union, 11
Welsh, Peter, 61–62, 64–65, 66, 101, 113–14
Weninger, Fr. Francis, 107
Western Watchman, 156
Whelan, Bp. Richard V., 34
Whipple, Gen. Amiel W., 57, 71

White, William, 63

Whittaker, Gen. Walter Chiles, 79

William Rosecrans and the Union Victory
(Moore), 156

Wilson, Col. William, 74–75

Wimmer, Fr. Boniface, 89, 110, 116, 129, 140

"woman order," 120

Wood, Bp. James, 105, 131

working-class Catholics: Fenianism and,
132; New York City draft riots, 109–16;
views on Civil War, 47–48; wartime
disaffection of, 110–11

Young, Bp. Josue, 42, 98

THE NORTH'S CIVIL WAR
Andrew L. Slap, series editor

Anita Palladino, ed., *Diary of a Yankee Engineer: The Civil War Story of John H. Westervelt, Engineer, 1st New York Volunteer Engineer Corps.*

Herman Belz, *Abraham Lincoln, Constitutionalism, and Equal Rights in the Civil War Era.*

Earl J. Hess, *Liberty, Virtue, and Progress: Northerners and Their War for the Union.* Second revised edition, with a new introduction by the author.

William L. Burton, *Melting Pot Soldiers: The Union's Ethnic Regiments.*

Hans L. Trefousse, *Carl Schurz: A Biography.*

Stephen W. Sears, ed., *Mr. Dunn Browne's Experiences in the Army: The Civil War Letters of Samuel W. Fiske.*

Jean H. Baker, *Affairs of Party: The Political Culture of Northern Democrats in the Mid–Nineteenth Century.*

Frank L. Klement, *The Limits of Dissent: Clement L. Vallandigham and the Civil War.* With a new introduction by Steven K. Rogstad.

Lawrence N. Powell, *New Masters: Northern Planters during the Civil War and Reconstruction.*

John A. Carpenter, *Sword and Olive Branch: Oliver Otis Howard.*

Thomas F. Schwartz, ed., *"For a Vast Future Also": Essays from the* Journal of the Abraham Lincoln Association.

Mark De Wolfe Howe, ed., *Touched with Fire: Civil War Letters and Diary of Oliver Wendell Holmes, Jr.* With a new introduction by David Burton.

Harold Adams Small, ed., *The Road to Richmond: The Civil War Letters of Major Abner R. Small of the 16th Maine Volunteers*. With a new introduction by Earl J. Hess.

Eric A. Campbell, ed., *"A Grand Terrible Dramma": From Gettysburg to Petersburg: The Civil War Letters of Charles Wellington Reed*. Illustrated by Reed's Civil War sketches.

Herbert Mitgang, ed., *Abraham Lincoln: A Press Portrait*.

Harold Holzer, ed., *Prang's Civil War Pictures: The Complete Battle Chromos of Louis Prang*.

Harold Holzer, ed., *State of the Union: New York and the Civil War*.

Paul A. Cimbala and Randall M. Miller, eds., *Union Soldiers and the Northern Home Front: Wartime Experiences, Postwar Adjustments*.

Mark A. Snell, *From First to Last: The Life of Major General William B. Franklin*.

Paul A. Cimbala and Randall M. Miller, eds., *An Uncommon Time: The Civil War and the Northern Home Front*.

John Y. Simon and Harold Holzer, eds., *The Lincoln Forum: Rediscovering Abraham Lincoln*.

Thomas F. Curran, *Soldiers of Peace: Civil War Pacifism and the Postwar Radical Peace Movement*.

Kyle S. Sinisi, *Sacred Debts: State Civil War Claims and American Federalism, 1861–1880*.

Russell L. Johnson, *Warriors into Workers: The Civil War and the Formation of Urban-Industrial Society in a Northern City*.

Peter J. Parish, *The North and the Nation in the Era of the Civil War*. Edited by Adam L. P. Smith and Susan-Mary Grant.

Patricia Richard, *Busy Hands: Images of the Family in the Northern Civil War Effort*.

Michael S. Green, *Freedom, Union, and Power: The Mind of the Republican Party During the Civil War.*

Christian G. Samito, ed., *Fear Was Not In Him: The Civil War Letters of Major General Francis S. Barlow, U.S.A.*

John S. Collier and Bonnie B. Collier, eds., *Yours for the Union: The Civil War Letters of John W. Chase, First Massachusetts Light Artillery.*

Grace Palladino, *Another Civil War: Labor, Capital, and the State in the Anthracite Regions of Pennsylvania, 1840–1868.*

Christian B. Keller, *Chancellorsville and the Germans: Nativism, Ethnicity, and Civil War Memory.*

Sidney George Fisher, *A Philadelphia Perspective: The Civil War Diary of Sidney George Fisher.* Edited and with a new Introduction by Jonathan W. White.

Robert M. Sandow, *Deserter Country: Civil War Opposition in the Pennsylvania Appalachians.*

Craig L. Symonds, ed., *Union Combined Operations in the Civil War.*

Harold Holzer, Craig L. Symonds, and Frank L. Williams, eds., *The Lincoln Assassination: Crime and Punishment, Myth and Memory.* A Lincoln Forum Book.

Earl F. Mulderink III, *New Bedford's Civil War.*

David G. Smith, *On the Edge of Freedom: The Fugitive Slave Issue in South Central Pennsylvania, 1820–1870.*

George Washington Williams, *A History of the Negro Troops in the War of the Rebellion, 1861–1865.* Introduction by John David Smith.

Randall M. Miller, ed., *Lincoln and Leadership: Military, Political, and Religious Decision Making.*

Andrew L. Slap and Michael Thomas Smith, eds., *This Distracted and Anarchical People: New Answers for Old Questions about the Civil War-Era North.*

Paul D. Moreno and Johnathan O'Neill, eds., *Constitutionalism in the Approach and Aftermath of the Civil War.*

Steve Longenecker, *Gettysburg Religion: Refinement, Diversity, and Race in the Antebellum and Civil War Border North.*

Harold Holzer, Craig L. Symonds, and Frank L. Williams, eds., *Exploring Lincoln: Great Historians Reappraise Our Greatest President.* A Lincoln Forum Book.

Lorien Foote and Kanisorn Wongsrichanalai, eds., *So Conceived and So Dedicated: Intellectual Life in the Civil War–Era North.*

William B. Kurtz, *Excommunicated from the Union: How the Civil War Created a Separate Catholic America.*